THE PEOPLE
v.
DISNEYLAND

HOW LAWSUITS & LAWYERS
TRANSFORMED THE MAGIC

By David Koenig

For my sisters
Michelle and Maryanne,
with love

The People v. Disneyland:
How Lawsuits & Lawyers Transformed the Magic by David Koenig

Published by
BONAVENTURE PRESS
Post Office Box 51961
Irvine, CA 92619-1961
USA
www.BonaventurePress.com

Cover art by Yannick De Smet (www.de-smet.me)

Publisher's Cataloging in Publication Data
Koenig, David G.
    The people v. disneyland: how lawsuits & lawyers transformed the magic / by David Koenig.
        p. cm.
    Includes annotated references and index.

ISBN-10: 1937878031
ISBN 978-1-937878-03-0

    1. Disneyland (Calif.) — History. 2. Amusement Parks (Calif.) I. Koenig, David G., 1962- II. Title.

791.0687949
Library of Congress Control Number: 2015907523

Printed in the USA
10   9   8   7   6   5   4   3   2   1

Contents

Lawsuit Citations: Allegations made in lawsuits are cited by the last name of the lead plaintiff. Dates listed are when the central incident took place, not when the case was filed. The vast majority of cases were filed several months to two years after the incident.

Use of the Term Disney: Within this text, "Disney" typically refers to the Disney company or representatives from its corporate, park management, or legal departments. For clarity's sake, Walt Disney is typically referred to by his first name.

Acknowledgments

WRITING ANY BOOK is a momentous task, even for an expert. Just imagine writing a book involving a topic in which one is far from even amateur, namely the law. Consequently, I have never relied more heavily on interviews, input and advice than I have with this project.

Chief among those was attorney Sharon Lowsen, who tossed me head-first into the middle of several lawsuits, where I could see the Disney lawyers up close and personal, and it was she who suggested I write this book.

Other attorneys who graciously shared their time, tactics and memories included Wylie Aitken, Drew Antablin, John Francis Carroll, Daniel Gilleon, Greg Hafif, John Lacklen, John Luetto, Barry Novack, David L. Price, and Amy Fisch Solomon.

Plaintiffs who shared their stories were Crusader (Andrew Exler), Julia Gillin, Dwight Palmatier, Victoria Penley, and devoted cast members Bob McDonald Jr. and Joanne Rowan.

For Disney's side of the story, I often relied on the insight of other long-time cast members, including Earl Archer, Nanci Coleman, Jan Doezie, Bill "W.C." Fields, Bob Gurr, Elizabeth Hayes, Kimberly Hensley, Robert Hill, Alan Howard, Rich Johnson, Larry Kaml, George Kissinger, Bob McDonald Sr., Tom Nabbe, Steve Odgaard, Ken Pellman, Ron Pogue, Glenn Raines, Bruce Turner, Garry Wood, and Mark Zimmer.

I also utilized quotes from prior interviews, including with Ella May Green, Larry Holmes, and Chris Perley.

The brilliant cover art was created by Yannick De Smet (Norke).

My fine editors were Sara Graves and the breathtakingly obsessive Hugh Allison.

Attorney Jack Burgin, an expert in both law and Disney, patiently pointed out several legal errors in an early draft, hopefully preventing me from looking even more foolish than I typically do.

Patrick Stibbs inspired the "modern dedication" on the back cover.

Adrienne Vincent Phoenix, MousePlanet.com, kindly provided use of a photo.

Family and friends provided untold measures of help. My gorgeous wife, Laura Koenig, did everything asked and more, assisting in research and, perhaps most valuably, locking me in the office for hours on end when it came time to do all the writing. She's the primary reason my books ever get finished.

Zach and Rebecca Koenig also provided keen insight while accompanying me on scores of trips to the Happiest Place on Earth. I also thank Anne and the rest of the Koenig, assorted Hamlins, David and the Keefes, and Uncle Brian.

Most of all, I thank my Lord Jesus, who—despite all the crazy conflicts in this world and a legal system that doesn't always provide true justice—offers matchless peace and the assurance of a victorious final verdict.

Preface

I DON'T CARE MUCH care for lawyers. I see most of them as professional intimidators often unconcerned about truth or justice; their sole job is, no matter who's right or wrong, to glorify their clients' side of an argument, tear down the opposition, and occasionally drag out the proceedings until the other side drops. As a result, the facts are sometimes secondary; the side with the savviest, most ruthless lawyer usually wins.

By that measure, Disneyland has some pretty good lawyers. They're charged with doing whatever it takes to protect not just a multi-billion-dollar corporation, but also its primary product and marketing tool: its "magic."

I first became aware of Disney's preoccupation with lawsuits back in 1987, during a visit with friends to the park's Golden Horseshoe Saloon. We were enjoying the "Golden Horseshoe Jamboree Show," an Old West music-and-comedy revue that included a fair bit of mingling with the crowd and audience participation. My group was a rambunctious one, so at one point in the show, the cowpokes wandered over to our table to recruit a few unsuspecting volunteers for a skit. They selected a pretty girl from our group and then motioned toward me. As I began to rise, another of the cowhands pulled my chair out of the way, then I was told to sit back down. I bent my knees and ended up on my rump. The audience howled. For a split second, the actor looked mortified. He quickly regained his smile and, between his teeth, whispered, "Are you okay? Are you okay?" I said I was fine, as he helped me up and led me to the stage. We participated in a silly skit about a traveling medicine show and at several points during the performance, the actor sidled up to me and whispered, "How are you doing? Still okay?" His paranoia struck me as a little out of proportion.

Soon after, I began my research for my first book, *Mouse Tales*, the

OUCH: My introduction to Disneyland's legal paranoia came in 1987 during my kerchief-wearing guest appearance in a revue at the Golden Horseshoe Saloon.

world's first unauthorized peek backstage at Disneyland. During my research, I discovered why the actor was so paranoid. In contrast to its idyllic facade, things do go wrong at the Happiest Place on Earth. There are unhappy guests and disgruntled employees. People get hurt, every single day. And many of them sue Disneyland because of it.

Mouse Tales covered Disneyland's legal dealings in general, but I made clear I was no legal expert (a status I proudly retain to this day). That didn't stop readers who were suing Disney or contemplating doing so from tracking me down for legal advice. Every month or so, I'd receive a call or email from someone who had fallen down in Fantasyland or tripped over a queue rope. I received a panicked call from the matriarch of the infamous "Prairie Family" (a brood of eccentric visitors who claimed they were ambushed and beaten by a half-dozen burly security guards and were now suing to get their annual passes back). Some time later I was tracked down by an ousted park security manager-turned-private eye. He'd been hired to investigate the death of a man killed at Disneyland while standing in line for a boat ride.

Then in 2000, I received a call from Sharon Lowsen, a tenacious fireball of a lawyer, whose unassuming office was a converted one-story house in Fullerton, five miles north of Disneyland. She had a former Disney security manager working as her secretary. The secretary was also a client, one of a growing number of ex-cast members who were convinced that they'd been terminated because of age. Lowsen wanted to hire me not only as a behind-the-scenes consultant, but also as what she termed "the world's first Expert Disneyland Witness." Instead of providing authoritative testimony on something medical or mechanical, I would testify as to how Disneyland operated in a historical context, minus the Disney spin, based on interviews with nearly 1,000 cast members.

Lowsen's co-counsel on a number of the cases, John Montevideo, was a tad skeptical, but agreed, I assume figuring if the judge wouldn't allow me on the stand, at least they could pick my brain. I pointed out inconsistencies in witnesses' depositions, referred them to other cast members in similar straits, and even provided a few confidential reports I had mysteriously ended up with. I provided consulting for about a year until, sure enough, the judge eventually ruled that there was no such thing as an Expert Disneyland Witness. But through and after the process, Lowsen suggested I write a book about legal dealings with Disney.

Unfortunately, several years later, when I committed to researching the topic more deeply, I discovered that the Orange County Courthouse, which had diligently retained every shred of paperwork filed in every O.C. Superior Court against Disneyland for the park's first 50 years, had begun going paperless. It scanned a small number of records in cases deemed important, warehoused a few others, and trashed the rest, assuming the case had been fully resolved for at least a couple of years. Nearly all the files and microfiches and microfilms—representing perhaps 1,000 Disneyland cases and in many instances the only surviving record of historic courtroom battles—were unceremoniously destroyed. Filings on ongoing cases can be viewed on computer terminals at the courthouse, but unfortunately there were files on numerous cases in the early 2000s that I never had the opportunity to view. Consequently, while this book draws upon research into 1,300 Disney cases, several hundred others are not covered. Statistics in this book, then, are based on an estimated 90 percent of all cases filed against the park in Orange County Superior Court, perhaps a quarter of the Superior and Federal Court cases filed outside of Orange County, and only the most intriguing of cases filed in small claims court.

Interestingly, despite a concerted effort of late to stem guest issues before they escalate to lawsuits, Disneyland continues to be sued about once a week—a pace that has held steady since the 1950s, despite the tremendous growth of the resort and, unfortunately, the ever-increasing tendency for the public to sue.

I

Home Court Advantage

DISNEYLAND WAS BUILT on a labyrinth of illusions. There are the self-evident illusions—of riding a flying elephant, of being under attack by pirates, of careening out of control on a runaway mine train. Then there are the deeper, larger master deceptions that hold together all the mini-make believes.

First, there's the greatest Grand Illusion—that you actually have stepped into a different place and a different time. Master illusionist Walt Disney wanted you to believe that you were no longer in present day Anaheim, California. You were truly in the Land of Tomorrow, or Fantasy, or Adventure. Through exacting attention to detail, right down to themed trash cans, nothing was to break the illusion. Cast members were trained to stay in character. Even plainclothes workers were themed—to disappear into the background; Walt had the Costuming Department supply every supervisor with the same, nondescript gray suit and orange tie, so the average guest would look right past them, yet he could instantly pick them out of a crowd.

The second master illusion is the perception that nothing ever goes wrong at Disneyland. Guests were entrusting not just their imaginations to Disney, but their safety as well. They were asked to suspend their disbeliefs, check their critical thinking, and give themselves over to the make believe. Visitors knew that while Disney might place them into seemingly harrowing adventures, ultimately the company was in control of everything. Their trust in Disney's omnipotence was so great, that whenever the weather got too bad, guests would line up to complain that Walt had allowed it to rain.

Walt and his successors reinforced the perpetual tranquility of the Happiest Place on Earth by working as hard as they could to keep the place clean, safe and fresh, and by having the workers responsible for the grunt work do so subtly, typically behind the scenes, so guests would never even be tipped off that anything conceivably could go wrong. Security guards wore unassuming Keystone Kops costumes. Attraction repairs were made after hours or behind neutral green barriers. Warning signs were few and far between.

But occasionally things did go wrong, oftentimes precisely because guests did let their guards down. Visitors tripped. Ride operators got distracted. Attractions malfunctioned. Guests and employees were mistreated. And sometimes those harmed sued.

Early on, Walt foresaw the potential harm high-profile lawsuits could cause in tainting public perception of his new venture, thereby jeopardizing his master illusions. The park had a lawyer working out of its administration building, who would look over lessee and construction contracts and farm out any civil cases, but he was more of a coordinator. To actually fight any claims, Walt didn't want a slick in-house counsel. It wouldn't fit the profile of a lovable Disney character. And a phalanx of suits from a giant Los Angeles law firm would seem too impersonal.

So Walt found a young, 31-year-old lawyer at one of the larger local firms and convinced him to set up shop on his own, with the promise that he'd get the bulk of Disneyland's business. A World War II veteran, W. Mike McCray was a born storyteller, with a razor-sharp mind and a gregarious nature atypical of a defense lawyer. In court, McCray usually tried to keep the mood light and, mimicking the cast member requirement, liked to call people by their first name, even the opposing lawyers.

His favorite tactic was taking juries on field trips to Disneyland, so, in his words, "they can benefit from seeing the operation." In reality, he hoped a little pixie dust would rub off on them. McCray had juries climb the maintenance stairway inside the Matterhorn, tour the Space Mountain building with the lights on, and ride the teacups. They'd have the place to themselves.

"We'd bus the jury from the courthouse to Disneyland at 8 a.m., before the park opened to the public," shared the park's court liaison, Jan Doezie. "But they'd enter through the front gate. The streets were glistening. The lights were twinkling. We'd enter a ride through the back, to see how it worked with the lights on and with the lights off. Oooh... ahhhh....."

Whereas Disney preferred to keep its dirty laundry out of the papers, McCray believed in occasionally airing the laundry, just in a sanitized state. He came across as open and honest with reporters, always ready with a quote or to regale them with war stories from the courtroom. He'd frequently mention his nickname in court—Perry McCray, or Iron Mike, or Mickey's Mouthpiece, he seemed to have a new one for every interview.

Unwittingly, those reporters were helping McCray to develop the park's third master illusion—that of Disney's legal invincibility. According to legend, Disney would fight every case, never give an inch, and always win. Publicly, McCray put out the word that the company rarely settled and lost in court even less frequently. Any losses were aberrations, once-in-a-lifetime oddities that could never happen again—to the point that the one attorney every other year who beat Disneyland in court was convinced they were the first ones to ever do so.

McCray figured the strategy was the only way to make sure 50 cases a year didn't turn into 500. If word got out that Disney was apt to settle, it might become an easy mark. And, certainly, Disney's deep pockets did entice a fair share of faux victims. Ride operator Earl Archer recalled, "One morning, just after the park had opened, I was standing back in the shadows, beside my turnstile of the Main Street Cinema, when a hippie-type couple appeared by the curb in front. I overheard him telling her to 'just kind of step off the curb and make like you twisted your ankle. Then we can sue this dump for big bucks!' I don't know what sets people off like that; but I suppose some people come out to make money while the majority come out to spend money and have fun while they're here. Thank goodness for the majority!"

McCray's confidence wasn't mere bluster. In its defense, Disney always had a lot going for it. Safety was a hallmark. Its employees were typically clean cut, well spoken, and made for believable witnesses. Everything was meticulously documented. Exhaustive note taking, according to nurse Ella May Green, "was important, but for a nurse it's not unusual. The legal profession says if it wasn't documented, it wasn't done."

That extended to the maintenance department, which used to check on every element of every attraction every night, replace parts well before they were expected to wear out, and chart it all. And, in the event of an accident, the obsessive documentation extended to all cast members. "We were told that whatever our assignment—the restrooms, an area, etc.—we should note slip and falls or any other possible guest injury, even if the guest refuses assistance and walks away," recalled sweeper Ken Pellman. "We were supposed to write down what happened, when, where, etc. That saves a lot of time. If someone has a legitimate claim against Disneyland, and the claims people can figure that from an incident report, then there's no need to drag it out or allow it to go to court. Conversely, it can protect Disneyland, too, depending on what happened."

The folks who knew best of Disney's reputation for perfection were the nearby residents of Orange County, California, a traditionally conservative area more prone to side with authority and family-friendly neighbors like Mickey Mouse. It didn't hurt that most people who sat on Orange County juries had positive, preconceived emotions favoring Disneyland and often knew someone who worked there. Subconsciously, they'd give Disney the benefit of the doubt.

Usually, emotional arguments worked in a plaintiff's favor. Disney stole that tactic from them. "It's tough to get a fair trial in Orange County," confirmed San Diego attorney Daniel Gilleon. "About half the juries are 55-year-olds working at McDonnell Douglas, and engineers are typically not good for plaintiffs. The rest are related to someone who works for Disney."

McCray frequented the O.C. Courthouse so often, that he found it easy to become good friends with a number of the local judges, privately calling them by their first names and suggesting good books they should read. His brother and partner, W. Patrick McCray, even became a judge.

Opposing attorneys quickly caught on to Disney's home-court advantage and began filing cases in Los Angeles and other plaintiff-friendlier counties. Disney would respond by moving to have the case transferred to Orange County, and was more often than not successful. Lawyers who were clever enough to find an exception, such as by also naming Burbank-based parent company Walt Disney Productions in the suit, on average found significantly greater success.

Disney follows a familiar pattern in dealing with aggrieved guests, hoping to dissuade them from suing. In the early days, injured guests were instructed to submit a written claim to Insurance Company of North America (INA)—the park's carrier and sponsor of its welcome center, Carefree Corner. Small claims were quickly settled. Anything INA deemed unreasonable or defensible was sent to McCray.

Nowadays, Disney claim agents initially play the extremely concerned friend. If that fails, they'll try buying injured guests off cheap with inexpensive trinkets, like free passes or T-shirts. "They might offer them a few tickets, so they could come back and hurt themselves again," cracked attorney John Francis Carroll.

If that doesn't work and the victim retains an attorney, Disney's attitude changes 180 degrees. Now, they're combatants. Disney will make sure you know of its legal prowess, hoping to intimidate you into backing down.

"My dad was an Imagineer, a conceptual artist who worked on Epcot, so my family (loved) the company, but the one thing was the talk of how vicious their law firm was," Gilleon said. "You'd meet with their attorneys and they'd say, 'We'll pay you $5,000 on a $100,000 case,' and many (plaintiffs) would accept it because they'd figure you can't get a fair trial."

No methods appear to be off limits. Disney has been accused of hiding eyewitnesses from plaintiffs. They've hired private detectives to spy on plaintiffs with cameras, searching for embarrassing behavior. They've had process servers bang on plaintiffs' doors in the middle of the night to serve documents. They've threatened to counter-sue, saying the plaintiff's accident cost the park money in attraction downtime and workers' cleanup time.

Disney has been able to get away with its hardcore stance because it has long been primarily—and at times completely—self-insured. There are usually no insurance adjustors at the negotiating table advising that it would be cheaper to settle early.

That said, if the plaintiff persists, Disney will calculate its odds for victory and the price of a possible defeat, and that will determine if they improve their offer. Settlements are common—but always confidential.

One afternoon in the early 1970s, ride operator Steve Odgaard was walking across Frontierland, when a little old lady, rushing to catch the Mark Twain, ran into him. "She weighed about 90 pounds. I'm 180," Odgaard recalled. "She fell down, banged up her elbow. About a year later, I got called into a deposition. I explained she blindsided me from behind. I wouldn't knock down a little old lady! Her lawyer asked me things like, 'What did you have for breakfast that morning?' I couldn't remember what I had the day before, let alone a year before. After her lawyer left, the Disney lawyers told me, 'We're going to settle with her.' I said, 'But it was her own fault! She wasn't looking where she was going.' 'Well, she's like 80-some years old, she's a missionary from Africa, it was her first trip to Disneyland, and she never asked for anything exorbitant. This we would not win in court.'"

In the early 1980s, McCray took on a young associate, Richard McCain, who appeared to have a similarly folksy nature and a willingness to wear Mickey Mouse ties, and he began grooming him to take over the firm. McCray was diagnosed with brain cancer in 1984, but didn't share the secret publicly. He didn't want to show a crack in the armor. He was dead a year later, and McCain took off on his own, retaining the Disneyland account. In time, Disney would hire large, prestigious mega-firms to defend high-profile cases and specialty cases, such as for discrimination or wrongful termination, but for the smaller, grind-it-out cases—the slip and falls, the minor ride mishaps, the "nuisance suits"—McCain would continue the McCray legacy and strategy.

McCray and McCain, ultimately, had always been subservient to whomever was calling the shots in Anaheim and Burbank. In the beginning, Walt was the final word and, in fact, his rule continued for several years after his death. Oversight for daily park decisions fell to the Operations executives, all of whom were marinated in Walt's philosophies and would continue running Disneyland exactly as they thought the boss would have. As new corporate management arrived in the 1980s, the power switched to the marketing department, which often found it easier to sell more and increase profits by ignoring Walt's obsessiveness with "Good Show" and long-term customer satisfaction. For the first time, Disney began settling cases if they thought it would be cheaper than fighting them. In the 1990s, when corporate growth slowed, the power was usurped by the accounting department, to control costs.

These days, there's a new Big Cheese calling the shots at Disneyland. Much of the power has moved to corporate's Legal department. A band of indistinguishable attorneys, with no park operational experience, no concern for history or traditions, and no understanding of what guests love about Disneyland, is now dictating major changes in the name of improved safety, security and access.

Certainly, if attractions or procedures proved inherently dangerous, Disneyland had always been willing to change them, at least secretly. "Disney will never admit that any changes were made to improve safety because that implies that safety previously had not been all that it could have been," charges attorney Barry Novack. "So they always have another, standard explanation." Innumerable press releases will attest that

Disneyland is "regularly reviewing its safety protocols" and "continuously improving its procedures." All changes, they would have you believe, are generated internally and should ever be attributed to any outside factors or incidents.

But the new lawyer-first mentality enveloping the park weighs potential for legal liability as seemingly its only criteria, never mind the cost or the impact on the guest experience or park's heritage. In 2013, a guest tripped stepping between Innoventions' slowly-rotating exterior and its stationary interior. The lawyers demanded the building cease turning.

The year before, Disney's Imagineers had the bright idea of reviving the old Flying Saucers ride of the 1960s. Guests loved the bumper cars on air, but they lasted just five years due to unreliable technology. Fifty years later, Imagineering had finally been able to perfect the mechanics and create a reliable, thrilling new version themed as Luigi's Flying Tires for neighboring Disney California Adventure. Yet Legal insisted the vehicles be so bulky and laden with safety mechanisms, that they were practically unmovable. When Walt Disney Imagineering (WDI) noticed during previews that the vehicles were creeping along like flat tires, they filled the arena with dozens of giant beach balls, hoping to preoccupy otherwise bored or frustrated riders. Five days after the ride's official opening, a woman was exiting her tire when she was hit in the head with a beach ball, hurting her neck (*Fong, 2012*). Within two months, Disney's lawyers demanded the balls be removed. The ride, which opened with two-hour lines, soon found itself a walk-on. Two years later, the ride was closed.

Disneyland's transformation would be 180 degrees, away from a time when few considerations were as important as putting on an incredible show.

II

Slips, Trips & Bumps

CONSIDERING THE MILLIONS of people who visit Disneyland every year and the variety of surfaces they have to traverse, from tricky cobblestones to slick tiles and steps, it's not surprising how frequently guests slip and trip. Such accidents have resulted in more than 500 slip-and-fall lawsuits over the years, making them the most common type of suit filed against the park.

In such cases, the burden of proof is on the plaintiff to prove that there was a dangerous condition that Disneyland or one of its employees either created or did nothing to remedy. Disney must be shown to either have been aware of the problem or should have been aware of, had they been taking proper care of their property. Disney's lawyers typically flipped the responsibility back on the plaintiff—that any hazard was created so recently that the park didn't have time to clean it up, but that a reasonable person should have quickly spotted and avoided the hazard. Or, that there was no dangerous condition and the guest fell due to his or her own carelessness.

Fewer than one in four slip-and-fall cases made it to trial, an ominous sign for any plaintiff, since Disneyland has won close to 95 percent of them in court. Yet the very first case did make it to trial and became one of only a handful to win.

In November 1955, Roy Mays was walking through the three-month-old park when he slipped on orange peelings and a banana peel. He argued Disney was negligent in allowing "debris and foreign matter" to remain on the ground, since it had reasonable time and notice to clean it up. All parties agreed to try the case in two parts: first, to determine if Disney was liable and then, if so, to determine damages. After the jury found Disney liable, park attorney McCray demanded a new trial, saying the evidence didn't support the verdict. The judge agreed and dismissed the jury. Mays then appealed, arguing that the judge erred not only in granting a new trial, but also in even considering McCray's request before the case was completed, since they never proceeded to the jury phase. The appellate court agreed that, yes, the judge was not permitted to hear or rule on Disney's request until the case was completed, but with the jury long since released, the court had no choice but to grant a new trial. By this point, eight years had passed since the accident, so the parties decided to settle.

One thing Mays had going for him was that Disneyland at that time was new; it took a while for its reputation for obsessive cleanliness to spread. In short order, the thought of Disneyland "cluttered with debris" would sound ludicrous to the typical jury, particularly in Orange County. Opposing lawyers knew, as well. "Certain kinds of cases had no chance, such as the vast majority of slip and falls, on ice cream or in a bathroom. Don't take those cases," said attorney John Luetto. "Disneyland has its SOP (Standard Operating Procedure), which dictates very specific ways they have to handle specific situations. It called for every square inch of Disneyland to be swept every 20 minutes. Legal theorem holds that a negligence case is judged by whether the defendant acted reasonably. Disney would put up its book, 'We sweep every square inch every 20 minutes.' Is that reasonable? Just because you fall down and get hurt, where you get hurt is not automatically responsible. That's not what the law is."

One plaintiff admitted to Disney that her shoes contributed to her fall on a rain-soaked boardwalk, but nonetheless insisted that the park was at fault, due to her mistaken understanding of the law (*Fry, 2006*). "If someone came to my house and slipped on my floor, I'd have to pay for them. That's what insurance is for," she said. Not surprisingly, she lost in court.

Yet there has been no shortage of lawyers willing to take such cases. Often the hazard is some sort of debris. One woman in her 40s claimed she injured her knee after slipping in a giant pool of "spit" on the Sleeping Beauty Castle bridge (*Lee, 2003*). Another insisted she slipped in a puddle of liquid that was oozing from a Frontierland trash can three feet away (*Khvann, 1988*). The jury couldn't envision it.

Equally common are claims that surfaces are inherently dangerous. Common targets include curbs (particularly the one surrounding the Hub), stairs, wet bathroom floors, waxed restaurants floors, the gravel pathway that led to the House of the Future, uneven porch boards, bumpy cobblestone walkways, rain-soaked surfaces, greasy parking lots, and the rough terrain of Tom Sawyer Island.

Plaintiffs who claim the pavement was too slippery are rebutted by the fact that the pavement is well within the coefficient of friction standards and is coated twice a year with an abrasive. And, Disney is always experimenting with different surfaces to find something more stable. In the late 1990s, Disneyland began replacing most of its vast acres of slurry-coated walkways with paving stones, which they thought would provide a more abrasive, less slippery surface, while making below-surface repairs easier. Underground work could be performed simply by temporarily pulling up a section of pavers, rather than jackhammering into the concrete and hoping the repairs didn't leave too obvious a patch. Yet the custodial crew thought the pavers could be even trickier to maintain and safely negotiate.

"To me, it was hard to beat fresh or relatively new slurry, which, for a time, covered what seemed like most of the park," recalled longtime sweeper Ken Pellman. "It was 'smooth' in the sense of not having anything that might catch or bump a heel or toe or wheel, but it also had a texture to it that made it less likely people would slip. Once the slurry was worn out, it wasn't as good. But then Disneyland started getting paving stones and stamped concrete. I don't know if those changed the statistics, but I do know that people using wheelchairs and other mobility aids didn't like that stuff as much, and there were times the pavers would come loose. The pavers definitely were more difficult for sweepers. Popcorn and other bits of debris were harder to sweep up. With slurry, a Dustex could be used from time to time to quickly sweep up large swaths of walkways and remove dust and tiny bits. Not so with pavers. Gum was always easier to remove from slurry."

At least one man handled his case out of court, after tripping over a sunken paver and landing on his face, giving him a bloody nose and a broken tooth (*Nguyen, 2002*). A 37-year-old paraplegic, however, lost at trial after the front wheels of her wheelchair became caught between the pavers leading into Tomorrowland and she was thrown forward, breaking her leg (*Miller, 2003*). In addition to $4,000 in medical bills, she also sought damages for pain and suffering caused by the break-up of her marriage, which she claimed was caused by arguments about the accident with her husband, who was pushing her wheelchair at the time.

In time, Disney would begin replacing many of the walking areas with a material that was equally attractive, but devoid of the gaps that could develop between pavers: stamped concrete.

Perhaps the most difficult area in the park to keep dry was the Cosmic Waves fountain, added during the 1998 rebuild of Tomorrowland. The fountain consisted of a series of ground-level jets surrounding a giant, slowly spinning granite ball. The idea was sort of a maze—visitors would attempt to dodge the five-foot jets while dashing to reach the ball in the center. Unfortunately, people thought the idea was instead to get as soaked as possible, and kids by the dozens would strip down to their skivvies and cavort in the new water play area. The area was protected by a rubberized mat, to cushion any falls, but that didn't stop water from sloshing out onto the neighboring pavement as children, soaked to the bone, ran off.

Disney knew it had a problem. A handful of slip-and-fall suits followed (*Marnadin, 2000*). Disney initially tried to alleviate the spread of moisture by limiting how high the jets would shoot up. In 2002, the jets were turned off completely. Soon after, the entire play area was cemented over, leaving a lonely granite ball.

Ironically, the most obvious site of slip and falls—restrooms—have generated comparatively few lawsuits over the years, thanks to an obsessive custodial crew. "It was always important to keep the restroom floors as dry as possible, and when people would use the sink but not a paper towel or hand dryer, the water would drip off their hands onto the floor," said sweeper Ken Pellman. "Of course, there were also toilet overflows. Every restroom supply closet has a check-in sheet with the cast member's name. The cast member signs in and out, checks off all of the things they did while there, writes down their next stop, and, importantly, notes the condition of the restroom ("Wet, messy," "Good, dry," etc.). If a guest claims a slip and fall in a restroom, I can guarantee you Disneyland's claims personnel will consult those sheets and possibly talk with the cast member who was on duty."

There have been almost as many suits filed by guests who tripped over floor mats, placed there to prevent slipping, than by those who slipped on restroom floors.

One 61-year-old man did get the park to settle after allegedly slipping in a bathroom in a pool of vomit (*Munushian, 1983*). He landed on his back and injured his head and neck so severely, he couldn't stand up. He laid on the floor for a half-hour before he was discovered by another guest, who called First Aid to assist with a stretcher.

Several guests have sued after blaming their falls on oil spills or potholes in the parking lot. One, 47-year-old Perlie Stone, admitted she walked over a darkened patch, thinking it was newly repaired asphalt (*1981*). It turned out to be an oil slick; she slipped and fractured her knee. Months later, after surgery, her weakened knee resulted in her fracturing her ankle. When Disney wouldn't give her $150,000, Stone asked the jury for $839,000. McCain reviewed the park's maintenance practices to ensure it took every precaution to quickly correct oil spills. He also had the woman testify that she intentionally walked through the hazard. The jury agreed, ten to two.

Another parking lot victim wasn't even a guest (*Collins, 1987*). He was a 63-year-old engineer attending a conference at the Anaheim Convention Center across the street. But the convention center's parking area was full, so he parked in Disneyland's lot. While he was at the conference, the park closed for the day and cast members strung a cable across the lot's entrance to keep cars from entering. Returning to his car that evening, the engineer found it dark, raining and hailing. So he hurriedly ran across Katella Avenue and tripped over the cable, breaking his elbow. He claimed the cable created a "concealed danger" to pedestrians and the area lacked sufficient lighting. McCain won over the jury by countering that the man was in a rush and shouldn't have tried to enter through the closed vehicle entrance—and he was jaywalking, to boot.

Another common defense is that plaintiffs were doing something or wearing something they should not have. A 56-year-old beautician didn't see the grape juice she slipped in because she was wearing sunglasses (*Adkinson, 1978*). A 22-year-old who slipped near the Haunted Mansion admitted she was skipping and wearing thick flip-flops (*Oliver, 1979*). When a 63-year-old woman blamed her fall near Carnation Plaza Gardens on the area being poorly lit and the cobblestones being unevenly worn, McCray persuaded a jury that she had actually tripped over her own feet (*Ferrington, 1980*).

An 80-year-old woman stumbled while walking through the park and broke her neck (*Cuzzolino, 1987*). She demanded $335,000. The lady insisted there must have been a hole in the sidewalk that caught her foot. But she admitted that she did not see any hazard before the fall and could not identify a defect later. She was too busy looking at "all the pretty things." McCain convinced the jury that she was not paying attention to where she was walking.

One woman fell down a stairway in the Great Moments with Mr. Lincoln theater when, she claimed, the lights were turned off before she could find a seat (*Jolly, 1973*). McCray insisted, however, "The lights were on at the time of the accident, and a spiel was given to watch your step. Apparently the plaintiff, who was accompanied and supported on both sides by her husband and daughter, somehow walked into a roped-off area and missed her step. She's blind in one eye and has trouble seeing out of the other." The case went nowhere.

Disney regularly uses park records to refute a plaintiff's testimony. A 53-year-old housewife wanted $129,000 to cover a twisted ankle and broken finger she suffered when she fell down the stairs from the City Hall restrooms (*Langley, 1976*). She claimed the steps were covered with dirt and debris thrown from an adjacent flowerbed by a small child. McCray simply showed the park had just opened—there wasn't really time for some mystery kid to bury the staircase.

A 63-year-old housewife from Washington was walking toward the Opera House, when she tripped over a curb and broke her leg (*Homier, 1985*). She alleged Disney had allowed so many "unrestrained" visitors into the park, she couldn't see the curb. The woman demanded $200,000. McCain responded that there were no defects in the sidewalk, curb or street, and he used attendance figures to illustrate that the crowds were light that day. Disney won, twelve to none.

Disneyland originally opened with few barriers or fences to keep guests off its grassy and planted areas; Walt just assumed people would know to stay on the clearly marked pathways. Yet as crowds grew thicker and some thought to take shortcuts, guests began trampling the plantings, and Disney countered by adding miniature fences and dividers. The park begrudgingly switched to three-foot-high metal fencing, after people starting tripping over the little ones. Disney usually won such cases, since people were often traveling into areas they shouldn't have when they tripped. But one man who tripped over an uprooted board of a small picket fence around hedges near the Frontierland Train Depot won $1,000 (*Duncan, 1959*).

A ten-year-old boy was playing around the antique Global Van Line truck that used to be displayed in front of the Main Street lockers, when he tripped over the crank, fell forward, and struck his noggin on the headlight cover (*Moss, 1964*). He claimed the crank was not visible at night. But because the crank was set back between the front wheels, the kid was more than likely trying to climb onto the hood. His family eventually dropped their suit.

In 1976, 43-year-old Rita Harris was trying to exit the park when she found her path blocked by a large crowd gathering to receive free Mickey Mouse posters. She tried to avoid the crowd by taking a shortcut through a flower bed, where she tripped on a sprinkler head, bruising her hip and head. After the case mediated for $15,000, Disney made a token offer of $500. Harris insisted on at least $10,000 and went to court, claiming the crowd was out of control and forced her into the flowerbed. The jury believed McCray—that the woman intentionally left the path to take a shortcut.

One woman tried to escape the crowds after Fantasmic by climbing over a rock planter near the River Belle Terrace (*Mohler, 1994*). She fell and broke her ankle. The lady claimed she struck her foot against a rock flower pot, because it was hidden behind a trash can. The jury, however, agreed she should never have been climbing behind trash cans.

Dozens of guests have sued after tripping over curbs they didn't see. Even more have injured ankles when they stepped off a curb or step not realizing there was one. A 53-year-old housewife was descending the stairway to board It's a Small World, when she failed to step down on the last step, because she believed she was already on the platform (*Bates, 1983*). She landed hard on her left foot, fracturing her ankle. Her lawyer argued that the stairway was negligently designed because the handrail deceptively ended at the last step, instead of the platform, giving the illusion that there were no more steps. McCain responded that the handrail was not designed defectively. The area was well lit. The steps had a non-skid coating in blue and, on the last step, a yellow caution line. The plaintiff was simply not paying attention and caused her own injury. Disney won the case, ten to two.

One lady blamed her fall in the Hub on the curb being too close in color to the street (*Smookler-McCole, 1990*). But the judge kicked out her suit upon the discovering the plaintiff was cross-eyed as a child and had corrective surgery that resulted in a lack of depth perception, which prevented her from distinguishing the curb from the street.

A 56-year-old Mickey's Toontown visitor fractured her knee when, as she stepped out of Mickey's House, she didn't notice the step down and fell (*Moshirobanhi, 1995*). She claimed the low level of lighting prevented her from seeing the bright yellow-and-white stripe across the step. The jury didn't buy it.

Several guests have sued after tripping over the trolley tracks that run down Main Street. At least two middle-aged women got their heels stuck between the tracks. The first, 65-year-old Ovella Lamb, was crossing Town Square during a visit in the late 1970s, when her Cuban heel lodged between the rails. She turned, fell and broke her hip. Although nearly all slip-and-fall trials must be held in the county where the accident occurred, at the time "diversity of citizenship" allowed a party from one state suing a party in another state to have the case heard in federal court. So since Lamb was from Oregon, her lawyer, John Francis Carroll, was able to have the case filed in U.S. District Court in Los Angeles.

Carroll alleged the track was a hazard and its groove should have been color-coded. And on cross examination, Disney's expert witness, a chief structural engineer for Imagineering, admitted the groove could be a hazard. McCray, however, argued that any potential hazard was "open and obvious"—anyone seeing it should recognize the potential danger and protect herself against it. "But," countered Carroll, "with the crowds, you're not measuring the size of your heel."

The first trial ended in a hung jury, but Carroll won the retrial, twelve to zero. Lamb was awarded the full amount she was asking for: $75,000. "I never would have won in Santa Ana," Carroll remarked.

During a Grad Nite in 2002, 54-year-old chaperone Nema Swank fell in a similar fashion, but tried a different argument in court. She contended it was too dark to see the tracks. She and her husband had seen the tracks earlier, as they headed for a student check-in at the Plaza Inn, just before the globe lights in the Hub were dimmed for the fireworks. But when the fireworks ended, she claimed the globe lights remained off and she was forced to make her way back across the Hub in the "pitch black." Her husband cautioned her to look out for the tracks. She looked down, took a couple of steps, caught her foot in the tracks, and fell.

At trial, Swank and several other chaperones insisted this Grad Nite was unusually dark, compared to previous Grad Nites they had overseen when there were twinkling lights in the trees and footlights. One chaperone even claimed that she spent a full hour in the Hub between fireworks shows, and the lights were off the entire time. Swank did concede that had the fireworks show still been on, they would have illuminated the tracks.

A Disneyland technical director then testified that the fireworks shows are programmed into the main computer, which also controls the lights. The computer is programmed to turn off the globe lights in the Hub ten seconds before the fireworks begin and turn them back on five seconds after the show ends—commands that cannot be overridden once the show begins. Other lights, including many trimming the castle, remained on during the fireworks. And right before the show began, a DJ warned guests that the lights were about to be turned off. The show was rehearsed twelve times before the first Grad Nite of the season, and a systems check was done every night before the park opened to make sure everything was running properly. After the show, no one reported the lights not coming on. Indeed, a Facilities manager said maintenance records did not show any work requests submitted for the Hub globe lights—something that would have happened had the lights not come back on. The jury believed Disney's witnesses.

Similarly, a 46-year-old woman severely fractured her leg when she stumbled off a curb trying to cross Main Street just before the Electrical Parade began (*Loesch, 1977*). She claimed she couldn't see the curb, because the lights were turned off with the parade moments away. McCray argued that not only should she have known where the curb was, because other guests had been sitting on it for the last half-hour, but where she attempted to cross was a roped-off "crossover" staffed by employees with flashlights. She lost.

Disney has long searched for efficient ways to deter guests from climbing or sitting on railings. A woman in her early 20s was leaning back against the railing in the Big Thunder Mountain queue, when it gave way and she fell to the ground (*Crespo, 1994*). McCain successfully convinced the jury that she was using the railing for other than its intended purpose.

A six-foot-tall accountant waiting in line for the Matterhorn got his foot tangled up in a chain link barrier, causing him to fall and cutting into his jeans and shin (*Webb, 2008*). At First Aid, a nurse applied a bandage to his shin to stop the bleeding, but apparently did nothing to prevent the ensuing infection.

Temporary rope dividers have accounted for even more accidents. In 1969, a visitor to Great Moments with Mr. Lincoln was leaning against a rope divider, when it snapped open, causing her to fall and hurt her hand and wrist (*Bullock*). Disney reminded her that the only way she could have fallen is if she placed her weight upon the rope, and while she was in line a safety message was being delivered over the PA system: "Please do not sit or lean against the ropes and handrails. They were designed only to separate the aisles and will not support your weight. (Pause) Again, for your safety may I remind you to avoid sitting or leaning against the ropes and handrails. Thank you." She quickly abandoned her suit.

More often, guests have sued—albeit usually unsuccessfully—after tripping over crowd control ropes or chains, often claiming they hung dangerously low, creating a tripping hazard. One particularly sympathetic victim—a five-year-old who ran into crowd control ropes set up for the Electrical Parade, fell and fractured her skull—did receive a settlement (*Digerose, 1980*).

In the park's earliest days, temporary crowd-control ropes were created by stringing a rope between metal poles on a circular base, like at a movie theater. But these stanchions were easier to knock over and, because they could be set up at varying distances between each other, the ropes between them often sagged to trip-level heights. So, early on, in an effort to make temporary stanchions more stable, Disney began drilling metal-ringed holes in the pavement, into which the poles could be quickly inserted. But when they weren't being used, the holes themselves could create a tripping hazard. One 52-year-old woman said she was strolling near the Rivers of America during a drizzle and slipped on a hole, which had filled up with rainwater (*Hubert, 1983*). The fall fractured her shoulder and knocked her unconscious. The jury agreed with Disney, eleven to one, that the holes were safe.

The mother of a mentally disabled 23-year-old blamed a similar hole for her son's fall on Main Street (*Covarrubias, 1999*). At First Aid, his mother told the nurse he "stepped off the curb and twisted his ankle." After being given an ice pack, he returned to the park. But three months later, he went to the hospital to remove a cyst on his spinal cord. The surgery left him a paraplegic. His mother filed suit against the park, claiming her son had tripped in a dangerous hole. As evidence, she identified on videotape the exact spot of the accident: a hole with a sleeve for a parade acrobat to insert his pole. She pointed out a graying area around the hole, which she argued showed the post sleeve was sinking. Disney, however, used maintenance records to show that the shadowy area was actually a repair made to the sleeve after a workman nicked it while drilling into the concrete a year after her son's fall. The supposed cause of the accident didn't exist at the time of the accident. The jury ruled for Disney.

Several guests have sued after the chairs they were sitting in collapsed—

FANTASYLAND'S Sword in the Stone display was patterned after the rectangular rock in the 1963 animated movie, but had to be chiseled down after a girl climbed up its side and fell off.

including folding chairs on the Mark Twain (*Musolf, 1958*), a redwood bench at Casa de Fritos (*Bailey, 1964*), a plastic seat inside the Captain EO theater (*O'Sorup, 1994*), and a toilet in Fantasyland's Princess restroom (*Hotzinger, 2002*). One woman tried to lean against a round table on the Village Haus patio, but the table spun and she went flying (*Fernandez, 1996*). Disney offered $5,000. She wanted $100,000. They met in the middle.

Occasionally, Disney discovers some seemingly safe elements could be made even safer. The park would use tall sprinklers to water shrubs in the planters, such as a brick-lined flower bed that ran around the back of the Matterhorn. "The line for the Matterhorn would extend back there and there was no crowd control, so you had guests sitting, standing and running on the planter. One guest tripped," said Disney's Jan Doezie. "We settled for like $3,000, and I told them to put in below-ground sprinklers that pop up."

The Sword in the Stone display in Fantasyland was originally modeled after its cartoon counterpart—a gold-handled blade set in an anvil sitting on a somewhat rectangular rock. In 1993, an eight-year-old girl climbed on top of the rock and fell off (*Stewart*). The park settled, but not before slicing the corners off the stone to create a near-triangular-shaped structure that's much harder to climb on.

In 2012, a young lady entered the Main Street Fire Station to view the old-fashioned pictures on the wall and the fireman's pole, but as she walked away, she tripped over a metal fire water bucket bolted to the floor (*Cox*). According to her suit, "The metal bucket was deformed, with sharp, jagged edges, and located in a relatively darkened location adjacent by the pole." She cut her left ankle, requiring stitches and leaving a scar. Disney quickly removed the bucket and paid her off.

The steep steps of the Swiss Family-turned-Tarzan's Treehouse could be particularly difficult to navigate. Attorney Amy Fisch Solomon nearly declined a case brought by a father who was carrying his toddler when he stumbled down the treehouse steps and broke his leg (*Smithour, c. 2002*). "Initially, I thought, 'Yeah, people fall down stairs all the time,'" she said. "But I went to investigate: The stairs are wood and they have been traveled. The stair risers were all eroded. Human nature assumes that there will be relatively even steps. The old rope handrail, left over the Swiss Family Robinson, was not effective. Disney really pooh-poohed me."

But, like the Ovella Lamb trolley track case more than 20 years before, Solomon was able to have the case tried in federal court in Los Angeles and swayed all twelve jurors.

The Favell family of Washington wasn't so lucky. In 1993, John Favell was stepping off the last car of the Disneyland Railroad onto the east bridge of the Main Street Station, his fourteen-month-old toddler Carley in his arms, when he lost his balance and began to fall. He instinctively reached out to grab the train's roof to stop his fall, but in doing so lost hold of Carley. She flew out of his arms and over the railing, and down eighteen feet to the pavement below, landing on the left side of her head. Her mother ran hysterically down to her child, only to pass out when she reached the base of the staircase. Carley had broken her skull and collarbone, and would develop a blood clot on her brain and suffer seizures.

In the aftermath, Disney raised the railing on the bridge to five feet—a height Carley would not have cleared had it been in place at the time of the accident. Nonetheless, the Uniform Building Code, which required railings to be 42 inches high, grandfathered in railings that were at least 36 high and had been installed before 1970. The old railing was 37 inches high. The company was cleared by eight of the twelve jurors.

In time, Disney began increasing the height of railings across the park, particularly those above bodies of water. In 2013, a boy stood up on one of

THE TRAIN STATION fencing was increased to five feet high in the section over the east entrance tunnel after a child fell over the railing.

the built-in stone seats leading to the castle, lost his balance, and tumbled into some bushes near the moat. Out came the tape measures. Disney discovered the stone walls along the bridgeway were only 34 inches high, so they added miniature railing extensions along the top to reach 42 inches—and jackhammered away all the built-in stone seats in the wall's alcoves, just in case.

Island of Adventure

Inch for inch, more falls have occurred on Tom Sawyer Island than anywhere else in the park. The rough terrain and primitive amusements— wobbly pontoon and suspension bridges, low-clearance caves, rock-shaped merry-go-round and teeter-totter—invited rambunctiousness with a hint of danger. But that was okay, because back in the Fifties, if a kid climbing a rock fell off, he might look upon his scrapes as a badge of honor and his parents would usually respond by telling him to be more careful.

Walt realized that with all the more complicated machinery and watchful attendants throughout the rest of the park, Tom Sawyer Island would be the one place without lines and specific rules; kids could basically run free.

"Walt said he put the paths on Tom Sawyer Island for the adults. He wanted the kids to explore," recalled Tom Nabbe, who played Huck Finn on the island when it opened in 1956. "Once in a while, you'd get an overzealous security officer who would enforce the kids on the paths. The only 'you do not cross the line' barrier was behind the fort—a barbed wire fence to keep you away from the burning cabin." Initially, there wasn't even any fencing along the waterline, just a perimeter of small shrubs and bushes; guests didn't have to be warned that if they got too close to the edge, they might get a little wet.

The island was patrolled by two or three security guards dressed as cavalry officers, primarily there to respond to any emergencies. Falls were frequent, leading to more than three dozen lawsuits. Disney settled a few of the more difficult cases for modest amounts—a girl who flew off Merry-Go-Round Rock received $3,000 (*Cummings, 1958*), and a boy who spun off and chipped a tooth got $750 (*Snider, 1960*). Undisclosed amounts were given to a doctor who injured his leg when a boy came running down from the opposite end of the pontoon bridge, causing it to overturn, throwing him in the river, and injuring his leg (*Rosenwasser, 1962*). As well, Disney struck a deal with two elderly women who claimed they were terrorized on the barrel bridge by several boys, who began rocking the bridge and knocked the ladies over (*Serradell, 1974*).

But for the standard stumble on the dirt or tumble off the rocks, Disney was prepared to go the distance. The dangers of running along a dirt path or climbing on big rocks were inherent and obvious, and victims were ultimately the cause of their own falls. Most plaintiffs begrudgingly came to this realization and abandoned their cases. Ten cases made it to trial. Disneyland won them all.

In 1958, a woman said she lost her footing on the loose gravel, so she reached out for a rock to steady herself. The rock turned out to be Teeter-Totter Rock, so she fell to the ground *(Stevenson)*. McCray convinced the jury that the fault for falling was her own—and that the purpose of Teeter-

Totter Rock was to teeter and totter, not to remain stationary.

Five years later, a woman stumbled while walking on a dirt pathway, as countless dozens of other guests had done that same week (*Howie*). Yet this lady claimed she was "violently thrown to ground" due to the "dangerous passageway." McCray successfully responded that an inanimate path cannot violently throw someone to the ground.

As time went on, Disney did make the walkways more defined and had security gently encourage guests to stay on them. It also used to have crushed seashells on the paths, for aesthetics and traction, but guests would cut themselves on the shells. So the paths were converted to decomposed granite, a softer yet more slippery surface.

With one merry-go-round case, Disney was unable to reach a compromise, so it was forced to go to court (*Makoutz, 1969*). A four-year-old boy flew off into the bushes, cutting his chin and requiring stitches. But dad's claims far exceeded the possibility of later scarring. He claimed his son had begun suffering seizures, periodic trances, and out-of-control behavior. He suspected the boy had suffered brain injuries, which would inevitably lead to retarded learning capacity, hyperactivity, speech defects, post-traumatic epilepsy, chronic brain syndrome with post-traumatic personality disorder, and an affected demeanor in his whole body. His symptoms were growing worse by the day. The father's claims were so outrageous, the jury sided with Disney.

In 1977, a 26-year-old school teacher and aspiring actress said that she had fallen in a hole in the middle of a dirt path, because employees had deviously covered it up with loose dirt to create a trap (*Salkin*). She sprained her knee, back and shoulder and broke a toenail. Disney responded that the woman and her friends had previously been detained on the island for violating park rules. No one witnessed the accident, and the "trap" could not later be found, so McCray convinced the jury that an accident never occurred.

In 1989, a twelve-year-old boy claimed he had gotten lost in Injun Joe's Cave and sought his escape in a roundabout way — across a steep embankment (*Greig*). He slipped and, while falling, grabbed onto an overhanging tree branch, but his grip gave way and he hit the ground, breaking his wrist. He required two surgeries and lost strength in his wrist. His lawyer demanded $50,000 in damages. McCain got the boy's mother to admit that her son was climbing the tree and fell, and that he suffered other accidents after the trip to Disneyland that aggravated his wrist. The jury

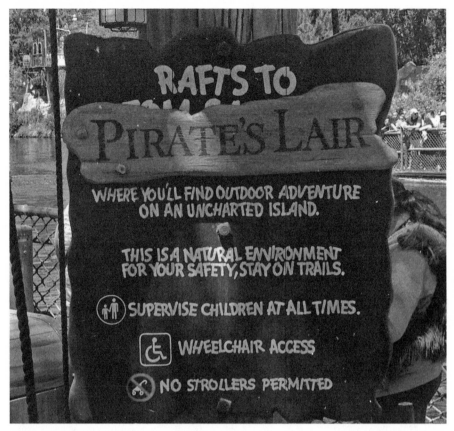

TOM SAWYER ISLAND was originally designed for kids to go "off road," free from their parents' watchful eye—the opposite of the area's current directive.

ruled for Disney, eleven to one.

Five years later, a 61-year-old woman fell 21 inches off a rock and landed on her back, suffering a compression fracture (*Pedersen, 1994*). She claimed that there were no warnings, barriers or handrails, and that 21 inches was way too high for steps on a pedestrian walkway. McCain argued that the area wasn't a pedestrian walkway, it was the "climbing rocks." Signs were posted urging guests to use caution when climbing. And there were alternate routes for her to take. She fell when she was back-pedaling outside the caves. The trial lasted six days, but the jury needed just two hours to rule for Disney, eleven to one.

Then in 2000, a 34-year-old woman hit her head on the low ceiling of the caves (*Patino*). Disney settled the case in mediation, but began taking a hard look at the island rockwork. Soon after, a six-year-old girl was playing with the toy rifle in the turret of the island's fort when she slipped—but a ring on her trigger finger got caught in the handle and the finger was torn from her hand (*Figueroa, 2001*). She was rushed to the hospital, but, because the tear was not a clean one, doctors were unable to reattach her finger. Disneyland temporarily shut down the island. Although the mishap was unique, the fort and its stairwells were a common site for falls. Disney removed the rifles and settled the girl's suit for $225,000 plus $20,000 in reimbursed medical expenses.

The following summer, a pair of accidents days apart—a girl sprained her wrist on Teeter-Totter Rock and another fractured her skull after falling off the climbing rocks—proved enough for park lawyers. They decided to fence off all amusements on the island. Teeter-Totter Rock was removed. (Merry-Go-Round Rock had already been torn out, a few years prior.) Low-hanging rocks and protrusions were chiseled down. Extra handrails were installed throughout the caves. The fort's doors were permanently locked. Mind you, guests were still allowed to visit the island during its neutering, they just couldn't touch anything.

Five years later, Disney tore down the termite-infested fort and rebuilt it as a no-guests-allowed dressing room for the Fantasmic actors. The rest of the island received a pirates makeover, with a ship's wheel to turn, bilge pumps to pump, and other interactive show elements. Now, with all activities regulated, Disney no longer had to station any security officers on the island. Every once in a while, a raft driver could give the island the once-over to make sure nothing was amiss.

In the end, the greatest thing Tom Sawyer Island lost wasn't its Tom Sawyer theming, it was its freedom. Kids used to be able to run wild, playing make believe, living whatever adventure their imaginations could dream up. From here on out, Disney would tell them exactly what and how to play.

Hard Hits

Several dozen guests have also sued after objects fell on them. In 1955, a customer at the Penny Arcade had a large wooden "door-like object" fall on her leg (*Pastor*). Two years later, a mannequin fell off a table at

Pendleton Woolen Mills and bumped a woman on the head (*Sloan*). Another Pendleton shopper was hit by a falling bolt of clothing (*Jalbert, 1966*). Several guests were struck by toppled trash cans. A middle-aged Club 33 diner won $15,000 at trial after an ice sculpture fell on her and broke her ankle (*Gribin, 1975*).

Less successful was a three-year-old Autopia passenger whose mother claimed was struck by a light pole that fell down next to the track (*Abbasyadeh, 1988*). Although no one saw the pole hit the boy, he started crying and his mother noticed a welt on his head and a red streak across his face. She said he subsequently began exhibiting erratic behavior, nervousness, hyperactivity, bedwetting and forgetfulness, and insisted her son was suffering post-concussion syndrome and brain damage. A cast member testified that he was the one actually hit by the light post. And spy work by McCain revealed that the boy's behavioral changes were due to a chaotic family life caused by major marital discord and that the red mark on his face was caused by allergies he had suffered since birth.

Disney did pay off a man who leaned back against a tree on Main Street and was electrocuted by loose wiring (*Perez, 2005*), as well as a woman who, while walking through New Orleans Square, had the end of a heavy string of lights fall from a building, strike her in the face, and flip her over a wall and into a planter (*Mays, 2009*).

Real trees have also been an occasional problem, due to their advanced age. Numerous trees in the park were left over from the property's prior life as farmland. Others were planted during construction, as already mature trees. In 1992, a woman sitting on a planter was struck on the head and shoulders by a limb that fell out of a tree (*Melcher*).

Nineteen years later, a day after particularly high winds, an entire 20-foot-tall oak tree toppled in front of the Golden Horseshoe Saloon, smashing a food cart and landing on top of a crowded walkway (*Madrijal, 2001*). A 73-year-old woman suffered a broken hip. In all, 27 guests and two cast members suffered cuts, scratches and bruises; eighteen were taken to the hospital. Within hours, maintenance crews chopped up the entire tree and pulverized the branches in a wood chipper. Two days later, a 20-foot ficus along the Jungle Cruise fell over, toppling another sixteen-foot-tall tree on the way down. Disney quickly went to work trimming back or entirely uprooting older trees throughout the park—and settled all claims.

Ten years later, a woman was sitting at the park's picnic area, when a six-foot-long tree branch fell on her head (*Pina, 2011*). The branch was so heavy, she was pinned under her daughter's stroller and pleaded for other guests to pull it off. She suffered cuts, bruises, sprained neck and back, and continuing dizziness, difficulty sleeping, and "mild nervousness." She blamed Disney for not adequately maintaining the tree or noticing that it was severely sagging, weighed down by massive fruit. In addition, her suit charged, "There are no signs posted in the picnic area warning patrons of falling branches. Trees are not at eye level, so the defendant cannot reasonably expect patrons to walk with their heads and eyes facing up to watch for potentially falling branches." The park settled.

The most common object guests are struck by are umbrellas. In 1978, a woman was dining on the Plaza Pavilion patio, near a row of umbrellas stands being used to anchor crowd control ropes (*Kemp, 1978*). A boy fell on the nylon rope, sending the umbrellas on top of the diner. Usually, injuries from such accidents are modest and Disney will settle (*Hurst, 1997; Boop, 2005; Narvaez, 2007*). Yet, one 32-year-old River Belle Terrace diner suffered a head injury after a large gust of wind swept up a table umbrella and sent its metal pole flying into her temple (*Harrison, 2009*). She developed a headache and was taken to First Aid, where she rested for about an hour. She'd actually suffered a microscopic brain injury, later not even detectable on a CAT scan or MRI. Eleven days later, she suffered a grand mal seizure. The jury agreed that Disneyland was negligent in failing to properly secure the umbrella and awarded her $546,000.

Accusations regarding objects that were blown into guests by the elements are a little harder to prove Disney was at fault because it has to be shown that Disney was negligent in not securing the objects. That wasn't a problem for a man who was struck in the chest and knocked over by a big metal sheet blown off the top of a popcorn cart by a gust of wind (*Davidson, 2010*).

Since Disneyland is responsible for the actions performed by its cast members within their normal scope of duty, when an employee inadvertently strikes or runs into a guest, Disney is pretty much on the hook. The park usually will settle, if it can reach a fair compromise, often a little more than the cost of their medical bills.

That was the case with at least a half-dozen guests who were run into by large metal carts, including one wheelchair-bound woman who was blindsided by a cart and then the worker who was pushing it fell on top of her (*Deturk, 1992*). Another woman was run over by a garbage bin pushed by a cast member (*Horning, 2002*). And a third settled after a custodian, out cleaning up debris after a parade, drove a giant motorized leaf blower over her foot (*Hancock, 1990*).

In 1976, a 56-year-old woman was waiting in line to ride the Jungle Cruise, when an employee came by, carrying several long poles and accidentally dropped them on her toe (*Silkiewicz*). She demanded not a penny less than $5,000. Disney offered $4,000. She refused, before later agreeing to a compromise.

Years later, a man was waiting for his stroller near Small World, when a cast member walked past him pushing a soda cart, which became tangled in a crowd-control rope strung between two light posts (*Gala, 2009*). A male employee arrived to assist her, but—against her pleas—began forcefully pushing the cart through the rope barricade with all his weight, causing the heavy light post to crash down on top of the guest. The visitor was immediately knocked to the ground and rendered unconscious. He later awoke, nauseous, dizzy, with cuts to his head, burning in his eye, and deep pain in his neck. The park quickly settled.

Inadvertent physical contact often occurs in the restaurants, as servers and busboys hurriedly attempt to navigate the crowds. A fourteen-year-old girl suffered second- and third-degree burns when a restaurant worker carrying a boiling teapot at the Plaza Inn accidentally spilled hot water on her hand, wrist and arm (*Norton, 1965*). A Blue Bayou diner was hit in the head by a plate that fell off a server's tray (*Lopez, 1991*). Another Blue Bayou diner had an employee moving an ECV (Electric Convenience Vehicle) out of the way drive into the back of her chair (*Peluso, 2004*). She alleged back pain—and a $20,000 bill to treat it. Another woman was walking through the Plaza Inn, when a waiter came running through the restaurant, while talking to a co-worker. He ran into the lady and knocked her to the floor (*Bays, 2005*). A Blue Bayou guest suffered second-degree burns when hot coffee was poured on his right arm (*Kwon, 2008*). Another woman demanded $10,000 after a Blue Bayou hostess pulled a chair out from under her, just as she was about to sit down, while she was carrying her child (*Crosby, 1999*). The jury awarded her the full amount.

The cases Disney does win are those in which they can prove that the guest was doing something he or she wasn't supposed to. In 1962, a woman wanted $50,000 after claiming a Golden Horseshoe Revue employee shoved her off the wooden boardwalk in front of the theater (*Prestia*). She testified that while she was waiting in line, the worker came out to inform the crowd that the next show was sold out. As he threw his arms in the air to signal for everyone to move back in line, he accidentally pushed her off the boardwalk, injuring her ankle and palm. Disney insisted there had been no contact. She walked backwards off the boardwalk by herself. First Aid records confirmed she was treated for moderate swelling, given two aspirin, and advised to get some ice and rest. The jury believed Disney.

An elderly woman said a sweeper whacked her in the ankle with a broom, causing her to fall to the pavement, scrape her knee, and throw out her shoulder (*Hernandez, 2001*). She admitted the custodian was blocking her path to the Plaza Inn, so she was trying to walk around him when she made contact with the broom. Another woman was heading for the exit of a temporary meet-and-greet, Baloo's Dressing Room, when an employee swung open the door into her (*Vlaovich-Ramierz, 1991*). She said she suffered four herniated discs in her neck and lower back, and racked up $500,000 in medicals costs. Disney convinced the jury that she should have seen the door coming. Similarly, a jury believed that a 43-year-old woman who collided with an employee rolling a giant umbrella through Frontierland should have been looking where she was going (*Schmidt, 1995*).

A 24-year-old man claimed he was watching the Mark Twain, when an employee pushed a four-foot-tall silver cart over his right foot, breaking his big toe (*Roberts, 1980*). He asked for just $2,600, to cover his medical bills, the loss of a couple days earnings, and pain and suffering. But this time, Disney refused to settle, because it had no report of any such accident occurring. At trial, McCain claimed the man must have broken his toe at some point prior to visiting the park, and the plaintiff was unable to identify the employee or the "phantom cart." Disneyland won a unanimous decision.

During the Main Street Electrical Parade's farewell season, a woman was sitting on a curb watching the parade when a driver allegedly lost control of a train float and ran over her foot (*Guenther, 1996*). She said it took three minutes for a group of men to roll the train off.

A few years later, Disney made the mistake of running the Christmas Parade in the rain. As the Aladdin float—a magic carpet/sleigh driven by a costumed Genie—tried to turn away from the crowd in the Small World mall area, its tires lost traction and the side of the carpet slammed into four guests along the curb. One woman, a 34-year-old immigrant from Guatemala, was knocked unconscious and suffered bruises to the face (*Perez, 2004*).

Inadvertent contact is even more likely for the costumed characters, who often have an impaired field of vision and are wearing bulky costumes with odd protrusions. A 49-year-old woman was watching the Christmas Parade from Town Square, when the Mad Hatter came marching by (*Gurll, 1960*). The old costume's gigantic hat and rubber head went down to the actor's hips and could be difficult to control, so that when the actor began to bow, his rubber face banged the poor woman in the head. She said "the sharp, unexpected blow to the top of the head" gave her a jolting pain to the head, neck and spine, down to her feet, and a sore, stiff back. Her neck was in traction, and she continued to suffer back spasms, numbness in her hands and arms, aggravated arthritis, and difficulty gripping objects and sleeping. The park settled.

Another woman was standing next to Darth Vader, when the actor tried to shoo away a bird by forcefully swinging his right arm (*Urlich, 2011*). He inadvertently hit her in the back, causing a strain and a deep bruise. When the numbness, tingling and difficulty sleeping continued, she sought $25,000 to cover her medical expenses. Disney settled.

The majority of character-related lawsuits occur as a result of playfulness gone horribly wrong. The actors are trained to act like their cartoon counterparts and interact with guests accordingly—a potentially troubling scenario if they're playing a taunting villain or an overly spunky character like one of the Three Little Pigs. A twelve-year-old girl said that, while posing with one of the bears in Frontierland, the character grabbed her around the neck and began strangling her (*Stormer, 1986*). She said she cried for him to let go and tried to break free, but "John Doe Bear" refused to release her. She sued for assault and battery, and money to cover her soft tissue neck and back injuries. Her case was mediated for $350, but Disney pressed for a trial. Three years later, the case was dismissed for "failure to proceed with reasonable diligence."

A man said he was walking hand-in-hand with his girlfriend, when either Tweedle Dee or Tweedle Dum attempted to break through their hands from behind (*Su, 2005*). The couple held fast, and the character continued to try to break the link, until the man felt a strange sensation in his left arm and elbow. He released his girlfriend's hand and cried for a nurse, as the character purportedly fled the scene. The victim complained of numbness and tingling, and was taken to the emergency room. Disney settled.

A tourist from Las Vegas and her eight-year-old granddaughter accused the Big Bad Wolf of stalking them down Main Street one night (*Sewell, 1995*). Grandma repeatedly told the wolf to stay away, but he kept coming back. She sat down on a bench, thinking the ordeal had ended, when the wolf snuck up behind her and suddenly jumped in front of her face. The woman was so terrified, she "jumped onto the bench in an attempt to escape the perceived threat and danger, and was caused to fall and receive injuries to her back, spine, shoulder, and severe shock to her nervous system." Employees supposedly refused to assist her. The eight-year-old also suffered soft tissue neck injuries in attempting to avoid the wolf, as well as emotional stress and strain, and "psychic injuries in the nature of damage to her fantasy expectations, images and illusions fostered by promotional plans and schemes of Disneyland."

Occasionally, guests are unknowingly too fragile to be played with. A 54-year-old woman said she was sitting in a chair, minding her own business, when Mary Poppins walked up and tried to lift her to her feet (*McClain, 1974*). She said the yank exacerbated a cervical fusion. The character denied everything, but the park nonetheless offered $1,700. The woman agreed to slightly more.

One visitor said she and two children stopped to have their picture taken with the Three Little Pigs, when, for no reason, Fifer Pig shoved one of the girls down (*Levy, 1980*). Mom saw her falling and tried to catch her, but lost her balance, tumbled and fractured her ankle. She wanted $75,000. Disney offered nothing. They insisted that Fiddler Pig was wiggling his nose and stomach, which got another guest laughing and the spectator backed into the woman, knocking her down. There was no way the company could have anticipated such an accident. All twelve jurors ruled for Disneyland.

Another lady claimed she was molested by Fiddler Pig (*Mick, 1976*). She was minding her own business, when the renegade pig ran up to her and grabbed her breast, then her arm and waist, pulling her closer and squealing, "Oh, mother! Mother!"—implying that the "plaintiff was mother to a pig." She cried for him to release her, but he held tighter. The crowd laughed. The woman was mortified. She fell into severe depression, and her weight ballooned to 240 pounds. She filed suit, seeking $150,000 for false imprisonment, assault and battery, physical pain, mental anguish, and humiliation.

Disney, though, knew the incident could not have happened as claimed, because the character's arms were inoperable stumps. Inside the costume's sleeves, the actors held round handles attached to the hardened hands. The plaintiff's lawyer learned this when he deposed the pig, played by Glenn Raines.

"Across the table, the plaintiff's lawyer claimed the pig pinched this woman," Raines recalled. "At that moment, the Disney lawyer took one of the pig's hands and dropped it on the conference table with a thud, showing how rigid and non-dexterous those things are."

Although the defendant claimed the attack occurred near It's a Small World, Disney insisted that at the time the pigs were appearing near First Aid, where lost children are taken to be reunited with their parents. "In the deposition, she said, 'The pig was running around calling me "Mommy, mommy."' I said there were probably a lot of lost children running around, looking for their mommies. I may very well have chased her and hugged her. That's the kind of thing we did with everyone."

The lawyer declined to continue with the case, and it was later dismissed for failure to bring it to trial within five years.

More often, it was the characters who took a beating from the guests. Kids took wild delight in pinching, punching, shoving and kicking the costumed actors, perhaps thinking they were indestructible Wile E. Coyotes. The actors would devise various maneuvers of self-defense to lessen the blows—perhaps twisting their bodies to lessen the impact or stepping out of the way.

Few were more adept at dodging blows than Robert Hill. Hill, who joined the Character Department in 1969, wasn't your happy, carefree cast member. He preferred playing the sullen donkey Eeyore, trudging about true to character and upset when other actors would play Eeyore upbeat, to get cheap laughs. The costume's large paws made it difficult to sign autographs, so Hill usually refused—resulting in several written reprimands. When he did sign, to be authentic he wrote, "EOR," as Eeyore did in the A.A. Milne books—baffling most of the guests.

Hill and his fellow characters were especially on alert on Sundays, which in the 1970s was the day of the week that attracted the highest percentage of Hispanic guests, who had a reputation for being more aggressive with the characters. Hill said cast members would joke that they would "go to church, confess their sins, then come to the park and beat the hell out of us so they'd have something new to talk about next week."

One summer day, Hill was greeting guests between the Plaza Inn and First Aid, dressed as Winnie the Pooh. On top of Pooh's head was a giant fiberglass honey pot that covered the actor's head and had subtle patches of black screening in the front and back, for the actor to look through. A tall, nine-year-old girl approached from the rear and socked him in the back.

"Boom! You might as well be in an oil drum," Hill recalled. He turned his head inside the honey pot, to look out the back while the girl thought he was still looking straight ahead. "I saw her winding up for a second run on me, so I spun around to scare her, but she was too close and Pooh's ear caught her in the side of her head. The ear was a fur-covered fiberglass shell. Her father said, 'Why did you hit my daughter for no reason?' Hit her? In this thing? My arms were hanging like something on a seal. I was harmless. But I could tell we had to get out of there."

The Pooh troupe hurried off stage, and Hill went to tell his lead what happened. He recalled, "The next thing you know, the family is at City Hall, where the situation multiplied. They registered an official complaint: you 'beat and battered my child.' My supervisor came and asked for my story. He saw no issue with it. At the time, the leads knew the limitations of the costumes, because they had all come up through the ranks themselves."

The girl's family filed suit, demanding $15,000 (*Lopez, 1974*). She said she spent about $160 on medication, to treat residual headaches. Both parties agreed to go to non-binding arbitration, where she was awarded $1,000. Disney said they wouldn't pay more than $500. The family said they'd already spent about $160 on medication, that the girl had suffered deep bruises, persistent headaches, and possibly future brain damage, so they wouldn't go below $1,000. The lawyer thought he was calling McCray's bluff. After all, did Disney want to risk the media attention of Winnie the Pooh slapping a little kid?

The case finally made it to trial six years later. McCray had wanted Hill to testify holding the Pooh costume, so he could point out its limitations. Hill refused. Disney had a strict policy to never publicly display a broken-down costume. If he was going to demonstrate the costume, he was going to be inside it.

So, he first took the stand as himself, to tell his side of the story—that he didn't slap her; he accidentally bumped her with a furry ear after being pushed from behind. Two things furry characters are never allowed to do are talk and retaliate. Then, after a brief recess, he reentered the courtroom—as Pooh. He demonstrated what he did at the park by skipping, dancing and nuzzling the court reporter.

"The plaintiff's attorney, when he saw me come out with the costume, I swear he did a facepalm. 'We're screwed,'" Hill said. "I skip out, the whole bit, you hear all the people: 'Oooooh.' Even the non-smiling bailiff was smiling. Meanwhile, I'm looking back at the jury room, and it's filling up with spectators. 'You're not gonna believe it—Winnie the Pooh's on trial!' It was standing room only in the back."

Finally, McCray asked Pooh how high he could lift his paws. Since the arms were inoperable stubs, he couldn't get them more than three feet off the ground—and the girl got hit in the head five feet high.

It took the jury 21 minutes to find Disney innocent. After the ruling, the bailiffs and other court staff asked Hill to put the costume back on, to pose for pictures with them.

It took nearly 30 years before another costumed character would get back on the stand. In 2004, 51-year-old Dwight Palmatier said he was walking, hand in hand with his wife past the Matterhorn, when an actor playing the Queen of Hearts, who reportedly was late for his lunch break, "came running as fast as he could," Palmatier recounted. "He ran directly into me. My foot embedded in his dress and, instead of stopping, he continued up the corridor, dragging me about five or six feet. My wife holding my hand and him dragging me by the foot, pulled my knees. When the individual was maybe 40 feet up the hill, he turned around and put one hand on his hip and pointed at me with the other and wagged a finger like a grandmother, making a gesture like it was my fault. My knees were so sore, I thought I'd better report it. So we went to the nurse. I told the gentleman what was going on, what happened. He put me in a wheelchair and had me taken to my room (at the Grand Californian). I had my wife take pictures of my black-and-blue knees."

His doctor advised surgery, but Disney refused to pay, denying the collision ever happened. At the time, he hadn't thought to talk to witnesses. And, unfortunately, by the time the case made it to trial, Palmatier had suffered two heart attacks and was on medication that affected his memory.

During the two-day trial, he said, "when they asked me questions, my reaction time was not the same (due to the medication) and I couldn't remember where the incident occurred. The person who was working at First Aid that day testified he didn't know me, that he'd never heard of me and didn't have record of me, even though he gave me a wheelchair. The (guy who played the) Queen of Hearts came up to the stand and lied. They showed the jury the costume. Alice in Wonderland came and testified in costume, as a character reference. The jury found her very sympathetic. They were going to bring in other characters from the Alice in Wonderland group, but they cut to the quick. My pain was real. The bruises were real. The operations I went through were real, but I could not identify the location, which undermined my credibility in the jury's eyes." They ruled for Disney and made Palmatier pay the company's court costs.

To maintain better control over guest-character interactions, Disneyland has increasingly prohibited characters from walking through the parks, where they used to randomly wander across, frolic with, and entertain the guests. Now, most characters spend their days standing in an exact, predetermined location, posing for pictures and signing autographs. Meeting characters is no longer a spontaneous event; guests know exactly which ones will be where and when, and head to the back of a nice, orderly line for their 30 seconds of face time (as a "character wrangler" stands nearby with a counter to make sure each character meets its quota of interactions).

Rambunctious kids have less opportunity to beat up on the characters, and, in the more sedate meetings, the characters have less opportunity to inadvertently beat up on the kids. Yet one family accused the White Rabbit of not getting physical enough with their children (*Black, 2012*). The African American Black family arrived at Disneyland to celebrate one son's sixth birthday. As they entered Town Square, they noticed the White Rabbit standing alone near City Hall. The boy reached out to hug the character, but the bunny allegedly "reacted in dramatic, forceful, physically intimidating, and coercive ways (shaking his hand to make Kobe lose his grip, turning his back, stepping away, etc.). This demonstrated that 'White' did not want to touch or be touched by Kobe, and to interfere with Kobe's attempts to interact with White in the same manner other children interact with other Disney characters." After his concerned parents snapped an awkward photo, their other children stepped up to greet the rabbit and "were rejected in the same discriminatory manner." The parents were appalled to realize White was treating them and their children "in a hateful manner, apparently because of their race and skin color." Their suspicions were confirmed when they saw him warmly embrace the non-African American children who had been standing behind them in line.

Since the incident took place directly in front of City Hall, the family walked right in and demanded to file a written complaint and speak with White's supervisors. As proof, the Blacks displayed digital photos they'd taken of the Rabbit uncomfortably posing with their children, along with a shot of White affectionately cradling an Asian child. The supervisors reportedly asked them to destroy all the photos. The Blacks reluctantly agreed to delete the one photo of the Asian kid, after being told they were violating the lad's privacy. The confrontation so upset the family, they left the park and started looking for a civil rights lawyer.

Their lawsuit—*Black v. White*—accused Disney of negligent training and supervision, and White of discrimination, intimidation, coercion and being unfit to portray the character because of his racial biases. But the real sore point, unmentioned in the suit, was how their concerns were brushed off by management.

Their attorney, Daniel Gilleon, recalled, "At City Hall, my clients were given the attitude: 'Here's a photo. We'll sign it, then go away.' If that doesn't work, the next step is, 'We'll give you four passes, then go away.' The next step is, 'We'll give you $500, then go away,' and then they dig in their heels. When one side has a legitimate complaint, they should just say, 'We're sorry. How can we make this right?' Instead their reaction is 'Go away. Pound sand. This didn't happen. But here's some park-hoppers.'"

Gilleon had little trouble drumming up media attention for his case—the racist White Rabbit discriminating against the black Black family—hoping to shame Disney into handling the case quickly. What the media attention did was bring a number of other guests out of the woodwork who claimed that their children had also been rebuffed by assorted characters.

To Gilleon's surprise, once the Disney lawyers got involved, the case was settled in short order, for "a fair amount." He said the quick resolution was "a combination of the media attention and the fact that the clients and I didn't care about the money. Once (Disney) got past this whole dismissive attitude and started talking to my clients respectfully, the steam came out of the bubble. They had been treated with complete disrespect. (Disney's) attorneys were respectful, professional and open to me saying there's a different way. If they handled it differently in the beginning, it would have never gotten this far."

III

Rides Gone Wrong

To CONVINCINGLY TRANSPORT visitors to faraway places and distant time periods, Walt insisted on every element of the illusion being as true as possible to the theme. His old-fashioned trains and boats and cars should look and sound and feel exactly like he imagined they did in their heyday. Now, that didn't mean he wanted to restore vintage vehicles. More often, he wanted replicas that looked and performed better than the originals. That way, he could customize their capacity, redesign them to theme park needs, and add modern safety enhancements, disguised behind the facade of antiquity. His horse-drawn fire wagon was designed to transport sightseers, not to fight fires.

Walt envisioned Main Street USA as a real street, from a real past, with a steady flow of vehicles trafficking down it. To be true to the turn-of-the-century setting, Main Street originally opened with strictly horse-drawn conveyances — surreys, streetcars, and the fire wagon. The greatest challenge was navigating them among the pedestrians. The surreys, the lightest of the vehicles, would prove the most dangerous. Ten surrey riders sued the park during the vehicles' decade and a half of operation. In 1957, a woman fell to the pavement when, just as she began to step off the surrey, the horses started walking (*Dossman*). She won her case and $1,000.

Less than three months later, seven surrey passengers filed suit when something frightened one of the horses and the team began to bolt down Main Street, toward Town Square (*Kohl; Ure, 1958*). The driver struggled to rein in the horses, as they sprinted between the pedestrians. Finally, he

was able to slow them down as they took the turn near the train station—
until a front wheel struck a curb and the surrey started to overturn, tipping
against a gas lamp. Several passengers were ejected from the coach; others
had to crawl out.

Because all the passengers were making the same claims over the same
incident, they were consolidated into a single suit. To lower their burden of
proof, their lawyers cleverly petitioned to have the surrey legally classified
as a "common carrier"—a novel idea for an amusement park ride. The
designation originated in the 1800s, to force operators of railways,
steamboats and stagecoaches to exhibit the *highest* level of care and
diligence in carrying passengers. In time, the stricter legal standard was
expanded to include taxicabs, buses, airplanes, even elevators. Since
Disneyland's surrey was functionally no different from a stagecoach, the
judge concurred, the park would be held to the heightened standard.

Attorney McCray opted for a two-pronged defense. First, he argued that
cast members did nothing wrong. The driver had worked with horses all of
his life and had worked at Disneyland since Opening Day, driving those two
horses nearly every day for three years. The horses were carefully selected,
well trained, gentle in nature, and, in those three years, had carried five
million passengers an estimated 15,000 miles without ever having shied,
been unmanageable, or run away. There's no way anyone could have
anticipated the horse would take off, since they still weren't sure what set
him off. The driver testified that there was a lot of activity on Main Street at
the time, including a workman on a ladder cleaning a gas streetlight. Some
horses are scared when they look up and see an object over their heads;
others are not. Yet, he'd never seen any of his horses frightened by the sight
of a workman or a ladder.

Second, McCray proposed that such mishaps were an assumed risk of
riding a vintage horse-drawn vehicle. Just as a person who climbs on a steep
roof assumes the risk that he might fall, so must someone who rides a horse
or a horse-drawn coach. The wild sprint down Main Street? The
overturning? They were part of the adventure! McCray even asked one of
the plaintiffs, a small boy, if he was scared during the mad dash. "No," the
lad responded, "I thought it was fun!" The jury bought it.

The plaintiffs were stunned. They appealed, arguing the verdict should be
overturned, due to the rule of "res ipsa loquitur," meaning that the cause of
the accident was under exclusive control of the defendant. Disney—and no
one else but Disney—could conceivably be seen as causing the accident, so

it must be held responsible. The appellate court responded that this doctrine required the defendant to explain the cause of the occurrence and rebut the inference that it resulted from its negligent conduct. But no one knew for sure why the horse bolted, and riders admitted that the driver appeared to have done everything he could have to try to bring them under control. The ruling stood.

A year later, another surrey rider filed suit after her horses became startled and began to run away, until they collided with a second vehicle (*Perry, 1959*). This time, Disney handled the matter out of court.

Gradually, Main Street began transitioning to more predictable, motorized vehicles. A pair of motorcars were introduced early on, followed by the double-decker Omnibus and a motorized fire truck. The one horse-drawn vehicle that remained—the trolley—was held on course by a rail. Its horses were much less likely to bolt, although it could happen. In 1965, 46-year-old Genevieve Marsh was riding one of the streetcars when up ahead the other streetcar collided with the Omnibus. Her trolley's horse was so distressed by the crash, it suddenly bolted, causing Marsh to bump her head and leg. She accused her streetcar driver of negligence. The jury ruled for Disneyland, reasoning that her driver didn't do anything that caused her horse to buck; the driver of the other streetcar did. So, Marsh's attorney convinced the judge to grant her a new trial, this time blaming the other driver. This time, she won $5,500.

Three Omnibus suits were filed over the years, all by females who fell off, into the street. In 1957, a five-year-old girl climbed up onto the front seat to sit next to the driver, but when the employee left to help guests from the back of the bus, the girl tumbled off the seat (*Yee*). An adult said she was thrown off the bus as it "jerked, swayed, lurched, stopped and started suddenly" along Main Street (*Walker, 1972*). Then, in 1974, a heavyset 60-year-old said she fell to the ground when, as she was stepping onto the double-decker bus, it started to drive away (*Coppock*). In court, McCray persuaded the jury that the woman would have been fine if she hadn't also slipped and hurt herself a few weeks prior, while walking through the nearby South Coast Plaza mall.

One fire engine case also made it to trial. An eighteen-year-old pizza delivery driver was walking down Main Street, talking to a friend on her right, when the fire truck ran over her foot, causing her to fall and fracture her ankle (*Brennan, 1987*). She claimed she racked up nearly $30,000 in medical bills. She was awarded $8,500 in mediation, but refused to settle for less than $15,000. At trial, she upped her demands to $25,000. Her lawyer argued that the driver of the fire truck was preoccupied and not focusing on the pedestrians in front of him. Attorney McCain, however, insisted it was she who was not paying attention to where she was walking. The fire truck was approaching her—from the front—at two to three miles an hour. She walked in front of him. In addition, despite claiming that the accident resulted in debilitating tendinitis in her knee, she admitted on the stand to such post-recovery activities as horseback riding, hiking, jet-skiing, and water skiing. The jury ruled for Disneyland, eleven to one.

Nonetheless, by the early 1990s, Disney stopped operating the vehicles by early afternoon, well before the start of each day's first parade and by which time the crowds on Main Street usually grow to unsafe densities.

Like Main Street, Frontierland also boasted a wealth of old-fashioned conveyances, from wagons and mules to boats and rafts. Yet its first rides were simulating a more freewheeling, Wild West atmosphere, with a greater hint of adventure.

In the park's earliest years, replica stagecoaches would roll across the back country of Frontierland, pulled by a team of four hearty steeds. Professional cowboys were in charge of taking of the reins and driving the coaches. Regular hourly cast members worked the boarding station. "We brought over a wooden step to help guests on and off the stagecoach and Conestoga wagons," recalled Opening Day coach-hand George Kissinger.

Unfortunately, one 33-year-old housewife tripped as she was stepping out, spraining her ankle and tearing ligaments. In court, she blamed the fall on a loose two-by-four—clearly Disney's fault for operating a dilapidated contraption that should have been scrapped 75 years ago (*Hungate, 1957*). McCray, however, proved that the stagecoach, while it looked like a dusty relic from the 1800s, was actually built new just two years ago and maintained in tip-top shape. The jury sided with Disney.

The stagecoaches' true flaw was that they were top-heavy. Every so often, the horses would cut a sharp turn, the stagecoaches would flip over, and the riders on top would be cast into the brush. The ride's fate was sealed on September 14, 1957. Midway through one trip, one horse became startled and gave a big leap, frightening the others. They all took off on a mad tear, galloping ferociously for a quarter-mile, before they attempted to make too wide a turn, and the coach flipped. The horses continued sprinting, dragging the coach on its side for another 200 feet, before they ripped the front wheels out from under it and finally slowed down after another 100 or so feet. Three riders sued. One woman who was riding inside settled (*Ruegsegger*). Two others—who were sitting on top of the coach—went to court. McCray resurrected his tried-and-true surrey defense: that the passengers assumed the "normal risk" of overturning when they boarded the stagecoach. The jury didn't buy it. A man who was struck his head and arm, suffering a five-inch cut over his ear, won $5,000 (*Horner*). Another rider won $17,500 (*Norton*).

Walt, meanwhile, had had enough. He ordered the ride shut down immediately. For a few years thereafter, more stable and considerably less thrilling covered wagons remained, sharing the rustic terrain with mule trains.

The pack mules offered among the most authentic experiences in all of Disneyland. Instead of a simulated trip on a pretend rocket ship or through a fake diamond mine, guests were actually riding real mules in an Old West setting. Consequently, the mules were a longtime favorite among guests, who opted to spend their precious E tickets on this old school classic rather than on some fancier, shinier, higher-tech marvel.

A professional wrangler rode the lead mule in each pack. Hourly cast members manned the boarding area. "Our job was to safely put guests in the saddle," said Bruce Turner, "like strapping them in a carseat."

The mules, however, had minds of their own, and would occasionally throw riders or suddenly decide they'd worked long enough—and unexpectedly drop to the ground and roll on top of their passenger. Fourteen lawsuits were filed over pack mule incidents. McCray quickly realized Disney wasn't going to win any of them.

One mule, in mid-trail, suddenly decided it wanted to sit down (*White, 1960*). The rider slid down its back and the mule laid on top of her. Disney offered $900. One mule strayed a little too close to the side of a trestle bridge and caught its rider's leg on the railing (*Williams, 1961*). So, the mule went down on one knee and tried to roll her off. Disney paid up. Another mule stumbled and fell onto its wee passenger (*Chew, 1962*). Disney cut a check for $750. About a half-dozen other guests were bucked off mules and then compensated for their trouble. One woman was thrown off into a fence, then rolled down the side of a hill (*Hammersley, 1971*).

Most settled. Yet Disney was unable to come to terms with four plaintiffs and reluctantly went to court. McCray's hopes of winning were slim; he just wanted to limit the damages. One woman who was thrown off won, but the judge reduced her damage claim and sent the case down to municipal court (*Steinbeck, 1960*). Another guest was on the last mule in the train, crossing over a bridge, when the other mules were instructed to stop—but his wanted to keep going (*Niemet, 1962*). So the mule began "jumping, lunging, rearing, shying and bolting," throwing the rider off to the side and dragging him through the bushes and over rough terrain, until the man was finally torn loose from his straps and fell to the ground. The jury gave him $4,000.

A decade later, a Berkeley fashion model had the misfortune of being assigned to ride the biggest, most temperamental mule, Ruth, who often irked the rest of the pack (*Eldridge, 1972*). The 8,000-pound beast was nipped by the following mule and went wild. It threw the woman to the ground and began stomping and kicking her. The guest was struck in the foot, leg, thigh and back so forcefully, she was left with a permanent hoof print on her back, endangering her modeling career. The episode also gave her and her son a newfound fear of animals, to the point where they would cower in fear whenever they saw a cat or dog. She began having nightmares and hallucinations of being terrorized by mules.

Disney, though, doubted there were any lingering injuries. They hired a private detective, who filmed the woman walking briskly around town and hopping on and off buses, with no visible handicap. Nonetheless, the jury found the park negligent for subjecting the public to such a violent animal and awarded her $41,084.

The ride reached the end of the trail in 1973, when a "rotten and rotting away" saddle cinch broke (*McKinney, 1973*). The rider tumbled to the ground, landed on his rump, and slid down a hill, seriously injuring his back. A jury would later award him $130,000. But just weeks after the accident, park management shut down the pack mules. At the time, they weren't sure exactly what they'd do with the winding trails. They let them grow over with weeds for four years before breaking ground on Big Thunder Mountain Railroad. But management finally realized the hard lesson Walt learned with the stagecoaches: the liability was too great to leave guest safety in the hands of unpredictable four-hoofed animals.

The closest guests would get to interacting with the wild would come a decade later, when the outskirts of the pack mule trail was converted to a petting zoo. There, children could play with always-docile critters, like baby goats and cows. With one exception. In 2006, the park brought in a large stray dog—a six-year-old male German shepherd/labrador retriever mix named Hemmingway—rescued from a local animal shelter. According to *Dickerson*, "Initially the dog was unlicensed, with no known history, and aggressive, not allowing anyone near him for approximately five days. The dog was noted to be 'not very social' and would 'not allow (the veterinarian) to pet.' The dog was adopted by employees of Disney. Disney failed to review the dog's history while at the shelter and failed to put him through a professional and comprehensive evaluation program to ascertain whether he could be safely placed in a petting zoo intended for small kids. They also failed to socialize the dog to children of all ages and in many types of situations. Disney placed the dog in a very high stress environment, putting him on a box in the ranch for hours at a time, where he was constantly approached by unknown children whose conduct was unpredictable. The dog was also walked in parades where fireworks were constantly exploding overhead."

Two weeks into Hemmingway's new role, a family from Illinois visited the petting zoo and walked up to the dog, as it sat on a box with a cast member holding his leash. The nine-year-old daughter began gently petting the dog's head and the five-year-old son patted its side, as the two-year-old daughter stood near its rear quarters. But when the two-year-old bent over to hug the dog, Hemmingway turned and lunged at the child, violently snapping at her face several times, before clenching down and holding its bite near her right eye. As the cast member stood back in shock, the father grabbed the dog's jaws and eventually was able to pry them open, pulling the fangs from his daughter's face. The children were hysterical. The mother, eight months pregnant, was so upset, she began hyperventilating and almost fainted. The girl was rushed to the hospital, bleeding profusely from her face and head. In addition to tens of thousands of dollars in medical bills, the family said they all were psychologically harmed and would require at least $500,000 in counseling, to treat post-traumatic stress disorder. The park quickly settled.

Historically, the Frontierland Shooting Gallery had been among the park's most dangerous attractions, because originally it featured a rack of sixteen real .22-calibre air rifles that shot lead pellets at metal targets. Fortunately, there were no reports over the years of anyone opening fire on others guests, though it would have been possible. A pneumatic cord kept guests from walking off with the rifles, but not from pointing them wherever they wanted. "The gun barrels initially were on a ring, then a U-harness, but guests could lean forward and aim the guns back," Bruce Turner recalled. "A lot of times I'd stand next to little kids to make sure they didn't turn the gun. Some guy once turned his gun and shot some windows out."

The original metal targets were angled forward, so that the pellets would be deflected downward. But after a day of direct hits, the targets would begin to bend back, and the ricochets would go flying throughout the gallery. Cast members regularly received little red welts from bounce-back bullets and would beg to wear sunglasses inside the gallery to protect their eyes. Occasionally, the pellets would ricochet all the way out of the gallery.

At least three guests sued over being hit by stray fire. The first victim said he was hit by his own shot and settled for an undisclosed amount (*Peyton, 1962*). The second, a 56-year-old woman who was merely walking past the gallery when a pellet struck her in the eye, accepted $1,000 (*John, 1965*). The third demanded his day in court after he was "struck in, to and above the right eye" by a lead pellet (*Petrantoni, 1968*). Yet by the time he made it to court, his injuries had healed and he was unable to prove any lasting effects. The jury ruled for the park.

Disney's initial response to the phenomenon was to make sure operators never used the term "ricochet." Anyone who was struck was hit by an "unidentified flying object." In the mid-1970s, high-powered overhead fans were installed to decrease the velocity of any ricochets. And, finally, in 1984, the gallery was closed and the real guns replaced with arcade rifles that fired infrared signals at electronic targets.

When Disneyland opened, the Mark Twain paddlewheeler had Frontierland's Rivers of America to itself. Walt, however, thought filling the river with as many watercraft as possible would bring the whole area to life. He celebrated the park's first Christmas Day by adding a pair of mid-sized Mike Fink Keel Boats. They transported up to 32 passengers at a time, about half inside the cabin, about half on top, without incident for 41 years—until the night operators, anxious to transport their final guests of the night, overloaded one keel boat, the Gullywhumper, by squeezing on 49. To make matters worse, the driver—convinced the boat was too stable to tip—began violently rocking the boat from side to side, to add drama. Just as the Gullywhumper was coming around the bend past Cascade Peak, the boat did overturn. Guests on top were thrown into the river. The passengers inside the cabin, including a grandmother, two pregnant women, and several children, were flipped underwater and hysterically clawed through the cabin's port-side windows to escape.

Fortunately, no guests suffered serious injuries, and Disney was able to keep most of them happy with gifts like free park tickets. But at least two families insisted on retaining lawyers. A mother sued, citing the emotional trauma of seeing her young daughter "swept from her arms and into the murky water" (*Martin, 1997*). And a married couple that was sitting inside the cabin said they were "trapped under water for a period of time," that only one employee jumped into the water "to aid panic-stricken passengers," and that, after they finally made it to land, they were forced to sit "for about 20 minutes, soaked wet, freezing and in pain" (*Davis, 1997*). They blamed the operators' lack of maturity, training and experience.

Disney responded that the husband had a preexisting back condition and that the boat didn't technically capsize, since it didn't overturn 180 degrees, only about three-quarters of the way. But, in short order, they reached settlements. The keel boats, meanwhile, were immediately pulled out of service and would never operate again.

By Disneyland's second summer, Walt opened Tom Sawyer Island. Motorized rafts were built to transport guests between the island and the mainland. Only a handful of raft suits have been filed over the years, mostly stemming from guests who fell when their raft came to a sudden stop.

For Disneyland's first Fourth of July, Walt introduced the Indian War Canoes. Again, he was taking a chance, because the boats would primarily be powered by the guests themselves. Sixteen guests were handed paddles and put to work, with the aid of two Indian guides, one who sat in the front and the other in the back. Three canoe cases made it to trial—a woman who was thrown to the floor of the boat when it took off before she could sit down (*Wilson, 1960*), a lady who slipped on a wet seat because she was given improper directions on helping to tie down the craft (*Walker, 1972*), and a man whose boat was rear-ended by a second canoe, causing a 250-pound fellow passenger to fall on his leg (*Gusman, 1995*). Disneyland won all three trials.

Disney would ferociously defend against passengers who slipped on the dock or in a canoe, since they could never admit that either was improperly maintained and operated. As a result, plaintiffs typically dropped their suits in frustration, such as a 27-year-old woman who said her canoe stopped too abruptly, throwing her from her seat (*Tamayo, 1964*). She struck her head against the seat in front of her and was knocked unconscious for a half-hour.

The cases that settled were ones in which something unusual happened, irrespective of any actions of the plaintiffs. Disney came to terms with a man who was standing on a wooden bridge near the canoe dock, when it gave way and he fell through (*Armendariz, 1979*). They also made good with two passengers who were flipped into the water after their canoe was rammed by a keel boat (*Maliszewski, 1992*). Keel boats were steered from the back of the boat, and the driver, who had the right of way, reportedly never saw the canoe. The rear canoesman did see the keel boat fast approaching, but only had time to try to push the keel boat away with his oar and holler, "Hang on, folks!"

In neighboring Adventureland, the Jungle Cruise generated far more lawsuits, but most of the incidents happened before or after the ride, rather than during. Of the roughly 30 Superior Court cases filed involving the Jungle Cruise, the majority concerned guests falling as they boarded or disembarked. Four times as many injuries occurred entering as opposed to exiting, since when boarding, guests step downward, onto a sometimes wet and wobbly surface. Starting from the ride's first day in 1955, Disney saw no use in securing the boat beyond having the loaders stand with one foot on the dock and one foot on the edge of the boat, steadying it as they assisted passengers on. Tethering the boat to the dock, they figured, wouldn't prevent the boat from rocking from side to side. The key was making sure the boats loaded evenly. Passengers entering from the rear were directed to sit on the far left side of the boat and passengers from the front were directed to the right. If too many passengers entered too quickly on the far side, the boats would tip back away from the dock, creating a gap that a guest could potentially fall into.

Seven falling cases made it to trial. Disneyland lost two—a woman who slipped and dislocated her right shoulder won $4,000 (*Griffin, 1968*) and a five-year-old boy who fell into the water (*1992*) won $21,120 after claiming the attendant became distracted. The five losers' arguments were familiar—the boat was rocking dangerously, it lacked handrails, and the attendants were negligent. But the juries instead believed Disney's arguments that loaders did everything they could to help all passengers safely enter and exit, and that all plaintiffs had been on boats before, so they knew that they swayed. That went for a man who said operators overloaded the boat on the far side, causing it to tip away from the dock, scraping his leg between the boat and dock, and forcing him to step into the water (*Larosa, 1995*). A 66-year-old grandmother demanded $175,000 after stumbling out of the boat while exiting and tearing her rotator cuff (*Parsonese, 1982*). She claimed the attendant hurried her out of the boat and shoved her down on the dock.

The jury unanimously thought she fell all by herself. A 65-year-old woman said she fell boarding and hurt her back, neck and shoulders because there were no attendants anywhere to be found to assist her (*Lasry, 1997*). Disney, however, wouldn't have permitted her to board the boat if there were no operators stationed at load. And faring no better was a father who severely fractured his left ankle, requiring two surgeries, when he slipped exiting while holding his eighteen-month-old daughter (*Kissee, 2006*). He was able to get a retrial after jurors admitted that Disney had been negligent in failing to properly secure the boat and hold it to the dock, but lost the second one, too, when it was determined that Disney's negligence was not a substantial factor in causing the injury.

Three passengers have also sued, claiming they were injured when their skipper fired his pistol at the charging hippo. The guns were real Smith & Wesson .38s, but they were loaded with blanks, which provided a nice, moderate pop. They were harmless—so long as the guns were pointed out of the boat at the lunging animatronic. Yet if too much powder were put in the shells, usually "double-loaded" by pranksters, the sound could be deafening. "It looked like fire shooting out of the gun," recalled one skipper. One man said he was "shocked" by the gunshot (*Daly, 1959*). A woman claimed the gun was fired directly at her, inflicting flash burns to her eyes, night blindness, photophobia, headaches and blurry vision for ten days (*Gardner, 1968*). Another lady said the gun was fired so close to her right ear, she suffered an "ear concussion" and the side of her face swelled up (*Tomino, 1972*). Disney settled all three cases.

The park also paid up to a man who suffered a gash when he hit his head on a shattered lightbulb on the underside of a boat's roof (*Wagner, 2000*).

Other suits have arisen as the boats neared the dock at the end of their journey. Passengers have left their arms dangling out the side of the boat, only to have them crushed against the dock. Disney's rock-solid defense is that passengers are continually warned to keep their hands and arms inside the vehicle at all times. One man was sitting in the back of the boat and, in trying to rest his right elbow on the stern, got his arm tangled up between the prop rudder assembly and a stanchion, injuring his arm, back and neck (*Richardson, 1966*). In the mid-1970s, the wooden rudder handle was replaced with a rubberized facsimile. Then, when the boats were replaced with a larger capacity fleet in 1993, they had no rudders at all. Disney also added handrails at the two boarding areas.

The Jungle Cruise's only complete safety overhaul came in 2012.

Bumpers were installed along the dock and the sides of the boats, to add stability and decrease any gap. Netting was placed along the perimeter at elbow-level, to keep arms from getting pinched against the dock. And skippers were finally instructed to tether the boats to the dock and gently throttle forward the engines, to keep the rope taut during load.

Collisions are infrequent, but were the cause of three of the most recent cases. A family of three suffered neck and head injuries after crashing into another boat (*Gillons, 2012*). Another passenger said she injured her back when, near the end of the ride, her skipper received instructions to stop and back up (*Jones, 1995*). He put his boat in reverse, full throttle, sending the boat off the rail and crashing into a partially submerged water buffalo. All riders were "bumped and tossed about."

And, in 2010, a 35-year-old man and his 25-year-old wife were on a boat that was going so fast as it approached the right turn near the hippo pool, that their boat derailed and kept going straight—crashing into the island and trees *(Lee)*. The couple was thrown from their seats. "In fact," they charged, "the crash was so substantial, the boat's radio normally used to call for help was broken. The boat's driver was forced to use the gun to signal that they needed help." Because all three crashes were clearly operator error, Disney was forced to settle.

Carnival Upgrades

Walt's vision for Disneyland was a carnival that wasn't a carnival, one that not only stressed cleanliness and safety, but was built on stories, with themed adventures in place of rides. Yet, ironically, his iconic "storybook" area, Fantasyland, would be built almost entirely from carnival rides in disguise.

That said, the land's welcoming attraction, the King Arthur Carrousel, wasn't even disguised. Walt bought an old carousel from the 1800s, then tore out all the benches and animals except for the jumping horses, and added a bunch of "jumpers" from other vintage carousels. That way, every kid could ride a galloping steed. Although the horses move up and down and the carousel rotates at a leisurely pace, riders are raised a fair distance above the wooden turntable and, if they're riding the outer edge, the neighboring pavement. So there's ample opportunity for clumsy riders to fall, particularly as they're climbing onto or off of their horses.

Of the dozen-plus carousel suits filed, three made it to trial and Disney won them all. In the first, a woman said she fell fifteen feet to the ground below—a claim easily disproved with a standard tape measure (*Stickler, 1959*). A 44-year-old homemaker boarded a horse in the down position, but at the end of her ride, it was in the up position, so she misjudged the distance to the ground, stumbled and fractured her foot and ankle (*Saatjian, 1993*).

After strapping on her grandchildren, a 55-year-old housewife decided she didn't want to ride after all and tried stepping off, after the carousel had begun moving (*Macherdchian, 1980*). She fell and broke her right hand. She argued that she wasn't given significant notice to get off before the ride started. Attorney McCain responded that an attendant had invited her to remain on, if she wanted, and that a warning bell had sounded in plenty of time to get off. The jury needed only an hour to unanimously deny her claim for $5,000.

In 2011, handles were added to the horses' center poles and additional stirrups were added to the outside ring of horses, to help riders climb up and down more easily. Six months later, a visitor from China tried stepping off a horse on the inside row—and missed the platform completely, tumbling into the center opening of the ride (*Duan, 2011*). She argued there should have been a barrier. She also wanted compensation for her daughter, who witnessed the horror. Disney settled.

The Mad Tea Party was basically a Tilt-a-Whirl with giant teacups that spun around on an also-spinning turntable. Yet Disney's version presented an extra challenge to safety experts, because the speed of the teacups would be, in part, up to the guests. As such, it would become one of Fantasyland's more prolific legal targets, generating at least 20 lawsuits. Initially, guests controlled the cup by rotating a circular metal steering bar. Within a year, the steering bar was replaced by a round metal platter that was easier to spin and less likely to strike the passengers.

Even though riders controlled their own speed, the ride could still be too violent for some plaintiffs even if they didn't turn the platter. In court, Disney's response was that the ride's turbulence was self-evident. Unlike a dark ride or a coaster that disappeared into or beyond a mountain, the Mad Tea Party sat right in the open, its dangers on display from 360 degrees. And, the option to increase the vehicles' velocity was entirely in the hands of the guest. The argument worked brilliantly, in court against a woman who attributed her injuries to being violently jerked around (*Henle, 1957*), and against a series of plaintiffs who gave up their suits before reaching trial, including one who said the centrifugal force threw her head back so violently, that she remained unable to straighten it (*Jensen, 1958*).

In 1989, mother and daughter manicurists said they suffered cervical and lumbar sprains when their teacup came to a sudden stop, jerking them around the vehicle (*Anderson*). They contended that loose rubber on a load wheel had become trapped between a drive wheel and the track, causing the abrupt stop. And that the cups should have been equipped with seatbelts. Disney claimed they had no record of any such accident occurring. The ladies demanded $50,000. The jury unanimously awarded them zero.

The time between rides could be equally dangerous. Initially, the teacups had no brake, so after the 90-second ride time, guests were expected to wait for their cups to stop spinning before exiting. And then there was the stampede to board. Ride operators would give the thumbs up to the first eighteen parties in line, and they would cut loose, racing to choose their favorite color cup. Ideally, everyone would be securely inside by the time the operator started up the ride. But Holly Smith went to court, claiming she was only halfway inside her cup when it started spinning and she was launched onto the seat (*1957*). The jury believed the park, that she had plenty of time to get herself situated.

Two years later, Elsie Brand contended that when exiting her teacup, she was unaware of the raised saucer beneath it, missed her step, and fell, suffering cuts, bruises and a broken arm. Disney convinced her that the saucer was unmistakable and the blame her own. She dropped the case.

In 1967, Anna Maresca said she was at the front of the line when the ride ended, and was pushed to the ground and trampled by the "unruly mob" hurrying to get the next ride. She suffered a broken hand and fingers, but also gave up on her case.

Years later, another woman suffered a similar fate, knocked down by the hordes that rushed for their teacups (*Thomas, 1996*). Her claim, however, was that Disneyland had intentionally permitted too large a crowd, because it had heavily advertised the day as the final appearance of the Main Street Electrical Parade and let through the turnstiles an unmanageable crowd "equal to almost double the normal capacity." And, specifically at the Mad Tea Party, operators allegedly "encouraged hysteria," by just throwing open the gates and letting guests run amok for an open teacup, forcing those who weren't quick enough to return to the queue and hope for better luck next time. The park, however, argued that operators always regulate crowd size and behavior, both in exactly how many guests they allow into the park and in how they assign guests for a particular trip, albeit not a specific teacup.

A 57-year-old school teacher was exiting the turntable and the high heel of her shoe caught in the gap between the turntable and the cement walk, causing her to fall forward (*Beck, 1981*). Her lawyer argued that, because there was no warning, the gap constituted a dangerous condition. Disney countered that the area was well lit and safely marked, and that the gap was necessary for the proper operation of the ride (so that the turntable could actually spin). The jury voted Disney twelve to zero.

One inherent danger of the teacups was their open doorway. Initially, it was covered with nothing more than a canvas strap. Usually, guests were safe if they were gripping onto the wheel, but if they weren't, and they weren't real heavy, and they were in a cup being spun real fast, anything could happen. In 1969, an eleven-year-old boy claimed the centrifugal force of the teacup threw him out the doorway, where he was "hit on the head numerous times with great force and violence by the opposite teacup and was knocked unconscious" (*Keidser*). He suffered bruises, swelling on his face, and had black eyes for two-and-a-half months. His lawyer argued the flimsy strap was an insufficient barrier. Disney settled for $1,500 and replaced the straps with sturdier metal chains.

In the 1970s, the metal chains eventually gave way to vinyl-covered chains. Neither provided an impenetrable blockade. In 1980, a four-year-old girl was launched out of the doorway and ended up completely underneath an adjacent teacup (*Schultz*). "A kid fell out," recalled longtime Fantasyland operator Rich Johnson. "I hollered to stop the ride. (Disney) immediately shut it down."

The plaintiff charged that the open doorway provided inadequate protection. Disney quickly settled and, according to Johnson, didn't reopen the ride until they installed latching doors on every teacup.

But even with a door, guests could conceivably still go flying out the top—as did one eleven-year-old (*Dosanjh, 1994*). According to witnesses, as the teacup spun faster and faster, the boy appeared to arch his back and slowly push himself out, despite the operator barking to sit down. He was thrown onto the turntable, where he was struck by a second cup. He suffered a broken back, injured shoulder, nerve damage to his arm, and headaches, and spent four months in a body cast.

During the trial, the plaintiff's attorney had a professor of physics testify that, based the boy's weight and the speed of the cup, the operator would have had 30 seconds to "Emergency stop" the ride—plenty of time to prevent him from being ejected. The boy's actions weren't out of the ordinary. The cause of the accident, he argued, was that the ride had no seatbelts, lap bars, or even basic hand holds—and was staffed by only one operator.

Disney argued the accident was the boy's own fault. Before his ride, the operator had recited a safety spiel, warning riders to remain seated and to keep their hands and arms inside the teacup at all times. As he started rising up the side of the cup, he was heard to yell, "This is cool!" And the operator testified that she never saw the boy ejected; she only hit the E-stop button because she saw his head tilting back and thought he was getting sick (despite a "protein spill" not being an emergency that typically elicits an E-stop).

The plaintiff's lawyer, however, countered that the safety spiel should not be given any weight, first, because it was inconsistent with Disney's own brochures, which regularly depicted riders with their arms in the air. Second, operators typically recite the spiel so rapidly that it was almost unintelligible against the crowd noise, the music playing, and the obvious lack of attention given by young riders such as the plaintiff who were primarily concentrating on obtaining a seat in the teacup. Whenever Disney witnesses were asked to recite the spiel, as typically delivered in the park, the court reporter would interrupt and ask the witnesses to slow down so that she could properly record it and, during deliberations, the jury asked that the court reporter re-read the spiel so that they could jot it down.

Nonetheless, the jury found Disney innocent. The judge was incensed. He called the verdict a "miscarriage of justice" and accused Disney's attorneys of hiding a key witness, improperly influencing the jury, and persuading them to give too much weight to the warning spiel, which the court reporter had read back much more slowly than Disney's witnesses had. The judge declared a mistrial. Disney appealed, and quietly worked out a settlement to avoid returning to court.

For years after, maintenance workers would occasionally tinker with the braking system and air pressure on the ride to regulate speed. The tinkering reached a ridiculous apex in early 2004, after a handicapped visitor lost his balance and fell out of a teacup. The guest didn't require medical treatment. He didn't hire an attorney. But Disney nonetheless panicked.

Maintenance tightened the steering wheels so severely, they were basically un-turnable. Unable to budge the steering wheels, most guests gave up trying and just sat there, as their non-spinning cups not-so-madly circled the turntable. Upset guests stormed City Hall to air their grievances, where clerks blamed any slowdown on a recent refurbishment and said the cups were sure to loosen up over time. A month later, the cups still weren't spinning, and a state Department of Occupational Safety & Health (DOSH) report surfaced, revealing the heretofore unknown accident. Still, it took the park several months to realize the ridiculousness of a Mad-Free Tea Party, that they had immobilized the fundamental, defining feature of the ride, before returning it to its spinning glory.

Walt's stories lent themselves particularly well to the carnival dark ride format. Yet Disney discovered that lawsuits involving the dark rides were trickier to defend against because nearly two-thirds of such cases involved entering and exiting vehicles, which are individually controlled by employees.

Although Disney typically played hardball, more often than not, they settled. With a couple of Mr. Toad's Wild Ride cases, they found extenuating circumstances. A 57-year-old man fell while trying to board, injuring his knee. But he didn't report the accident until two days later, so he was unable to prove it happened at Disneyland (*Knutzen, 1994*).

A 37-year-old father holding his infant son was exiting a Mr. Toad's Wild Ride car, when it started up, catching his foot and dragging him for several yards (*Bilal, 1984*). He claimed operator error twisted his foot and inflicted him with the terror of almost seeing his baby "dashed to the ground and crushed by the cars." His case appeared solid—until it was dismissed two years later, after the man was shot to death by a California Highway Patrol officer when he showed resistance after being stopped for running a red light.

Only one Mr. Toad case made it to trial (*Todd, 2000*). A woman was halfway out when her car started back up, throwing her onto the track. "As she was falling," recalled her attorney, John Lacklen, "she saw the next car coming right for her and thought it was going to crush her head, but her brother pulled her out of the way at the last minute. She did not suffer serious physical injuries, but she did suffer a serious case of PTS (post-traumatic stress). She was screaming in her sleep night after night, experiencing horrible nightmares. She developed breathing problems for which she was hospitalized. She had to go to therapy. It affected her speech. She was really debilitated. She had been a movie producer and a writer. She was a hiker, very outgoing, very active, and suddenly she'd lost all ability to function."

Lacklen lined up a string of credible witnesses who could testify to the woman's previous state, plus two psychiatrists and a psychologist. But he had no eyewitnesses to the accident. "It came out in discovery that when there's an accident, there are people at Disneyland who come out and their whole job is to make sure the witnesses leave," he said. "They don't take any names or numbers. They attempt to disperse witnesses, so the plaintiff has no witnesses. 'Everything's okay here, you can go on with your vacation.'"

Worse, he contends, cast members lied about what really happened, and the Orange County judge and jury were predisposed to swallowing whatever line Disney fed them. "The employees were expected to cover up," Lacklen said. "The verdict was decided five days into the three-week trial. They had already decided my client's claims were bogus. I later found out the jury had been discussing the case during the trial, although they had been instructed not to. I was told early on the foreman told them how to decide the case. One of the jurors didn't speak English. The judge said he spoke it well enough. I demanded a mistrial, but the judge refused."

In fact, Lacklen felt as if he'd lost the trial before it ever started. He said, "The judge was against me from the very beginning. Every single dispute went in favor of the defendant. Every time I had a witness, I had to hurry up, I was wasting time. Everything I did, he threatened to shorten my time. He did not do the same for the defendant. (Disney's) attorney was a friend of the judge. One time during a break, they were discussing what books to read; they knew what the other would like."

On the whole, Disney preferred staying out of court in dark ride cases. No Snow White's Scary Adventures or Pinocchio's Daring Journey trials reached verdict. The only one to make it to trial, involving a Snow White car moving while the rider was stepping in, was settled halfway through (*Lindstrom, 1996*).

Five Peter Pan's Flight cases made it to trial; Disney lost two of them. Juries awarded $5,000 to a 65-year-old woman (*Sims, 1967*) and $13,370 to a 30-year-old disabled clerk who were thrown out of vehicles while trying to exit (*McAdoo, 1994*).

Disney bested a 28-year-old general contractor who claimed that while he was exiting, his Peter Pan vehicle suddenly jerked forward, throwing him back in, wrenching his back, and bruising his elbow (*Huff, 1983*). He said other guests had seen the ride having problems and Disney "maintained a dangerous condition by allowing the cars to jerk." McCray insisted no such operation problems or accident occurred.

As well, a man and his three-year-old daughter were halfway out, when their Pan vehicle started back up, "bucking" the father in the back and ejecting him (*Gentile, 1993*). His child was still in the boat, so he and his wife chased it down and tried to pull her out, not realizing her arm was stuck inside. They argued that the boat's giant sail blocked the view of the ride operator at the console, so she couldn't know if passengers were safely out of the vehicle or not. Disney, however, revealed that some years before it had installed a giant mirror near the exit area, for just such a purpose, and that the daughter's injuries were caused by her parents. She would have been fine if they'd let her proceed back to the boarding area. Disney won the case.

Alice in Wonderland has generated about twice as many lawsuits as any of the other dark rides, resulting in two trials. But while there would still be some falls at load/unload, those cases would be in the distinct minority, because Alice's caterpillar vehicles, unlike the cars on all the other dark rides, didn't have a lip at the base of their doorways to potentially trip over. Instead, the wide opening allowed riders to dangle their feet outside of the vehicle—only to have their limbs run over or crash into scenery. Disney typically put up a tough fight against such cases, arguing that riders were responsible for keeping their feet inside the caterpillar.

Two Alice suits made it to trial, and both involved straying left feet. A fourteen-year-old boy was riding with three friends, when their vehicle made a sharp turn and his foot was thrown out and under the vehicle, breaking a bone in the top of his foot (*Glenn, 1978*). He claimed the ride was poorly designed and lacked restraints. Disney responded that the only way the boy's foot could have ended up underneath the ride was if he had been attempting to get out of the vehicle and purposely put his leg out to release a safety catch between the car and the floor. The jury sided with Disney, eleven to one.

Nineteen years later, a woman who had been unable to bend her left knee for five years was forced to ride with her left leg extended out of the car (*Dukin, 1997*)—parroting a claim made by an earlier rider who said she was allowed to ride with her left leg poking out because her foot was in a cast (*Pierson, 1971*). At trial, the jury determined damages of $52,000, but considered Dukin 55 percent liable for the accident, reducing her award

NO LIP along the base of the doorways on Alice in Wonderland's caterpillar vehicles meant there was nothing for passengers to trip over, but also nothing to prevent them from sticking their feet out during the ride. It took 45 years and numerous foot injuries before Disneyland finally added new lap bars with a triangular guard plate to keep feet safely inside the cars.

proportionately.

In 2000, a fifteen-year-old from Arizona stuck his leg out while he was traveling down the exterior "Vine" (*Borbeck*). His foot caught between the underside of the car and the rail, breaking his foot and tearing muscles in his knee. He didn't win his case, but he did attract a lot of publicity. Then in 2002, a woman from Utah claimed her left leg was dragged about fifteen feet through the boarding station because her vehicle took off before she could get fully inside (*Messick*). Soon after, Disney replaced Alice's T-shaped lap bars with L-bars featuring a triangular metal guard plate that kept feet inside the vehicle when the bar was lowered. The foot accidents stopped.

Usually, malfunctions on the dark rides cause the cars to simply roll to a stop. But not always. Three months after Mr. Toad's Wild Ride opened, a 55-year-old housewife was passing by the scene in which a stack of barrels lunges forward as if they are going to fall on the rider, when the safety cable broke, and the barrels did crash on top of her, injuring her head and back (*Fowlkes, 1955*). Disney settled—and immediately closed the ride until Imagineering could design an entirely new barrel contraption.

A few months later, a Snow White car suddenly lost power and was rear-ended by a second car, injuring the first rider's back and neck (*Jordan, 1956*). His car was bumped off the track and began to smolder. A third car then struck the second, knocking its occupant out cold. Disney broke out the checkbook.

In 1963, a power failure suddenly shut down all the vehicles on Alice in Wonderland and plunged the ride into darkness. The sudden stop sent an eight-year-old rider's head smashing into the back of her car, reportedly fracturing her skull (*Duarte*). Trapped in the pitch black, the girl and her two siblings went hysterical. After the ride, she started vomiting and behaving oddly. Disney settled for her doctor bills: $737.35.

Years later, an Alice car ran off the track and crashed into a wall, starting a pileup of cars behind. A woman in the second car to ram the first agreed to settle, but then had second thoughts—and sat on the offer for five years, until the case was dismissed for lack of prosecution (*Bankhead, 1977*).

Fantasyland's aerial spinner ride features two distinct differences from the typical carnival spinner—one, the vehicles are themed as Dumbo the Flying Elephant and, two, a joystick in each cabin allows passengers to control how high they want their elephant to rise. Originally, a host in the control booth had two joysticks, each operating half of the elephants, but Walt preferred placing guests in control of their own destinies. For its first decade, the ride proved relatively incident-free—apart from having to cut an open doorway into the elephants about a year in, to make it easier for kids to climb into the vehicles. Then came a pair of incidents in 1968. A woman claimed she was thrown out of her vehicle and into the concrete pit below, as a barrage of flying Dumbos pummeled her in the head, shoulders and back (*James*). At trial, the jury believed Disney, that the woman could only have escaped from the vehicle by her own effort.

Less than five months later, a lady claimed that the operator started the Dumbo ride before she and her daughter had a chance to settle into their seats (*Green*). Her child was thrown forward, splitting her lip against the console, while the woman, who was pregnant at the time, ended up straddling the ride. During interrogatories, she revealed that she had suffered permanent whiplash on the Mad Tea Party during a visit to the park seven years earlier. Despite the woman's history of questionable complaints and the mildness of the latest injuries, Disney realized operator error was to blame in the Dumbo case and settled for a token amount.

The only other Dumbo lawsuit occurred outside the ride. A 28-year-old housewife was standing watching her daughter ride Dumbo, but had chosen an inopportune vantage point: directly in front of the iron exit gate (*Hill, 1978*). The first person to exit the ride swung open the gate, right into the victim, causing her to fall and break her ankle. An arbitrator awarded her $2,250, but Disney insisted on going to trial. There, the plaintiff demanded $15,000, arguing that Disneyland should have had markings on the pavement indicating the potential danger, that the gate lacked a sign that specifically warned that it would swing out, and that no employee warned her of the danger. Disney attorney McCain responded that the plaintiff was standing directly in front of a gate clearly marked "Exit," that the gate was painted a different color than the rest of the fencing, and that she had sufficient time to notice that it swung outwards. The jury took one hour to rule for Disneyland, eleven to one.

The Casey Jr. Circus Train was originally envisioned as a roller coaster, but the designers feared that the train cars would be at risk of overturning on the undulating track, so it was slowed down and made a modestly quick scenic cruise. Still, the riders would not be strapped into normal train seats, but would instead sit inside cages or on benches salvaged from the original carousel. So for the ride's first few months, in addition to the conductor driving the train, a second ride operator rode in back with a whistle that he was to blow if he saw anybody fall off.

Fortunately, the ride continues operating to this day, with minimal carnage. Years ago, a pregnant woman had second thoughts about riding and demanded her cage be unlatched so she could exit (*Williams, 1961*). Displeased with the operator's response, she decided to unhook it herself, and in doing so tripped and fell out of the car. The judge deemed all the wrongdoing her own and dismissed the suit.

Another lady said that as the train was approaching the station, "the brakes didn't hold and there were repeated jerks as (the conductor was) attempting to get the train under control" (*Shelton, 1969*). The rapid starts and stops caused her to bang her head against the side of the car and her upper arm against a railing. Disney settled.

Ironically, the Skyway gondola ride was statistically safer in its original, rickety state, in which two passengers sat on plastic patio chairs bolted to the floor of round metal buckets, than in the sturdier, rectangular, four-passenger cabins with molded-in benches introduced in 1965. The original version generated zero lawsuits. Admittedly, even the new models encountered relatively few problems. If something was going to go wrong, it typically occurred in the loading station. There, cast members pulled the gondolas off the cable onto a U-bar, so they could be brought to a stop to unload riders while the cable kept moving. Operators would then board new riders and slide the cabins back onto the cable, for a trip to the other station. Four riders filed suit when their buckets moved unexpectedly as they were trying to board.

One suit made it to trial (*Cummins, 1987*). The 28-year-old rider, who coincidentally worked as a claims representative at competing sky-bucket operator SeaWorld, had just boarded at the Fantasyland Station, when she felt her cabin being struck from the rear. Her husband, who was just entering, was knocked to the gondola's floor. The woman felt immediate pain to her shoulder, arm and neck. She reported the collision to an attendant at the Tomorrowland Station. An arbitrator ruled she deserved $30,000. Disney refused. In court, her lawyer argued operator error: while the buckets were on the U-bar, their movement was controlled solely by the cast members, and they had failed to follow company guidelines by allowing the gondolas to crash into each other. McCain, though, got the woman to admit she neither saw nor heard any collision. There was no collision. The only jolt would have been the light pop as her cabin popped back onto the cable. She merely experienced a normal ride on the Skyway. The jury ruled unanimously for Disney.

The Skyway's final lawsuit was the only one that took place outside of a station (*Charles, 1994*). In 1994, a 30-year-old rider from San Bernardino County tumbled through an open Skyway doorway and plunged 20 feet until he landed in a massive tree near the Alice in Wonderland ride. The man claimed he had been launched through the open door and, although visibly unharmed, suffered permanent neck and back injuries. He wanted at least $25,000.

Disney was immediately suspicious. The cabin doors had a two-step locking procedure that required an operator to flip both a lock and a handle from the outside. Maintenance records showed the doors on every gondola had been inspected that morning. And, coincidentally, the victim plunged out of the cabin when he was directly over the only spot on the Skyway's route where the fall wouldn't have killed him.

Nonetheless, for eighteen months, the man stuck to his story, insisting he wasn't doing anything improper. Then, three days before the case was to go to trial, faced with mounting evidence that his story was baloney and threats from Disney's attorneys that they would countersue for costs, he dropped his suit and quietly admitted that he "came out" of his cabin, and that his suit was "ill advised." Disney's greater loss was that seven months after the incident, it had closed the Skyway for financial reasons. Now the public was convinced it was shut down because riders were falling out.

Safely operating the Storybook Land Canal Boats offered challenges similar to the Jungle Cruise, but has resulted in far fewer lawsuits, perhaps due to the ride's significantly lower capacity. Operators don't tether the boats for boarding; they simply practice balanced loading. "When you begin loading, you step onto the raised edge on the side of the boat. That brings the boat into the dock," said former Storybook guide Nanci Coleman. "The first guests are loaded on the front left side of the boat. This somewhat secures the boat at the dock, so there is less of a gap between the boat and the dock. The boat is loaded from front to back, with about six guests on each side. Children are often seated on the bow to be 'lookouts for whales.' That expands capacity."

The first four Storybook Land suits proceeded to trial. Disney beat the first—a 200-pound woman who fell while boarding (*Wallace, 1958*). The next case, however, involved a woman from Montana who tried boarding as a gap opened between the boat and the dock (*West, 1959*). She stepped into the gap, catching her leg between the boat and dock, badly bruising and cutting her ankle. She demanded $60,000. So, attorney McCray took the jury to the ride to show how difficult it would be to get one's leg between a boat and the blue dock, which had recently been painted with a white stripe to accentuate its edge. The jury reimbursed the plaintiff's claimed medical expenses: $660.18.

Disney won the other two trials—a woman who tripped on the edge of the dock as she was exiting (*Farabee, 1961*) and a lady who said she hurt her leg when the boat suddenly "dipped and jerked" (*Pittman, 1969*).

Disney handled all future cases out of court, including a lady who stepped in before the seat cushion could be moved and slid on the "slippery mat" (*Rance, 1978*), a 57-year-old woman who tripped while boarding because the cast member had carelessly allowed a large crowd to shove her (*Williams, 2002*), and a man whose hand was crushed between the dock bumper and the boat as it returned to shore (*Villalobos, 2003*).

Future Worlds

The original Tomorrowland was best symbolized by the TWA Moonliner, a 76-foot-tall spaceship that marked the entrance to a movie-based Rocket to the Moon attraction. Yet the area's most popular ride was considerably more grounded—real gasoline-powered cars that kids could drive along miniature highways, foreshadowing what would be their very real future. The construction of the Autopia ride, in fact, coincided with the construction of the Santa Ana Freeway right outside Disneyland's gates. Walt saw the attraction as a fun way to teach children safe driving. His fear was that they instead would mistake his highway for a racetrack or a demolition derby course. Just in case, he had each vehicle's body and wheels fully encircled by massive aluminum bumpers, selected because Kaiser Aluminum was one of Tomorrowland's first sponsors.

As expected, riders—accustomed to the bumper cars of other amusement parks—delighted in smashing into each other, only to discover the aluminum bumpers, instead of springing back, would take the full force of the impacts and crumple. As well, the original roadway was two-cars wide, so cars could pass each other. But that also left room for guests to ram each other from the side and, if they turned sharply enough and drove up on the curb, to make a U-turn and head back in the wrong direction, leading to several brutal head-on collisions.

With all the abuse, the cars started dropping like flies. Park mechanics worked furiously to get them back into service as quickly as possible. The guests also suffered. On the park's third day open to the public, a girl smashed her Autopia car into a curb, slamming her face against the bare metal steering wheel (*Marshall, 1955*). She fractured two teeth, cut her mouth and lips, and hurt her jaw. Disney defeated the guest in court, arguing she drove herself into the curb. But as similar accident reports piled up, Imagineers went to quick work, adding foam-rubber padding to the metal steering wheels and replacing the aluminum bumpers with springier steel bumpers.

Nonetheless, Autopia would produce more injuries—and lawsuits—than any other Disneyland attraction. Well over 80 Autopia lawsuits have been filed, with the vast majority arising from one car rear-ending another. Disney quickly identified the most common site of impact: the loading zone, where wild-eyed drivers saw the parked cars being boarded as sitting ducks. Worse, guests were entering and exiting the vehicles, making them more prone to injury when their cars were struck. In 1956, the Imagineers embedded a power-operated flap into the track at the end of the ride. When cars drove over it, the flap would automatically trigger their brakes. But then ride operators would have to manually re-set the mechanisms on every braked car, leading to even more rear-endings than before. The system was quickly abandoned.

A year later, Disney narrowed the width of the track, to make it more difficult for cars to turn around or to strike other vehicles from the side. Still, there was nothing to keep the cars pointed forward. One woman plowed into a curb and suffered bruises, cuts to her face and chest, and a broken wrist (*Corsch, 1958*). She said her car wouldn't start, so an employee arrived to power it up—with the wheel pointed toward the curb, basically directing her to doom. McCray successfully argued that the car initially conked out because she slammed into the curb. The ride operator then restarted the car and straightened her out, but she steered back into the curb anyway, causing her injuries.

The car designs also continued to evolve. In 1959, the new Mark V Autopia car debuted, featuring a one-piece fiberglass body, shock-absorbing bumpers, and heavier side bumpers. But the biggest change came in 1965 with an entirely rebuilt track. Gone were the curbs and in was a center guide that prevented cars from straying more than a few inches to the right or to the left. Autopia had been averaging about five lawsuits a year; the addition of the guide rail cut that number in half. But while the rail eliminated crazier maneuvers, side swipes, and front-end collisions, it didn't eliminate rear-endings. If someone in front of you were driving too slowly, you no longer had the option of passing—only to wait or to plow right into them.

Over the years, Disney would continue tweaking the ride to cut down on the rear-endings—stationing cast members along the track as lookouts, adding "No Bumping" signs, giving ride operators a PA system to warn guests, and redesigning the cars yet again with flexible outer bodies and spring-loaded bumpers. Yet the rear-endings remained constant. As a result, Disney had no chance but to vigorously, publicly fight all rear-ending suits. To admit rear-endings were an ongoing, hazardous feature that Disney had created, was aware of, and allowed to continue, would be to admit the ride was inherently flawed and dangerous.

The park settled a minority of the cases, usually when they could get the victim to accept a token offer. An eleven-year-old rear-ended the car in front of him, causing his mouth and front teeth to smash into the dashboard, cutting his lip and chipping a tooth (*Donath, 1964*). Disney argued that not only did the boy cause the collision, his dental condition caused his injuries. According to the accident report: "Operator heard boy crying in one of the cars... the boy's teeth are very crooked. This is not a result of the accident." Nonetheless, Disney paid a minimal settlement to resolve the case quickly.

Disney was more likely to settle when a cast member was directly involved, such as when guiding a car into the loading zone and accidentally rear-ending the plaintiff's vehicle (*Olson, 1967; Blackshear, 1978; King, 1981*). A few cases were settled in mid-trial, after Disney lawyers sensed the jury seemed to be more sympathetic to the plaintiff.

Twenty Autopia lawsuits proceeded to verdict; Disney lost only three. The first two losses were typical rear-endings, but the plaintiffs apparently found sympathetic juries; a woman was awarded $10,000 (*Barron, 1961*), while a four-year-old boy and his mother took home a combined $2,500

Lawsuit Magnets

Most frequently sued Disneyland attractions, according to more than 1,200 Orange County Superior Court cases filed from 1955 to 2015.

1. Autopia
2. Matterhorn Bobsleds
3. Space Mountain
4. Haunted Mansion
5. Jungle Cruise
6. Pirates of the Caribbean
7. It's a Small World
8. Splash Mountain
9. Mad Tea Party
10. Alice in Wonderland
11. PeopleMover
12. Big Thunder Mountain Railroad
13. Pack Mules
14. King Arthur Carrousel

(*Wyatt, 1963*). Disney attorneys then went on an uninterrupted 40-year win streak defending the Autopia.

Disney usually argued that, although cast members were trained to deter "bumping," collisions were commonplace and an obvious, acceptable risk to passengers. A family of five riding in four consecutive cars claimed they all suffered whiplash when they were rear-ended in a chain reaction by an "inexperienced" eight-year-old boy (*Hakes, 1976*). They claimed he was too young to be driving, and Disneyland was negligent in allowing him to do so. McCray successfully argued against proximate cause; the boy was to blame, but not because of his age or inexperience. Guests carelessly rear-ended each other constantly on Autopia, regardless of age or driving experience.

Disney would cast doubt about plaintiffs' injuries, explaining how low impact any crashes were (the cars were governed to speeds of no more than seven miles per hour) and consequently how insignificant any injuries would have been. A 29-year-old executive secretary and her six-year-old son were riding Fantasyland Autopia, not long after a storm had left a tree branch strewn across the roadway (*Varela, 1975*). About ten cars were backed up behind the branch, so the woman hit the brakes to avoid the vehicles in front of her—and the following car smashed into her. Her son's forehead was thrown into the dash, and the woman tweaked her lower back and neck. The boy required stitches. The woman demanded surgery, but afterwards her neck felt worse, so she demanded another. And another. And another. She would be hospitalized seventeen times, undergo eight operations, attempt suicide once, and rack up $123,000 in hospital bills.

The woman demanded $750,000. Disney offered $10,000, to avoid a trial. It didn't work. McCray laid out his case: family problems and an unscrupulous doctor had persuaded this "psychologically neurotic, hysterical woman" to undergo a series of operations, all of them unnecessary, that turned her into a "surgical invalid." The trial lasted 24 days. The jury took two-and-a-half hours to unanimously absolve Disney.

A 63-year-old retired professor took his six-year-old grandson to Disneyland, where Autopia was his favorite ride (*Tatangelo, 1991*). They'd already ridden the Autopia four times that morning, about eight times the day before, and about eight times on a vacation earlier in the year. But on their fifth trip of the day, they were rear-ended so forcefully, the man suffered trauma to his spinal cord, exacerbating a pre-existing condition. He demanded $225,000, since operators habitually failed to control traffic and prevent bumping. Disney's McCain responded, however, that after 20 rides in six months, the man was aware and presumably used to Autopia's risks. Plus, there was no medical proof that any particular rear-end bump caused the man's bulging discs.

Disney lawyers, whenever possible, would take jurors to the Autopia, to show them how much fun everyone was having, and how safely the ride was operating. Or on several occasions, they brought Autopia cars to the basement of the Orange County Courthouse, where jurors could view the pint-sized vehicles, which looked like harmless toys, and Imagineers could point out their myriad safety features.

A 37-year-old pregnant woman and her three-year-old son claimed that they were forced to plow into the back of the car in front of them because, due to improper maintenance, that car stopped suddenly, after derailing (*McClean, 1991*). The crash injured the woman's lower back and created complications in her pregnancy; her son suffered whiplash. She demanded $35,000. During the three-day trial, however, McCain demonstrated that such a derailment was impossible. The accident never happened. The jury took less than fifteen minutes to unanimously rule for Disneyland.

As he was slowing down near the end of the ride, a 42-year-old truck driver was rear-ended and pushed into the car in front of him (*Thompson, 1982*). Then he was rear-ended again. He suddenly went numb in his hands and legs. Confused and unable to speak, he had to be helped out of the vehicle by a cast member. He figured his symptoms would go away, but, when there was no improvement after three hours, he reported the accident to First Aid and was taken to the hospital. He was diagnosed with a herniated disc, slight concussion, and possible central cord syndrome. He demanded $150,000, claiming the cars were dangerous and should have been equipped with headrests. He cited records showing 1,000 injuries suffered on the Autopia over the last ten years, of which 230 were neck-related. Disneyland was aware there was a problem, he charged, and should have remedied it.

McCain countered that the vehicles were safe; only an imperceptible fraction of the 3.5 million Autopia riders a year claimed any sort of injury. Headrests were unnecessary due to the low level of impact (3 to 4g) and would block the vision of children. The plaintiff's injuries were strictly the result of an accident suffered two years earlier and the normal aging process. Disney won the trial nine to three, but a decade later did redesign the cars yet again—with high headrests to cut down on the whiplash claims.

Unfortunately, the headrests were to blame for a serious accident before the rebuilt ride even opened to the public. During a "soft opening" a few days before the official opening in 2000, Susan Fesler and her daughter boarded, unaware the ride was still being tested. During the ride, she was repeatedly rammed by the car following her. When she complained to ride operators stationed along the track, she was ignored. She begged one operator to tell the driver behind her to stop ramming her car, but he laughed. Fearful the crashes were becoming more severe, Fesler wrapped her arms around her daughter to protect her from injury—just as their car was struck again, throwing her head back into the fiberglass headrest. By the time she reached the loading zone, her head and back were severely injured, and she told the cast member she couldn't exit without assistance. As he gingerly helped her out, he mentioned the "ride was being tested," "things like this happen," "you take your chances on a new ride," and "all of the bugs had not been worked out."

Fesler found her own way to First Aid, where a nurse asked why no one had helped her get there, as it was readily apparent that she was in distress. She was taken to the hospital and underwent surgery to treat a skull lesion. Fesler also expected to undergo back surgery. She subpoenaed First Aid reports that showed 22 similar neck/head injuries during the new Autopia's first 21 days of operation. The park settled.

At even greater risk than drivers are pedestrians, who have been struck by vehicles in the loading zone. A ten-year-old Egyptian boy stepped off the sidewalk and into the path of an oncoming vehicle *(Sawires, 1991)*. The car ran over him and fractured his shinbone. His lawyer argued that the ride had inadequate supervision and should have had guardrails or some sort of barrier to prevent children from stepping into traffic. McCain responded that the boy was seen spinning and dancing, and his parents and friends weren't paying any attention to him. The boy would have been safe had he been properly supervised. Disney won, twelve to zero.

The problem of pedestrians on the track worsened when Autopia was completely remodeled in 2000, doubling the number of lanes and introducing parallel loading zones, further confusing the exit route. Cast members reported that kids running on the track became a daily occurrence. Mostly, guests inadvertently exited the car on the wrong side or were overanxious to board before the prior guest had exited. Other times victims were retrieving a dropped souvenir drivers license or were just kids out for a joy run.

In 2001, cerebral palsy sufferer James Stein said he was trying to climb out of his vehicle when the next riders began crowding him, giving him less room to be sure he was stepping out squarely on to the curb. He wasn't, and slipped off the curb and down to the pavement. His attorney, Amy Fisch Solomon, recalled: "This family lived in Arizona, and they were absolutely Disney addicts. Their daughter's nursery had been all Disney. Her onesies were all Disney. And every birthday, they'd spend like three days at Disneyland. The husband was a middle-aged accountant with slight cerebral palsy, which gave him a little bit of an awkward gait. There was no handicapped assistance. They were forcing new people on before getting the old people off. They went to disembark, and the dad tried desperately to get out, but there was no one to help him, so he took a tremendous fall and fractured his hip. Nobody helped, nobody said they were sorry, it was just sort of 'get out of the way.'"

Solomon filed the case in Los Angeles and when Disney was unable to have the case moved to Orange County, both parties agreed to waive a jury and proceed to a "bench trial," in which a judge alone would determine the verdict. Solomon argued that Autopia's design created an unreasonable risk to patrons, since it forced arriving and departing riders to share the same small platform. She got a park manager to testify that waiting guests often milled about closer to the cars and would try to climb in before prior passengers had exited. Plus, there were no physical barriers separating the two groups of passengers, and only three cast members were left to oversee eight loading points. Disney responded that Stein caused his own injury. Crowd control was sufficient and physical barriers weren't necessary, since they don't exist for most means of transportation, such as buses, subways, trains, elevators, or for ingress and egress into buildings.

What Disney didn't bring up during the trial was that during the three years between the time of the accident and the time the case made it to trial, it had been continually changing the ride to correct any problems that may have contributed to the accident. Requiring at least three cast members to oversee the eight zones didn't go into effect until ten months after the accident. At the time of the mishap, each platform was manned by just two cast members. Based on recommendations from Cal/OSHA, Autopia could send out only six cars at a time with cast members watching the platform. Then, in 2003, after a small boy was struck by a car after wandering on to the track, the company quickly designed and installed safety gates at the loading zone.

The judge found Stein 55 percent and Disney 45 percent at fault, and set an award of $150,000 for damages (of which he received 45 percent) and $30,000 for loss of consortium (of which his wife received 45 percent).

Disney also upped its determination to do whatever it takes to keep Autopia lawsuits from ever being filed. The rear-endings continue, but these days very few Autopia victims end up filing suit.

In 1957, an aquatic version of Autopia opened in adjacent Fantasyland, but with the hope that the Motor Boat Cruise would operate free of the car ride's accidents and lawsuits. The boats ran on underwater pipes, so they couldn't be steered too far to either side, and their gas pedals were inoperable. The engines ran perpetually, at a constant speed, so cast members used long poles with loops on the end to hook the boats as they approached the dock, then held them steady as guests entered and exited. Boats could still catch up with and rear-end each other, but since they were both moving at slow, controlled speeds, the impact was never more than a light bump.

Still, there was some room for mischief, particularly by guests who were able to work the rollers on the bottom of their boats off the rails. In addition, operators did not enjoy struggling to hold the boats steady, and one lawsuit surfaced. A guest tried entering a boat that was bobbing, causing him to fall into the vessel and cut his leg on a rusty nail under the dashboard (*Saperstein, 1958*). Disney settled.

When the surrounding area was redone in 1959 to accommodate several new rides, Disney used the opportunity to rebuild the Motor Boat Cruise. They installed underwater air gates to hold the boats in place during loading, as well as new boats featuring inoperable steering wheels, a more confining rail that boats couldn't wriggle off of, and a metal windshield frame. The windshields didn't have any glass in them, but they did act as a nice handhold for guests climbing into and out of boats—as well as a psychological barrier to deter teens from climbing onto the bow when their boats entered the un-patrolled backwoods of the river.

Consequently, the ride enjoyed three-plus decades of relatively litigation-free existence, with only two other lawsuits arising. Since the ride had such a sterling safety record, Disney insisted on taking both to trial. The jury awarded $4,331.14 to a 64-year-old woman who fell when her boat moved as she tried to enter (*Zikmund, 1961*), but sided with Disney over a twelve-year-old girl whose own carelessness led to her falling off a boat and into the water, injuring her chest and ribs (*McAlister, 1965*).

Tomorrowland's Satellite View of America exhibit consisted of a replica of the American continent, as viewed from 50 miles in space. To make sure guests didn't bunch up in any one spot, they walked along a slowly-rotating circular platform. A tourist in her seventies said the rotating floor threw her to the ground (*Schilkey, 1958*). Disney argued that she was responsible for losing her balance, because the ride had thick, continuous handrails and the platform moved extremely slowly. The jury found for Disney.

Not long after, the attraction was replaced by the circular Circarama theater, which would show the 360-degree movie *America the Beautiful* on side-by-side screens encircling the room. Because Disney wanted visitors to view the film at all angles—and to maximize capacity—the theater would have no seats. Instead, rows of railings were installed to give guests something to rest against for the 20-minute movie. That left operators to constantly warn guests not to sit on the railings and place themselves at risk of falling off.

A 28-year-old woman said that watching *America the Beautiful* created such a "circular motion in the premises" that she became extremely dizzy and decided to leave the show early (*Hovespian, 1971*). But while she was making her way through the exit, she began to swoon and tried to lean against a metal railing to keep from falling. Instead, she fainted, fell backwards over the railing, and hit the back of her head on the concrete floor. But when she was in First Aid, her husband confessed to the nurse that his wife didn't want to walk through the maze of empty crowd-control lanes, so she tried to climb over the railing, tripped and fell. According to the nurse's report, the woman even apologized, saying the accident was her own fault. At trial, the plaintiff's lawyer knew the nurse was on the witness list and her notes were Exhibit A. So, he admitted in his opening statement that although his client's actions led to her injury, he thought Disney's dizzying movie was the underlying cause. McCray promptly asked the judge to throw out the case as a "non-suit," since the opposing attorney already admitted his client was to blame. The judge agreed.

The theater is currently the site of a dark ride, Buzz Lightyear Astro Blasters, which generated a couple of suits, both in 2008. A woman was stepping from her car to the moving conveyor belt, when her foot struck a guard plate and she fell (*Gates*). Her trailing foot then became caught on the vehicle, shattering her thigh bone. Disney quickly settled. Less than three months later, a man claimed he hurt his right hand when his Buzz Lightyear car jerked rapidly to the left, as he was trying to buckle his seatbelt

(*Brown*). He demanded $4,500 for enduring two months of pain, suffering and Disney harassing him about his injury. When he discovered the company wasn't budging, he dropped his case.

Tomorrowland's earlier carnival attraction was a Dumbo-style spinner, but instead of flying elephants, the vehicles would be themed as spaceships. The Astro-Jets experienced just a handful of accidents, and Disney proved victorious in the lawsuits that followed. Unlucky plaintiffs included a nineteen-year-old who cut her mouth and cracked two teeth against the safety bar (*Ridinger, 1965*), a 36-year-old who banged her knee while boarding (*Murphy, 1965*), and a nine-year-old who hit his head when his rocket launched upward (*Reed*, 1988).

The earliest incident, months after the ride opened in 1956, involved a nine-year-old girl who said the violent spinning threw her face against the inside of the vehicle, breaking off her two front teeth (*Lyle*). Her lawyer contended that Disneyland was negligent in not installing seatbelts, handholds or padding around the lip of the cockpit, and for failing to provide safety instructions to help avoid such an accident. Cast members had also allowed the small girl to ride behind a same-sized friend, because the rule at the time was you only had to ride with an adult if you were under eight years old. Her father, who rode with her little brother in the jet behind hers, had cautioned the girls to "sit down and be quiet" and to be "careful." The girl testified that she was holding on to the right, "inside" edge of the cockpit to keep from sliding toward the outside, but her hand slipped.

At trial, McCray pointed out several inconsistencies between the girl's version of what happened and her father's, such as whether she was moving her head and if her friend was yanking the control bar. A park safety engineer testified that centrifugal force kept riders back in their seats, so restraining devices were unnecessary, and would prevent heads from striking the sides of the cockpit—unless the guest made some voluntary movement. The operator testified he did recite a warning spiel before the ride for passengers to remain seated at all times. The jury ruled that the girl had caused her own injuries, and their decision was upheld on appeal.

Ironically, in 1958, as the case was being litigated, a woman rider was killed after flipping out of an identical spinning rocket machine at the Pike amusement park in Long Beach. Imagineer Bob Gurr was asked to design a safety cage for the Astro-Jets, but Walt refused to go for it. Seatbelts, however, were added by 1967, when the ride was rebuilt atop the PeopleMover boarding area. Now rising to 90 feet in the air, the newly renamed Rocket Jets promised a more thrilling ride—especially for one family of three (*Haynes, 1977*). As they were climbing into a rocket and the operator was delivering the warning spiel from his console, two mischievous twelve-year-old boys reached behind the employee and hit the button to start the ride. Up went the jets. The young daughter had time to sit down, but her parents weren't so lucky. Mom had begun stepping in with one foot, so she was jolted back to the platform. Worse, dad was halfway in the vehicle; he was thrown chest-first into the cabin and spent the entire 92 seconds of the ride clenching the jet, as one leg dangled out the side. Both parents claimed the premature takeoff strained their backs, gave them "horrendous headaches," and caused the wife to lose a $2,000 pair of earrings.

The man demanded $50,000. Disney agreed to $6,500. He lowered his demand to $20,000. But Disney refused to go above $7,500. At trial, he asked for $15,000. His argument was that the operator was inattentive and negligent in allowing the boys to press the button. But McCray countered that over 30 million people had ridden the Rocket Jets without any serious accidents. The ride didn't malfunction, and the ride operator did exactly what he was supposed to do. There was no way to anticipate the accident, since nothing like it had ever occurred before. McCray also disputed the nature and extent of the couple's injuries. The jury deliberated just 90 minutes before unanimously finding for Disneyland.

The last ride introduced to the original Tomorrowland lasted just five years in the early 1960s, but it's a wonder the injuries weren't greater in number and severity. In 1961, the Flying Saucers landed, a ride that was basically bumper cars using hovercrafts. Bumper cars are typically the most injury-causing rides at an amusement park or carnival, because their express purpose is to get guests to ram into each other as forcefully as possible. Consequently, Disneyland never seriously considered a bumper car ride, but instead encouraged designs of "duck bump" rides—bumper boats that were basically inner tubes that a guest could lean in a certain direction and the boat would float in that direction, without ever achieving the speed or the impact that a car ride would. By the early 1960s, the space race was all the rage, so Disney designed a Flying Saucer ride with inner-tube-encircled hovercrafts. To lift itself off the ground, the first prototype craft had a giant spinning blade underneath it—an amputation nightmare in the making. Disney instead opted to place massive, high-powered fans underneath the ride surface, which would propel the motorless hovercrafts in whatever direction the riders leaned.

But while the Flying Saucers never generated tremendous velocity, they could severely jostle riders who weren't braced for the impact. Over the ride's five years, five women would file suit over collisions, with varying degrees of success. The first won $1,100 at trial (*Behar, 1962*). The second settled for $1,500 (*True, 1963*). The third had an even stronger case, since she was hurt when an operator pushed her saucer into the wall (*Gonzales, 1964*). She too settled. Juries found for Disney in the last two cases (*Lundin, 1964; Cusimano, 1964*)—guests who blamed their injuries on the saucers being "propelled erratically," one of whom smashed into the railing so hard she lost her earrings—because they were the ones who were in control of their own crafts.

But Disney had had enough, and yanked the unreliable ride as it began dreaming up plans for a whole new Tomorrowland.

The First E Tickets

Every year, Walt added new, increasingly elaborate attractions to increase Disneyland's capacity and appeal. So many unique, high-profile rides debuted in 1959, that Disney referred to their unveilings as the park's second grand opening and introduced a new, higher category to its ticket books: the E ticket.

Perhaps the most iconic addition was the Monorail, the country's first. Walt wanted his to be more than a theme park ride; he saw it as a viable real-world transportation system. As a prototype for future city planners, his Monorail would provide the ultimate in smooth, high-tech, trouble-free operation, and, for its entire 55-plus years of operation at Disneyland, has done exactly that. For one thing, no other attraction's vehicles have been completely redesigned as frequently. Disney has produced seven different Monorail models, each of them improving on capacity, aesthetics, durability, reliability, performance and safety.

As well, unlike its sister fleet in Florida—with its six stations and twelve trains traversing three separate lines that cover nearly five miles—Disneyland's single rail accommodates a maximum of three trains at a time across half the distance, typically at lower speeds. At Walt Disney World, the Monorail is more akin to busy public transportation, handling an average 150,000 riders a day, than at Disneyland, where it's more an amusement, transporting a small fraction of that total. Consequently, Disney World's fleet has suffered rear-endings, fires, a fatality and other mishaps—along with resultant lawsuits, while Disneyland's Monorail has been involved in fewer than ten cases, all lower profile.

In fact, the first three cases, which all arose during the ride's first year of operation, involved not the Monorail itself, but the escalating ramps that transported guests to and from its second-story station in Tomorrowland. Evidently, the three plaintiffs—all elderly women—were unfamiliar with or insufficiently spry to remain upright on the ramps. Two of the cases made it to trial. The first was a sweet old lady who was thrown to her knees on the downramp (*Campbell, 1959*). She wasn't exactly sure how it happened. She was probably pushed down by the crowd, but she couldn't remember. The jury gave her $4,500 anyway.

The second plaintiff's toe became trapped in the metal forks at the top of the moving upramp (*Bensley, 1959*). McCray argued that the ramp moved so slowly, patrons exhibiting even the minimum of caution could safely maneuver the system. Disney won the case.

Some years later, another woman said she fell on the exit ramp because the Monorail itself was "defective," because "patrons were caused to be brought out into the bright sunlight" and then forced to board a dangerous ramp (*Carlson, 1967*). She eventually dropped the action.

The Monorail's sparkling safety record was spotlighted in the case of a ten-year-old boy from Illinois who had the tailcone doors slide closed on him as he was exiting, trapping him by the head, until the doors could be yanked back open (*Hookham, 1999*). Although no medical personnel visited him at the scene, after the family returned to their hotel, they requested the Disney nurse come to their room. She noted a quarter-sized bump above his right temple and no marks to the left side. The boy seemed alert and denied losing consciousness. So she prescribed ice and aspirin. Convinced his injuries were more serious, the family drove him to the emergency room. There, doctors examined his bruised head, but found nothing further.

The family sued Disney for product liability, alleging the company had created an inherently dangerous ride. To try to prove the Monorail was plagued with problems, the family demanded copies of all maintenance work orders involving the attraction in the weeks leading up to and immediately following the incident. Disneyland turned over copies of 104 work orders. The plaintiffs thought they had the goods—until they realized that most of the reports were for regular maintenance and inspections, rather than illustrating problems with the doors or recurring complaints of things breaking down. Repairs were typically for items like a malfunctioning intercom, or the microphone in the station being too loud. The most interesting item: over a three-week period, three times maintenance men had to be sent to retrieve dead crows that had been electrocuted on the Monorail beam. The case was later dismissed.

The rickety wooden roller coaster was one of Walt's least favorite features of the amusement parks of the day, yet he knew that, due to audience expectations, eventually he would have to add a true thrill ride. So he insisted that his would be less rickety and highly themed, so that it didn't look like a roller coaster. Just as he discovered the idea for the Skyway during a trip to Switzerland, on a later visit he found his theme for a coaster—a bobsled run down the majestic Swiss peak, the Matterhorn. To make the ride more family friendly and more like a sled run over snow, he insisted on a smoother ride, which led to the track being the first ever designed of tubular steel, instead of wood.

Traditional coasters sent down cars linked in trains, to increase capacity. The Matterhorn's bobsleds, to imitate the luge design, would go down the mountain individually, with two seats that accommodated two riders apiece, by sitting in each other's laps. Ride operators would have to try to distribute the weight evenly among bobsleds, and the attendant in the control tower was charged with dispatching them at safe intervals, so a heavier sled didn't catch up with a lighter one. As a precaution, about two dozen spinning tires, called "boosters," were installed at strategic points along the track, such as longer uphill sections or after the big splashdown finale. The boosters rotated at the average velocity of how fast a sled should be traveling at that point in the mountain, helping to speed up lighter vehicles and to slow down heavier vehicles. In an emergency, the tower could also deploy several large skids pads installed along the track, to suddenly brake the sleds. And, as a last resort, the nose of each sled was filled with two feet of impact foam, in case of a collision.

When the Matterhorn Bobsleds opened in 1959, it had no minimum age or height requirement. Walt wanted the whole family to be able to enjoy it together, figuring no matter how small the child, he or she would be sitting safely in the lap of an adult. (Eventually, he'd impose a three-year-old age requirement, but no height limit was mandated until 2000 and, even then, it was only a modest 35 inches.) It didn't take long for the first incident on the

Matterhorn to trigger a lawsuit. One week, to be exact. An elderly woman sued not because she was injured, but because she was frightened (*Mogul*). She alleged she would never have taken the ride if she had known it was a "roller coaster" because such rides terrified her. The case made it to trial. Disneyland won, arguing that the nature of the ride was evident just by looking at the 147-foot-high mountain, and that the woman incurred no permanent damage.

But most of the 65-plus lawsuits involving the Matterhorn were filed by guests who claimed they received too rough a ride. Back in the days when operators dispatched the sleds, about half the cases centered on collisions. Disney lacked a strong defense; because the tower was in charge of maintaining appropriate spacing between the sleds, it was apparent who was at fault in the event of any impact. Consequently, Disney quickly settled the vast majority of Matterhorn crash cases.

During the ride's first summer, one bobsled stalled and a second smashed into the back of it, injuring all riders. Four passengers filed suit and Disney quickly settled (*Mann, Paiz, Rawson*). A few weeks later, a man was climbing out of his sled, when another sled barreled into the back of his, throwing him against the side of the sled (*Hicks*). The next day, another man was in a sled that stalled on an incline (*Mingus*). Ride operators had to give it a push, but moments later, it stopped again and a second sled plowed into the back of it. A week later, a man was attempting to board a bobsled when it was rear-ended, causing him to fall over the front seat and onto another guest sitting in the back (*Freed*). Disney settled with all three men.

The company was equally likely to settle other types of accidents that could be traced to the actions of the tower, such as bringing the sleds to too quick a stop. Beneficiaries included a little girl who was sitting in front of her father when the ride jerked, causing her mouth to strike the side of the sled and chip a tooth (*Schultz, 1960*), and a man who fell on the tracks after his sled dispatched as he was stepping into it (*Howard, 1975*).

In all, nine Matterhorn cases made it to trial. The only one Disney didn't win was the only one involving a collision. A woman stepped into a sled and was still standing when another vehicle smashed into the rear, throwing her from the front to the back seat (*Root, 1960*). Disney realized it was at fault, but the woman refused to settle. They went to court, and she won $4,200.

During the other trials, McCray and McCain were able to blur the line between operator error and injury, or dispute the injury entirely. A woman hurt her spine on the ride, but couldn't explain how (*Rubey, 1961*). Another lady claimed whiplash when her sled lurched to a stop at the top of the first hill (*Wegner, 1961*). A man said he endured the same rough stop, but his head was thrown back against the seat and his wife's head was thrown against his chest (*Polin, 1961*). Yet he admitted both of them were leaning forward at the time. A woman fell on her knee while exiting (*Webster, 1963*). A couple was jostled as their sled returned to the station (*Johnson, 1971*). A 56-year-old maid wanted $2,999 after stubbing her toes on the abrasive bobsled interior (*Avila, 1981*). McCain successfully argued that she cut her toes because she was wearing flip-flops and must have kicked the side of the sled in her excitement.

And, a 37-year-old woman alleged that as her bobsled was leaving the splash pool, another vehicle rear-ended it, crushing her right hand and wrist (*Bennett, 1987*). She failed to alert the park at the time of the accident. The first time the park learned of the injury—or the supposed collision—was when she filed her suit. An arbitrator awarded her $60,000. Disneyland refused to pay. So, she increased her demands to $138,000. But at trial, McCain convinced the jury that the accident never happened.

When Walt Disney World opened its first coaster, Space Mountain in 1975, Disneyland management immediately took note of how much more efficiently Florida's new computer-controlled system operated compared to the Matterhorn. But because the Matterhorn was the only thrill ride Disneyland had, it couldn't take it out of operation for an extended period to rebuild it. It had to wait until it added its own Space Mountain in 1977, before being able to shut the Matterhorn down late that year for a seven-month rebuild. As on Florida's Space Mountain, the new bobsleds would have two sleds linked together, to increase hourly capacity by 70 percent. Each vehicle would have redesigned bumpers, higher backrests to guard against whiplash, and a padded holding bar in front of each seat. But most importantly, two Program Logic Control computers would now oversee the operation of the sleds and emergency systems, automatically shutting down the ride if it determined two sleds were getting too close to each other. Operators in the loading area would now dispatch the sleds using computers on four computer kiosks, while the tower position would oversee a monitor that tracked the location of all moving sleds and two IBM printers that recorded all functions and abnormalities.

The Matterhorn benefited from having all its computer's bugs worked out during Space Mountain's breaking-in period, so mishaps were few.

Bobsled lawsuits plummeted; instead of guests lodging about three such suits a year, the computerized system cut the rate to one suit every other year.

Accidents, however, occasionally did happen—a number of them blamed on the Matterhorn's seatbelts. The bobsleds used long canvas straps that slid through the buckle and then the buckle clamped on to the strap. The slide-through "friction fasteners" made it quicker to strap in different-sized guests, but more difficult to check to make sure they were snug. Particularly at risk were the "lap" riders, whose belts pulled them down, but not back, because they were sitting in front of their friend instead of a rigid seatback. In 1980, a woman claimed she was ejected from her bobsled when her seatbelt "failed to hold" (*Mora*). She suffered a broken jaw, two fractured teeth, and a cut lip and chin. Disney settled.

Then, in 1984, 48-year-old Dolly Regene Young was thrown out of her bobsled and fatally run over by the next sled. Her seatbelt was found unbuckled, crossed on her seat. Her estranged husband and two adult sons filed suit, demanding $5 million. They contended that ride operators had failed to ensure that the belt was properly fastened before dispatching her sled. She must have stood up to gain access to the seatbelt so she could buckle herself in. Disney, however, suspected the woman had unfastened her belt, leaned forward, and rose to calm to her special-needs son in the seat in front of her, who had begun panicking as the bobsled entered the dark tunnels. But even if somehow the belt was left unbuckled, Disney alleged, the woman remained at fault for standing up.

The bobsleds carried about five million passengers a year and the only other serious accident the park would admit to was 20 years earlier. In that case, fifteen-year-old Mark Maples unbuckled his seatbelt, stood up, and his face smashed into part of the mountain. The impact fractured his skull and he was thrown from the sled. He never regained consciousness and died four days later. His father and stepmother filed suit, claiming the park was at fault for allowing their son to "be thrown, propelled, slipped or fell" from the Matterhorn. But Disney refused to offer a dime, insistent that their reputation was on the line. The boy alone was at fault. Discouraged, the Maples went into bunker mode. They stopped answering their phone and refused to return all calls, including from their own attorney. The lawyer ultimately was allowed to be relieved from the case, and the suit faded into oblivion.

The Youngs' case was trickier. Their victim wasn't a reckless teenager, and their attorney was all in. He sought permission to inspect the bobsleds for safety defects and planned to introduce at trial photographs of the bloody accident scene and the victim, after the bobsled had been rolled off her. Most powerfully, he discovered that not long after he filed the suit, the park changed the bobsleds' seatbelts to snap-in buckles, which would be easier for ride operators to check at load. Disney denied the change had anything to do with the lawsuit. They claimed they were forced to switch because their previous seatbelt supplier had gone out of business. Nonetheless, just as jury selection was to begin, the parties settled.

Although the new seatbelts buckled, their length still needed to be adjusted properly and the lap-seating arrangement ensured riders would never be fastened too tightly. Seven weeks after the Young settlement, another woman blamed not being "properly secured" in her seat for allowing her right knee to smash against the inside of her bobsled, causing bruises and tearing ligaments (*Smith, 1988*). Another woman alleged a rotator cuff tear because her seatbelt was not properly secured (*Enriquez, 2002*). Two years later, a heavyset tourist from Pennsylvania said ride operators, hurrying to rush on the last riders before closing up for the night, forced her to share the smaller front seat with another large adult, instead of allowing her to ride alone or with a child or other "proportionally sized and weighted person" (*Christy*). Their combined weight was "in excess of reasonable safety." In addition, she said, attendants failed to make sure that she was safely secured by the seatbelt and that her seatbelt functioned properly.

The last straw was in the summer of 2011, when a man from Las Vegas was directed to sit behind his considerably larger companion—despite a warning sign that stated: "Larger Passengers Enter First, Slide to Rear of Seat" (*Shorey*). Their friends, still standing in line, questioned cast members whether the men should switch places due to their size, but allegedly they were told everything was fine. The attendants also supposedly failed to confirm that their belts were fastened correctly. Shortly after they dispatched, the momentum of the ride pushed the larger passenger back against the smaller passenger, causing the back rider's head to strike the metal bar behind him. He began screaming in pain and begging to get off, but the ride continued. Once the sled returned to the station, the victim could exit only by crawling out on his knees. He collapsed in the unload area, where he remained until a park nurse arrived and contacted paramedics. He was placed on a gurney and transported to the hospital, where he was found to have suffered severe neck, lower back, and shoulder injuries. The park settled.

The following January, Disney shut down the mountain for more than five months to reconfigure it for all-new bobsleds. The new sleds would have locking seatbelts and no more lap seating. Instead there would be three single seats in each sled, with two cars linked together. As well, the ride's minimum height requirement was increased to 42 inches—second only to the Indiana Jones Adventure. Disneyland's original thrill ride, which became the first roller coaster millions of kids ever rode because for 45 years it had no height requirement, now had the one of the most severe.

The Submarine Voyage would be the most incident-free of all the signature attractions added in 1959. The vehicles moved less than two miles per hour, rarely started before all passengers were safely seated, and never encountered anything they could crash into—except occasionally each other, when one inched up a little too close pulling into port.

One wealthy passenger was stepping out of a sub just as a second boat bumped hers from behind, causing her to lose her balance (*Sherwood, 1960*). Although she had no visible injuries, she demanded to go to First Aid to treat her severely sprained back and neck and numerous cuts and bruises. The Disney nurse, however, couldn't find any cuts or bruises, so suggested the indignant victim go to the hospital. She promptly hired flamboyant San Francisco attorney Melvin Belli and his partner, Seymour Ellison, who staged a big show in court and convinced the jury to award the ailing victim $36,500.

The ride did have a couple of potential minor hazards. For one, because quarters were so tight inside the vessels, the seats had springs so they would automatically flip up and out of the away when not in use. Children, in particular, would leave their seats to push their faces up against a porthole, then lean back only to discover the hard way that their seat was no longer where they left it. One nine-year-old girl tried to sit back down, fell to the floor, and hit her head (*Sye, 1964*). Her lawyer demanded a list of all similar injury reports during the ride's first five years of operation. Disney provided two names: a woman who wiped out in 1960 and a five-year-old boy in 1961.

Potentially more hazardous, passengers entered the boats by crossing a loading ramp that flipped down across the top of the craft, stepping through a flip-up hatch, and traversing a tight spiral staircase—on a ride surrounded by water. The occasional stumble was inevitable. One woman testified that she was exiting through the hatch right behind her young son, just as cast members dropped the loading ramp into place (*Fitzjerrells, 1961*). Terrified that the gangway would sever her son's head, she quickly pulled him back into the sub, "causing her body to bend in an abnormal position and pinching her right hand against the side of the hatch." She demanded $500 for medicines, medical appliances, doctors, X-rays, and other expenses for the care and treatment for her injuries, plus $50,000 in general damages for her pain and suffering. Disney agreed to reimburse her medical expenses, but she was only able to furnish $32.50 worth of receipts. And, during the trial, the park nurse testified that the woman had confessed to pinching her right palm between the railing and the gangway as she was disembarking. Still, the jury ruled for the plaintiff—for $32.50.

The jury did rule for Disney in the case of a man who claimed that "a volume and quantity of water" suddenly began gushing through the entrance hatch, prompting him to dive out of the way to keep from getting wet and striking his back (*Mulhern, 1970*).

Handled out of court was a woman who was entering a sub when the hatch prematurely closed on her head, "knocking her practically unconscious" (*Kohl, 1987*). Her hair got caught in the hatch as it slammed shut, and for a brief period she was left dangling by her hair, allegedly causing headaches and a spinal injury.

Although the subs were among the park's safest rides, they were also among its lowest capacity and most expensive to maintain. So the attraction was "temporarily" decommissioned in 1998, despite disingenuous promises from management that the ride would reopen within five years. It took nine years, a change in management, and the idea of adding the marketable *Finding Nemo* cartoon characters to get the go-ahead for it to resurface. A year later, a woman entering a rebuilt submarine slipped on a wet top step and fell down three more steps. She landed on her side, struck her head on the side of the sub, and suffered a concussion, bruises, cracked tooth, and injuries to her eye and leg (*Hamilton, 2008*). Disney handled the case out of court.

Massive Movers

The main limitation on Disneyland's early growth had been ride capacity. Walt's initial response was to keep building more and more attractions. But he realized there was a better way after being hired to create four major attractions for the 1964-1965 New York World's Fair. The fair would draw more than 50 million visitors—ten times the number who'd annually visit Disneyland—and most of them would want to visit Disney's pavilions. Walt needed more efficient methods for moving larger quantities of guests through each attraction. The answer lie in continuously moving cars and multi-row boats. Instead of rides that several hundred people could enjoy in an hour, Imagineers began designing rides that cycled through several thousand people an hour.

Disneyland's first high-capacity "people-eater" was It's a Small World. By the time the ride was imported from New York, cast members already had two years of operational experience with the ride system. Consequently, when it opened in Anaheim in 1966, there weren't the problems typical of a new ride's break-in period. The exact same flat-bottomed bottoms floated through the exact same fiberglass trough, using basically the same track and boarding area layout, so there were few surprises.

Still, the ride did require operators to time the dispatch of boats properly. On its first Fourth of July, one of the busiest days of the year, a dispatcher sent a boat before a woman had a chance to sit down, throwing her against the seat (*Scott*). Disney stubbornly demanded to go to trial. On the stand, the dispatcher admitted to accidentally sending the boat too early and, afterwards, apologizing to the woman for his mistake. McCray decided to settle mid-trial.

Disney usually tried to settle similar instances of "premature activation," as one suit called it (*Iturralde, 1994*). But the park stood firm when there was no operator error. Close to 30 cases were filed involving Small World, most of them involving falls while boarding or, in a few instances, disembarking. Four such cases made it to trial; Disney won them all. In one, a 39-year-old secretary who weighed 280 pounds twisted her knee and ankle when the boat took off as she tried to step in (*Helland, 1988*). Her right leg caught between the dock and the moving wall, dragging her into the water. Her husband had to fish her out. She wanted $295,000 to cover her injuries and loss of future earnings. McCain argued, though, that operators had told her and her group to wait for the next boat, but her husband told her to get into a boat that was already fully loaded and had begun moving. Her injuries were attributable to her obesity. The jurors sided with Disney, ten to two.

A minority of Small World cases were caused by a second boat rear-ending the plaintiffs', either in the station or along the track, usually as the boats backed up near the end of the ride, waiting for there to be room at the unload station. Disney usually went to battle over collision cases, because boats bumped into each other every day, all day long, and, assuming the riders were properly seated and safely inside the boat, the impact would be negligible. Collisions in the station, however, more likely merited a payout. A thirteen-year-old rising to exit placed his left hand on the back of his seat to push himself up, when a second boat plowed into his thumb, tearing the nail off (*Davis, 1976*). Disney agreed to pay $976.95 in arbitration. A six-year-old was steadying herself on the rail of the boat, when an attendant "forcefully pushed" her boat against the side of the flume, breaking her arm in two places (*Miller, 1991*). The park settled.

Pirates of the Caribbean opened in 1967, using a similar boat and flume system as It's a Small World. It has generated more than 30 lawsuits, the majority stemming from either slip and falls while boarding or collisions. The boats were dispatched by an operator in the control tower, and if the operator launched before guests were fully in or out of their boat, Disney would usually end up settling. But those who slipped of their own accord, Disney would fight those to the death. In time, Disney would install an "enable" system, requiring operators working unload to activate a green light before the tower could dispatch a boat.

All three Pirates cases that made it to trial involved falls in the station. One woman said as soon as she sat down, she realized she was on top of a puddle of water, so she stood up, just as the boat lurched forward (*Tuckness, 1973*). She was thrown backward, injuring her arm and "violently seating her." Disney successfully convinced the jury that the woman stood up of her own accord, and operators had no way of knowing she would suddenly do so.

A 35-year-old mother holding her two-year-old son lost her footing while boarding, breaking her ankle and bruising her child's jaw (*Garcia, 1985*). She spent six weeks in a cast and her boy developed headaches, a sleep disorder, and hyperactivity. She argued that no one helped her into the boat, the area was poorly lit, there were no handrails, and the boat had a dangerous bump on the floor that caused her to fall. McCain responded that there was ample light, handrails right to the edge of the dock, and no bumps on the boat's floor. If she needed assistance, she should have asked. She merely lost her balance and fell. She wanted $165,000. She won nothing.

Another woman slipped in a puddle on the floor of a boat and, after pulling herself onto her seat, asked to see the park nurse (*Osorio, 2009*). But the nurse would take a while to arrive, so in the meantime she was sent through the ride, where she experienced "roller coaster-like drops and climbs." Ten minutes later, when her boat returned to the station, the nurse still hadn't arrived, so the attendant "requested that she complete the ride a second time." In increasing pain, she refused and demanded to be rescued from the boat. The nurse finally arrived, and she summoned paramedics to rush the woman to the hospital. In court, the woman testified that the anti-skid coating on the bottom of the boat appeared to have rubbed off, leaving a smooth, slippery surface. No matter, the jury sided with Disney.

The other common Pirates problem was collisions—and these were the ones Disney usually took out its checkbook for. Several rear-endings occurred in the station, but most occurred at the bottom of the first down ramp, where either a boat got caught up on the side of the flume or when a heavy boat was dispatched too quickly and caught up with a lighter boat in front. The first such accident happened four days after the ride opened in 1967, when a man's boat smashed into the boat in front of his and then was rear-ended by the next boat (*Illions*). Similar suits would be filed every few months for the next five years, until sufficient brakes and sensors were added to keep the problems in check.

But in 1994, Gary and Donna Neubauer from Los Angeles filed suit for $2 million after their boat bumped another boat that was backed up at the bottom of the first drop. Seconds later, a third boat came careening down the falls, rear-ending the Neubauers' boat, splintering and climbing over the rear of the boat, and injuring the husband's lower back. Their attorney, Drew Antablin, contended that, with all the cameras in the ride, cast members were aware that boats were backing up, yet continued to send boats down the ramp. To strengthen his case, he insisted that Disney be held to the higher standard of a common carrier, since they were transporting guests in a vehicle. Disney argued that the transportation was incidental. Guests weren't taking a trip to reach a destination; they exited in exactly the same place that they began. The judge ruled for the plaintiff, citing as precedent a mule ride at Smoke Tree Ranch that provided similar round trips. Soon after, Disney settled.

Antablin suspects the case settled so quickly afterwards because Disney had lost its common line of defense. He explained, "Without the heightened duty of care, generally speaking, a defendant, whether it was Disneyland or someone else, would always argue: 'We exercised *reasonable* diligence in maintaining and operating the facility, and what happened was a freak kind of thing.'"

A couple of plaintiffs complained they were injured on the chain lift at the end of the ride. A 69-year-old man said his boat lurched to a stop on the ramp, then suddenly jerked forwarded, whacking his back against his seat (*Kane, 1972*). A woman suffered a similar fate, as recounted that evening in the cast member log book for the ride: "A female guest claims her boat started up the upramp only to slide backwards half-boat length and jerk. Just happens she had back surgery five years ago. She comes up to the unload dock with $$ in her eyes. (The supervisor) came right over to assist with this one." Sure enough, she promptly filed suit, but Disney stood its ground, arguing that the plaintiff had a pre-existing condition. They finally agreed in arbitration to reimburse her medical bills of $204.30 (*Poche, 1975*).

T omorrowland had always been a patchwork of quick fixes and corporate exhibits. So as soon as the construction finished up on New Orleans Square, Walt got to work on an entirely New Tomorrowland. He would not live to see it completed, but when the area opened in 1967, it was exactly as he had intended. Its most noticeable addition was an elevated, constantly moving tramway that would add an overhead kinetic element and serve as a prototype for Walt's dream of an Experimental Prototype Community of Tomorrow in Florida. At Disneyland, guests ascended an escalating Speedramp to the second-story boarding area, then walked across a slowly-rotating turntable to enter the still-moving PeopleMover cars, which were linked in fours.

Walt envisioned the revolutionary ride system—pioneered as the Magic Skyway at Ford Motor Company's World's Fair pavilion—as a safer, more efficient alternate to automobiles. Nonetheless, several accidents occurred during the PeopleMover's first weeks in Anaheim, as Disney worked out the bugs. A couple sued for being "thrown about" on the ride (*Griffith, 1967*). A 60-year-old lady said she struck her foot on the ride (*Rosario*). A woman claimed she was rising to her feet in the last car of a four-car train when the ride suddenly shut down due to a power failure, but the following car kept going and rear-ended hers, causing her to strike her head on a metal bar and knocking her unconscious (*Broyles*).

The ride was so slow, running two to seven miles per hour, that rambunctious teens figured it would be fun to jump from one cabin to the next—not realizing that the cars occasionally sped up and that, should you fall between the vehicles, they would not stop for anything. One night during the ride's first summer, fifteen-year-old Ricky Lee Yama slipped while trying to hop from car to car, fell between the two vehicles, and was dragged and ground to an unrecognizable pulp. Before the ride's second summer, designers affixed metal bars around each car to deter guests from climbing out. Afterwards, fewer guests would attempt an escape, although one who wriggled out and also slipped, met the same fate as Yama (*Gonzalez, 1980*). Another teenager, who jumped onto the track to retrieve her Mickey Mouse ears as the car passed through a dark tunnel, was somewhat more fortunate (*Ogle, 1972*). As she chased back after the car,

The *What* Ride?

Plaintiffs don't always display a profound grasp of Disneyland operations in their legal filings. In some cases, they don't even know the name of the attraction they were injured on.
Here are a few of the choice misnomers:

The Jungle Book Ride
(Jungle Cruise; Lasry, 1997)

The Haunted House Amusement Facility
(Haunted Mansion; Shoshan, 2002)

Cup and Saucer Ride
(Mad Tea Party; Steiner, 1956)

Richfield Futurama Car Ride
(Autopia; Haynes, 1964)

Utopia
(Autopia; Hurt, 1981)

The Senior Autopia
(as opposed to the old Junior Autopia, perhaps? Donath, 1964)

Mickey & Friends Roller Coaster
(Gadget's Go Coaster, Humphrey, 2014)

Inspector Gadget Roller Coaster Ride
(Gadget's Go Coaster; Petrick, 2006)

she ran out of the tunnel, tumbled out the exit, hitting a stair railing and then the concrete 30 feet below. The impact crushed her leg, hip, pelvis and the right side of her buttocks, forced her to spend three months in a body cast, and left her with a limp. In court, the families of all three falling victims lost, because their injuries were caused solely by their own actions.

Another factor designers didn't anticipate was how the PeopleMover would react to rain. They found out one evening, exactly four months after the ride's grand opening. "It started raining," recalled PeopleMover foreman Tom Nabbe, who had that day off. "The cars were going up an incline, lost traction, and started rolling backwards. The cars behind wouldn't climb out of the valley. We had cars banging into each other."

Because the ride was designed to run continuously until it was manually turned off, cars continued to smash one into the next. "We were in the last car of a train of cars," said passenger Larry Strauss. "As our train came around a bend and up an incline, the train of cars in front of us rolled back toward us. We were hit from the front and then from the back by other trains. (After the first impact,) there was chaos, and there was a yell that, 'Here comes another one,' and as soon as that was out, the second collision hit. There was a lot of screaming." He and his wife suffered cuts that became permanent scars.

Another rider said she was thrown out of her seat, her face striking a metal pole and knocking her unconscious (*Noll*). Thirteen other passengers were treated at First Aid and, in all, 23 total riders would seek compensation from Disney. All agreed to settle except one, a woman who said her head banged into her daughter's head, cutting her cheek on the girl's wide metal barrette (*Frederickson*). She was also knocked to the floor and suffered a cut lip and lingering pain to her neck, back, shoulders, head and knees. At trial, Disney admitted the accident was its fault, but disputed the extent of the woman's injuries. The jury awarded her $37,740, but then several jurors confessed that they hadn't been given sufficient time to discuss the case. The judge agreed that the amount was excessive and told the woman to either accept $25,000 less or face a new trial. She refused. Disney, hoping to avoid a second trial, raised its offer to $17,000. Privately, they were prepared to go as high as $20,000. The woman wasn't budging. She got her new trial—and this time a judgment of $4,720.55.

Inside the park, Disney acted quickly to fix the problem. "First of all, we stopped running it in the rain," Nabbe said. "They installed mechanical lifts on the drive motors, changed the tires to a treaded, pneumatic tire, and changed the platens on the bottoms of the train so it wouldn't slip." All five operators that night and the foreman were fired, for not reacting quickly enough.

A final change would come reluctantly. In 1972, the five-year-old son of comedian Dom DeLuise was climbing out of a PeopleMover car when his left foot got caught under the next car's front metal wheel, severing his three middle toes. The following summer, a car ran over a five-year-old girl's foot (*Franklin*) and seven months later a twelve-year-old lost the tips of two toes in an identical accident (*Sparks*). Disney settled the latter two cases for about $16,000 apiece and then installed a protective flange along the track, to keep toes away from the the bottoms of the vehicles during load and unload. DeLuise's lawyer had hoped to handle the matter without filing suit, considering it a freak accident, but Disney's actions suggested a pattern. He finally did file suit—days before the seven-year statute of limitations was to expire. During discovery, the attorney researched First Aid files and found more than 75 similar accidents during the PeopleMover's first five years. After an arbitrator ruled DeLuise was due $80,000, the park quietly settled.

The PeopleMover was hit by several more suits related to injuries caused by rear-end collisions (*Martinez, 1987; Ahlers, 1993; Canty, 1994*), all of which were settled for modest amounts, before the ride was mothballed in 1995.

The most notorious feature of the New Tomorrowland of 1967 was Adventure Thru Inner Space, a trippy dark ride that pretended to shrink guests to the size of an atom. To ensure guests' attention was directed precisely at the right scenes, Imagineering designed a tram system that continuously moved like the PeopleMover, but featured clamshell-shaped cars that shielded guests from viewing unwanted areas of the ride. The vehicles, though, also gave the riders inside a sense of privacy, as if *they* couldn't be seen and, encouraged by the psychedelic images around them, would engage in all manner of illicit behavior.

Two weeks after the ride opened, a fourteen-year-old girl tried to jump from one car to the next, stumbled and was crushed beneath the two cars, shattering her pelvis and breaking both legs, one of them in five places (*Blakely, 1967*). She suffered a permanent deformity to her left foot, ankle and hip area, and accused Disney of creating an unsafe condition. Yet Disney fought back, arguing—as it would when Yama was crushed under the PeopleMover just three days later—that the girl was wholly responsible for leaving the vehicle. But, to make sure no one else tried to climb out of their vehicle—and to cut down on other mischievousness—Disney began stationing a lookout in the dark, to spy on riders during the most common trouble spots.

After eighteen years of constant mischievousness but few lawsuits, Inner Space was closed to make room for a *Star Wars*-themed flight simulator, Star Tours. It continues to enjoy a similarly litigation-free existence, although two months after it opened, a 43-year-old high school teacher was lured into riding by students she was chaperoning for their last ride of the night (*Costles, 1987*). At five-foot-four and 280 pounds, she did not enjoy the "more active" rides. But the students promised it was "rad." She didn't see any warning signs and assumed it was just a movie, like Circle-Vision or Mission to Mars. The turbulence sprained her neck and back, and prevented her from returning to work. Her lawyer blamed Disney for failing to warn guests of the ride's true nature and for designing defective seatbelts. McCain responded that there were, in fact, ample warning signs and the ride itself, including seatbelts, operated properly and safely. She had been willing to settle for $12,000, but asked for $78,000 at trial. The jury unanimously awarded her zero.

The Haunted Mansion copied Adventure Thru Inner Space's OmniMover ride system, with constantly moving clamshell vehicles that could be reoriented to any angle to keep guests' focus on specific elements—critical to the success of an attraction that relied on illusions. The continuous ride systems on Inner Space and the PeopleMover loaded and unloaded riders onto a turntable, moving at the same speed as the vehicles. But the plans for the Mansion dictated riders would load and unload in different rooms, and there was no room for two giant turntables. Instead, Imagineering designed moving sidewalks that would run alongside the vehicles at both load and unload. Unfortunately, guests could not seem to get the hang of stepping off the cars and onto the conveyor belt, and vice versa, made more difficult by the dim atmospheric lighting and the use of a black walkway. A week after the ride opened, a woman stumbled trying to climb into her Doom Buggy (*Georgiou, 1969*). The park settled, but as the bodies and lawsuits piled up, McCray knew he would have to mount a tougher defense. Roughly two dozen lawsuits would follow involving wipeouts on the moving walkways. Eleven would make it to trial, of which Disney would win nine of them, often because it could identify extraneous circumstances that contributed to the fall and, whenever possible, the jury would be invited to Disneyland to see the innocuous walkway in action. One plaintiff claimed that as she was exiting, her car moved forward unexpectedly, causing her to become dizzy, so she needed to be helped out by an attendant (*Libertone, 1969*). That's when she struck her foot on the ledge of the car and tripped. Disney was able to prove that the cars didn't move unexpectedly; they run continuously at a constant, predictable speed, so the cause of her tripping and falling was likely her own inexplicable dizziness.

A 55-year-old guest said she twisted her leg and bruised her knee when she was "thrown" out of the vehicle and onto the moving walkway (*Burke, 1970*). Disney was able to demonstrate that there was no force to eject her; she fell due to her own clumsiness. A 49-year-old woman said that while alighting from the vehicle, her foot "became entangled in Haunted Mansion's mechanism," knocking her over and dragging her several feet (*Byers, 1970*). Disney illustrated there was no mechanism to catch unsuspecting feet, just a smooth rubber walkway. A 77-year-old who fell and fractured her hip was shown to have fallen not from a dangerous condition of the ride, but from her own unsteadiness (*Long, 1974*).

The first of two Mansion plaintiffs to beat Disney in court was a 57-year-old woman who made the case that she fell only because an attendant, trying to assist her out of the vehicle, instead pulled her onto the walkway. She won $2,800 (*Swearingen, 1973*).

Eight years later, a 72-year-old immigrant from Ecuador fell onto the conveyor belt at load and broke her hip (*Murillo, 1981*). She argued that the ramp was hidden behind a darkened corner, there were no warning signs of the imminent danger, and no employee available for assistance. Disney countered that there were ample warnings—signage, audio recordings, and instructions by the hostess, who stood at the beginning of the ramp. The woman missed them all because she was blind in one eye and spoke no English. But, she didn't appear as if she required any assistance. If she did, it should have been apparent to any of the members of her large party. The plaintiff simply wasn't looking where she was walking.

The plaintiff had asked for $35,000 at the pre-trial settlement conference, scaled back to $30,000 at the start of the trial and to $25,000 while the jury was deliberating. Privately, she would have gone down to $20,000, but Disney wouldn't exceed $15,000. The jury, meanwhile, was in a quandary. They found the plaintiff sweet and sympathetic, but couldn't identify anything specific Disney had done wrong. After deliberating for five hours, they agreed ten to two to find Disney innocent, but still give her the $25,000. They submitted the verdict form finding in favor of the defendant, with the typewritten proviso, "However, we find that Disneyland has some responsibility and therefore award plaintiff $25,000." The judge was dumbfounded. He explained that the only way they could award her money is if they found against Disneyland. They filled out a new form, but McCray was livid. He got a juror to admit, "The majority of jurors wanted to find for Disneyland, but award money to the plaintiff." McCray demanded and was granted a retrial. The plaintiff agreed to a compromise before the case could be reheard.

Particularly early on, Disney made a number of changes to the loading and unloading process to reduce the number of injuries. They had extra operators at unload to help passengers out. They smoothed out an unnatural lip on the vehicles to provide greater clearance. They painted white dots and arrows on the ramp. They later added a fanciful yellow pattern, to make it even more unmistakable. The wipeouts gradually decreased to a trickle.

Although most of the Haunted Mansion lawsuits involved falls on the moving ramps, there have been about a half-dozen cases involving lap bars crashed onto knees or ankles, and a couple on the elevators. One woman was leaning against an elevator wall that turned out to be the door (*Miranda, 1999*). It opened unexpectedly, she lost her balance, and struck her head on a guard rail. After Disney settled the case, attendants were reminded to make sure all guests in the elevator were instructed to move to the "dead center" of the room.

The Race for Thrills

By the 1970s, the amusement park industry, particularly in Southern California, was beginning to change. Just as moviegoers began to look down on Disney's old-fashioned movie characters and franchises, parkgoers began comparing Disneyland's family focus to competing parks' younger, hipper audience of thrillseekers. In 1971, Magic Mountain opened 60 miles northwest, and quickly began adding bigger, faster, more extreme roller coasters. Just seven miles away, the once-tame Knott's Berry Farm added its first true coaster, the inverting Corkscrew, in 1975. That same year, Florida's Magic Kingdom opened its first coaster, Space Mountain. It was a hit out of the gate, and Disney knew it had to quickly bring the ride to California to keep up with the competition.

Disneyland, however, lacked the Magic Kingdom's luxury of space, and was forced to build its Space Mountain in a significantly smaller building.

There would be room for only one track, instead of Florida's dual track layout. So, to make up the loss in capacity, Anaheim's rockets were designed wider, so guests could sit side by side instead of single file. Now, each two-car train could hold twelve guests instead of eight. And, Disneyland's track was made ten percent longer, so it could accommodate up to twelve trains at a time, instead of eight. As a result, California's snugger Space Mountain ended up with same capacity of about 2,000 riders per hour.

Most importantly, Space Mountain's computer-controlled operation system was light years beyond the Matterhorn's manual system. The system automatically dispatched cars every 18.5 to 40 seconds, the interval constantly adjusted based on the number of rockets running and the weight of each load. Heavier cars were held back a little longer than lighter cars. If one car was gaining on another, safety brakes along the track would automatically slow it down. The operator in the tower would also be notified if two vehicles were getting too close to each other and entered the same brake zone, so he or she could hit the brakes. The brakes were all placed at the top of inclines, so if the ride had to be evacuated, cast members would head to each sled and, instead of forcing the passengers to walk back with them along the track, they could release the brakes one at a time, and the sleds would coast back to the station.

Although the operators in the control tower didn't manually dispatch vehicles, they did have plenty on their plate. They looked down on the loading area to make sure all rockets were ready to safely proceed, while studying a bank of computers and TV monitors to make sure all was well inside the ride. The computer actually increased the pressure and intensity of the environment, because operators were constantly on the clock.

"If you're working the tower, you've got a whole variety of things you're watching at the same time," said Larry Holmes. "You're watching the progression of each vehicle through its brake zone. You're watching the loading procedure inside of the Spaceport. You're making sure that no vehicle is getting too close to another vehicle and all of the vehicles are moving in the same time frame. If there's a delay, you have to buy time by bumping back what's going on before and what's going on after. Now, the computer will help you with that, but essentially it's a judgment call. It's up to you to inhibit this vehicle for a couple seconds because it's heavily loaded and the vehicle in front of it's lighter. If it caught it, it would start a ride cascade, and management's going to want to know why. Safety's really important to them, but at the same time, they want to make sure things flow smoothly. If you have a breakdown, it's gonna be a minimum of ten, fifteen, 20 minutes for you to get up and running. The whole ride stops. Everybody on the ride is going to have their experience changed. Everybody waits longer. Employees are going to have to go physically up into the ride to each vehicle. That can be dangerous."

The key position on the platform, "console," oversaw the loading process. The console position made sure new riders were safely seated inside their rocket, lap bars were lowered and secure, and everyone outside the rocket was a safe distance away. Console then hit a button to advance the rocket into the dispatch position, where the computer would decide how quickly to launch it into the mountain. At non-peak times, the position in the station before load was unmanned. Guests would remain seated until the rocket ahead of them was dispatched and the computer would automatically advance them to the load position, where they would exit. When it got busy, guests would unload at the earlier position and a second console would have to advance the empty rocket to load.

Disneyland did enjoy the advantage of having had the Magic Kingdom work out most of the kinks in the system, although Anaheim did have its own breaking-in period, filled with frequent breakdowns. Because of the computer monitoring, collisions were rare. Two cars in the same train did collide during Space Mountain's second summer, after they became uncoupled. The computer sensed a mechanical problem and stopped the front car, and the back car rammed into it. But since the riders suffered only minor bruises, Disney was able to dodge any lawsuits.

More often, sudden emergency stops, braking from a top speed of 32 miles an hour, kept trains from rear-ending each other. Yet the stops were so immediate, they occasionally resulted in whiplash claims—the most common complaint among the close to 40 Space Mountain suits filed over the years.

In fact, the first Space Mountain case to ever make it to trial concerned a 26-year-old psychiatric aide who claimed that as his sled was slowing down at the end of the ride, a second rocket rear-ended his (*Barton, 1981*). He demanded $10,000 for whiplash and a back sprain; an arbitrator awarded him $7,500. But Disney suspected he was lying. The plaintiff subpoenaed a copy of the ride computer's print-out for the time of the accident, which showed one of the brakes "overtrimming" or drastically slowing down the rockets. McCain argued that the ride, by design, drastically slowed down rockets as they came into the station. The computer's sensors and brakes made a rear-end collision impossible. The jury unanimously ruled for Disney.

The second most common complaint on Space Mountain was that passengers were injured due to the violent nature of the ride—although such claims were far fewer than on the significantly rougher Matterhorn. Space Mountain's problem was that it operated in the dark, making it more difficult for riders to anticipate and brace for twists and turns. Two families claimed Space Mountain's sheer intensity led to death.

In 1979, 31-year-old Sherill Anne Hoffman went to ride Space Mountain with her husband, ten-year-old son, and seven-year-old daughter. As soon as she was seated, she began slumping over, so that an operator allegedly had to "force" the lap bar down over her head. During the ride, her condition deteriorated, to the point where when her rocket returned to the station, she was too weak to climb out. Employees told her to remain seated, and that her sled would be diverted on to a spur track, where she could be slowly helped out without having to shut down the whole ride. Unfortunately, the dispatcher missed his cue and Hoffman's rocket was launched back into the mountain. By the time operators realized what had happened, they figured the woman would return to the load area more quickly by letting her just finish the second trip. When her sled returned to the station, she was nearly unconscious.

Cast members helped her out, and had her sit down for a few minutes, until a nurse and a security guard arrived to take her in a wheelchair to First Aid. There, she was advised she probably wouldn't need a doctor; people faint on Space Mountain all the time. When she passed out again, her husband demanded she be taken to the hospital. There, doctors discovered that she had had a tumor in her heart which broke loose during the ride, flowed through her blood stream, and pieces entered her brain. She remained in a coma until dying a week later.

Disney argued that there was nothing they could have done to prevent the death, since the woman's fate was sealed once the hidden tumor dislodged. Yet the husband's lawyer contended the wrongful actions by ride operators and the nurse exacerbated her condition and cost precious minutes that could have been used to properly treat her. Disney settled.

In 1992, a ride on Space Mountain twisted 32-year-old Antonio Burnistine's head and neck so violently, it tore a vertebral artery and he fell into a coma. En route to the hospital, he suffered a stroke. An Air Force master sergeant who had served in Operations Desert Shield and Desert Storm, he suddenly found himself a quadriplegic. His family sued both Disneyland, for the injury, and the hospital, for insufficient care. Two years later, they dropped their suit against the hospital, after his father-in-law was charged with criminal neglect for causing him malnutrition and removed from his care. A year later, Burnistine died of pneumonia. Disney settled with his wife and mother, and improved the head and neck support on its rockets.

A third victim barely escaped with his life—but Disney was determined to pay out nothing. In 1983, eighteen-year-old James Higgins and two buddies consumed eight tall cans of Magnum malt liquor before arriving at Disneyland. But when an attendant noticed one of the teenagers urinating in the parking lot, he instructed them to leave. So, they drove out of the lot—and then minutes later returned and re-parked their car. They headed straight for Space Mountain. Higgins was seated in the rear seat and, as his rocket took the final curve, he flew out of the vehicle, smashed into a wall, and crumpled to the ground five feet below the track.

Elizabeth Hayes was working load as their sled returned to the station. She recalled, "A young man got out of his rocket and walked over to the person on console and said, 'My friend jumped out of the rocket.' What? She looked at me, unsure what to do. I said we should E-stop the ride, but she called the lead. I said, 'We really need to stop the ride.' (The lead) said, 'No, no, no.' He walked the ride—with the attraction running—and when he arrived at brake zone 10, he saw the guy lying there. He left him there and told us to cycle out the attraction. 'We don't want any of the guests to see him lying there.' The nurse arrived, then an ambulance. (Higgins) squirmed out of the bar and tried to stand up. There's a dip right before that, then a really fast curve as you're coming around to the re-entry tunnel."

His buddies were taken to the park security office and interrogated by police for five hours. They finally fessed up to Higgins' daredevil antics. "He was 6-foot-5, 137 pounds, like a pencil with hair, and he lived to go to amusement parks, climb up the back of the seat, and sit there during the ride," remembered Jan Doezie, the park's court liaison. "Space Mountain is basically six circles to the right and then—whoop—to the left. That's where he fell out."

Higgins spent a month in a coma, only to awake paralyzed and with some brain damage. The last thing he remembered was boarding the ride. All he could figure was that his lap bar must have come up and maybe his outstretched arms struck a low-hanging beam. His buddies suddenly started claiming ignorance, as well.

Higgins' attorney told Disney he wanted $6 million. Nothing doing. Because operators cycled through the ride before shutting it down, Disney couldn't be sure which rocket Higgins fell from, so they disassembled and examined every rocket, inch by inch. Everything, including the lap bars, was in perfect working order. Disney knew the teen had somehow worked his way out of the restraint.

At trial, Higgins' lawyer upped his demands to $7.2 million. He pointed the finger at everyone. Cast members working the front gate, parking lot, and security were negligent for allowing three drunk teenagers into the park. The Space Mountain crew was negligent for improperly operating the ride. The Imagineers were negligent for creating a defective design that allowed his client to be ejected. And, the maintenance crew was negligent for signing off on a faulty lap bar. (The only cast member he didn't single out was the only one who actually did screw up—the lead who refused to immediately stop the ride. The lead was promptly demoted.)

The lawyer had an engineering consultant testify that he examined the rocket soon after the accident and determined that the only way Higgins could have fallen or jumped from the vehicle was if the lap bar had been raised. He also noted a ring-type safety mechanism inside the car that permitted passengers to unlock their own safety bars. Disney quickly replaced the device with a T-bar that made unlocking the restraint extremely difficult.

McCray countered that the ride was structurally sound, defect-free, and completely safe. In fact, he challenged, you can ride the attraction safely without a lap bar—but please don't. The only way for someone to be ejected was for them to intentionally wriggle free from the lap bar and raise his center of gravity. Under cross-examination by McCray, the plaintiff's expert even admitted that if Higgins would have stayed seated and kept his hands and arms in the vehicle, he would not have been thrown from the ride—even if the lap bar were raised. McCray then brought a rocket into the courthouse accompanied by a ride operator who was the same size and weight as Higgins.

"I had to go through all these cast members to find one who was also six-foot-five and pencil thin," said liaison Doezie. "I told him, 'I need you to get in that seat, I'll put down the lap bar, and I need you to wriggle free.' He spent 45 minutes to an hour practicing. He couldn't get out. Well, finally he figured out this puzzle and got out. So I said, 'Do it again, this time faster.' Then again, even faster. We had to get down to 35 seconds, or whatever the time was that it took from when (Higgins) got out of camera range to when he reached the top of the ramp. We got to where he could do it easily, smoothly every time I asked."

On the stand, McCray asked the ride operator to demonstrate how effective the lap bar was. Indeed, the restraint was formidable. Then he was asked, if a rider were persistent enough, could he work his way around it? "The plaintiff's attorney didn't think it could be done," Doezie said. "He was looking down at his notes when, wham, the cast member was out. The attorney said, 'I was looking downward and I missed it. Can we see it again?' We were thinking, 'Sure, you just lost the demonstration and you want us to repeat it?' This time the attorney walked up, took the lap bar, and shoved it down on the cast member. But this time he got out even quicker, in just a few seconds." The jury ruled for Disney, nine to three.

Space Mountain's unforgiving metal lap bars would be the subject of several more unsuccessful lawsuits. One man bruised his thigh when he slammed the bar down too forcefully (*Ohe, 1981*). Years later, a six-foot-four auto painter who weighed 270 pounds claimed his left thigh was severely bruised by a lap bar and wanted $200,000 for his trouble (*Sederberg, 1995*). But the man didn't make any mention of the injury until an hour later and, in court, delivered conflicting testimony. McCain suggested he may have been hit by an automobile.

Another recurring claim is guests, usually teenage boys, who leave their arms dangling out the side of their rocket as they return to the station, only to have their appendage crushed between the side of the rocket and the load platform. It usually occurs when no one is working the unload position, so their rocket is automatically advanced to load. The employee at the load console is so concerned with safely loading the guests, they don't notice the wayward arm in the next rocket.

Disney settled at least one of three such cases (*Cortes, 1993*). An earlier case, they played hardball against. A young teen's arm became wedged between the load dock and the rocket, and the operators rushed to try to manually shove the rocket backwards. Loader Elizabeth Hayes recalled, "One cast member suggested bleeding the brakes, but I said, 'You'll tear his arm off! Get everybody out of the rocket and rock it a little.' This gave us a little play and we were able to work his arm out. I had him sit down and hold his arm until the nurse arrived. His arm at the wrist was badly mangled. There are signs everywhere to keep yours arms inside the vehicle. I asked him why he put his arm out. He said, 'I thought the ride was over.' I asked, 'Was the rocket still moving?' 'Yeah...'"

Although his parents didn't want to pursue legal action, the accident permanently messed up the boy's wrist and derailed his participation in sports. So, as soon as he turned eighteen, he filed on his own. But after meeting with Disney's lawyers and discovering the uphill battle he would face, he quickly withdrew his suit.

In all, ten Space Mountain cases made it to trial, although several involved one-of-a-kind accidents. A 28-year-old dog groomer bent forward as her sled pulled into the station and struck her face on the seatback in front of her, chipping two front teeth (*Crowe, 1981*). McCain argued the victim bent forward not due to the forces of the ride, but of her own will. And, she had an extensive list of prior accidents (at least thirteen on record) and was claims conscious. She didn't get her $25,000.

One time, a rocket had to be diverted onto a spur track due to crying children. In the storage area, cast members began evacuating the rocket. While stepping out, a 39-year-old school teacher bumped his head on the low ceiling, spraining his neck (*Bennett, 1991*). He demanded $9,500, arguing there was poor visibility in the evacuation area and no warning of a low ceiling. McCain responded that the plaintiff was angry that his vehicle was sidetracked, and impatiently stalked off, without paying attention where he was going. He had also had prior neck surgery. The jury ruled for Disney, nine to three.

As he was boarding, an electrician found a plastic soda bottle on the floor of his rocket (*Rivera, 1997*). He picked it up and set it on the platform. A cast member then allegedly threw the bottle back into the sled, rudely shouting that "it was not his responsibility to throw trash away." Not only did the dressing down cause the passenger "to suffer humiliation, mental anguish, and emotional and physical distress," but in reaching to retrieve the bottle, he jammed his right middle finger on the vehicle floor, fracturing it. He asked for $1,693 to cover his doctor bills plus $250,000 for the harsh treatment. He didn't get it.

Another man said a kid sitting in the front of a Space Mountain rocket threw a Coke cup, causing him to turn his head so quickly, he twisted his neck (*Miller, 1948*). Disney won on appeal. And yet another man said ride operators who were helping him board a rocket caused him to fall by pulling away his cane (*Mayes, 2000*).

As the coaster packed on the years, mechanical failures became more frequent. But because the ride was so popular, Disney didn't want to leave it out of service any longer than it had to, so Space Mountain never received rehabs as long or as frequently as the Matterhorn. The addition of heavy speakers to accommodate on-board audio in 1996 also contributed to the ride's premature deterioratation, and welders were increasingly called in to patch cracking rails and beams.

In 2000, midway through a ride, a wheel hub assembly broke off from one rocket, activating the emergency shutdown system and halting all cars. But the damaged rocket buckled and its front wheels derailed. The sudden stop injured all ten passengers, one couple most severely (*Woodcock*). The husband was propelled forward and his jaw, shoulder, neck, head and chest slammed into the seat in front of him. His wife's foot became entangled in the wrecked rocket seat. Stranded in the dark, bleeding and suspended 40 feet in the air with the front end of the sled dangling over the edge of the track, she began screaming for help. For nearly 45 minutes, none arrived. During the interminable wait for rescuers, the couple witnessed cast members climbing on to the track and collecting pieces of the shredded rocket and track. They also alleged maintenance personnel began repairing and welding the track before rescuing any passengers. Disney medical and Anaheim fire department personnel finally arrived to administer treatment on the scene. The fire crew was shocked at the gravity of the situation; a ride operator had nonchalantly reported it as "We have a guest in the Space Mountain attraction with a foot injury."

Nearly 90 minutes after the accident, the couple was finally transported to the hospital. There, the husband was found to have suffered thirteen bulging discs, nerve damage from the base of his neck to the bottom of his spine, a dislocated jaw, cracked teeth, torn rotator cuff, and a painful joint disorder. The wife sustained a collapsed arch in her foot, permanent damage to her knee, hip and shoulder, and two herniated discs. Disney settled quickly.

Over the next two years, Disney began drawing up plans to rebuild the entire ride, incorporating all-new sleds and track. Months before they could initiate the rebuild, a rocket blew through the brake zone in the re-entry tunnel and smashed into the back of a vehicle that had been stopped just before the station. Seven guests were injured; four were taken to the hospital. One, an eight-year-old girl, suffered neck, back and shoulder injuries, and her family filed suit *(Sharp, 2002)*.

DOSH had Disneyland shut down Space Mountain for two days, to figure out what went wrong, repair the damages, and make sure they would hold. The following spring, the ride closed again—this time for well over two years, to gut the building and replace all mechanical parts, including track, beams and sleds.

By the 1980s, water-based thrill rides were becoming all the rage at amusement parks, and Disneyland finally began construction of its first—Splash Mountain—in 1988. Workmen targeted a January 1989 completion, but ran into a problem. The flume ride's climax, a 52-foot-drop at upwards of 40 miles per hour (the fastest ride in the park), left test riders soaked. Disney had no problem with some riders getting a little moist—after all, the word "Splash" in its name should tip off guests of the possibility—but drenching all passengers was not an option. They wanted everyone to be able to ride, not to have guests decline to accompany the rest of their group because they didn't want to get wet.

Disneyland postponed the ride's opening and began work redesigning the log boats and the flume. The original eight-person logs were replaced with seven-person logs made of lighter fiberglass and fitted with an underwater scoop to help deflect water. The bottom of the big drop was redesigned to further divert the splash around rather than into the logs.

The ride opened six months late, but the splash remained, albeit in significantly lighter volumes. Not long after the ride opened, a 30-year-old warehouse worker, Sandra Lucero, got so wet on the ride, water was spilling from her sandals when she climbed out. Because her sandals were so soggy, she slipped and hurt her legs, knees, back and neck. She was awarded $20,000 in non-binding arbitration, but Disney demanded to go to court. There, she increased her demand to $50,000, arguing that Disney should have either further redesigned Splash Mountain to make sure it didn't soak riders or provided a "dry-access" alternative. McCain countered that a ride called Splash Mountain could reasonably be expected to create a splash, and that the woman fell out of her own sandals, all by herself. The jury unanimously sided with Disney.

One problem was how freely guests could move within the logs. Instead of seats, riders straddled a long bench, single-file, with two narrow backrests for larger passengers to lean back against. The others sat in their neighbor's lap, none of them with a seatbelt. Momentum kept everyone seated as they were plunging down the big drop, but passengers were defenseless in the case of a sudden stop. Two days before the Lucero fall, another woman was thrown forward when her boat stopped suddenly *(Tupaz, 1989)*. She struck the seatback in front of her, bruising her chest and injuring her neck.

As on other flume attractions like Small World and Pirates, rear-endings were a worry, particularly in areas where boats were prone to back up, namely in the loading area and before the final drop. Disney typically tried to settle such cases, if the injuries were readily provable and could be linked to the operation of the ride, and the asking price was easy enough to swallow. They paid off a woman who whacked her head on a seat, suffering a broken nose and a concussion *(Freund, 1996)*; another who fell when her boat took off as she was stepping in *(Guyaux, 1995)*; and a third who suffered double whiplash, first when her log bottomed out at the end of the drop and later when it was rear-ended as she waited to disembark *(Hennings, 2000)*.

But if Disney sees an out, they'll take it to the mat. Seven Splash Mountain cases have made it to trial; Disney has won them all. A 40-year-old dentist suffered a broken hip and leg, when her husband fell on top of her during the climactic drop and she was thrown against the inside front of the log *(Chao, 1994)*. She argued that the ride lacked proper restraints and warnings of the considerable risk. McCain responded that the logs had sufficient handholds, and that it was near impossible not to be aware of the ride's five-story drop. The victim also admitted that her vulnerability to injury was related to her pre-existing rheumatoid arthritis. The jury agreed.

A 42-year-old electrician claimed his log took off before he had the chance to be fully seated, throwing his back against the seat and his son against his chest *(Haberman, 1994)*. He said the fall aggravated his congenital case of Scheurmann's curved spine disease and would require him to undergo future surgery to repair slipped discs in his back. The jury sided with Disney, believing the man's problems were caused by a pre-existing condition.

A woman and two children claimed they suffered strained backs, headaches, and emotional distress when their log came to a sudden, unexpected stop *(Garibay, 1998)*. The jury didn't buy their story. A 41-year-old doctor suffered whiplash after a rear-ending *(Avants, 1998)*. Again, the jury ruled for Disneyland.

In 1996, seventeen-year-old mechanic James Eubanks hung his left hand outside the log as it approached the lift, when his gold engagement ring caught on a screw head protruding from a hatch. A split-second later, the lift jerked the log on its journey, tearing his finger off from above the socket. As soon as operators learned of the accident, a maintenance worker rushed to the scene to retrieve his severed finger—and to tighten the screw and clean up the blood before photos could be taken. Ultimately, jurors believed Disney, that the teen was at fault for disobeying numerous signs and recordings warning passengers to keep their hands inside the vehicle at all times.

In 2010, Splash Mountain operators crammed too many heavyset passengers into the same boat, which caused it to become stuck in the flume at the top of the drop. Attendants had no choice but to evacuate the boat. But as one passenger, Steve Wilson, was climbing out, the log moved, causing him to slip and fall back into the log, striking his back on the top of the seat and aggravating a pre-existing back problem. He filed suit, asking for $1.3 million, to cover past and future medical costs, lost wages, and pain and suffering.

He retained Barry Novack, who earlier had seduced large settlements out of Disney in two other Splash Mountain cases—a woman suffering head, neck and back injuries (*Lynn, 1999*) and a 69-year-old whose diabetic condition was complicated when her log started before she could fully sit down (*Traina, 2000*). Novack charged that Disney was culpable for violating two of its own operating guidelines. First, Splash Mountain vehicles held a maximum load of 1,190 pounds. The five members of the plaintiff's group weighed a combined 1,475 pounds. Cast members, said Novack, "overloaded the log. The plaintiff was like 420. His friend was about 450. His wife was about 300. The ride broke down and had to be evacuated just at the top of the drop. And even though their operating manual says logs, when being evacuated, should be tied off, the ride operators didn't. They had never been trained to. My client stood up, the water started moving around, he fell back and was injured."

Novack contended that in the wake of the accident, Disney "began training cast members to tie off logs during evacuations. It's always been on the books; now it's in the training." As far as potentially overloading boats, he admitted that calling attention to an individual's weight could be uncomfortable, but suggested that in cases of doubt, perhaps Disney could install unobtrusive mats that guests could stand on before they boarded, to be weighed collectively.

Novack was able to have the case tried in Los Angeles, but the jury proved no friendlier. They ruled that Disney was negligent in not following its own rules, but that the negligence didn't contribute to Wilson's injuries. As in all seven Splash Mountain trials, the plaintiff took home zero.

Splash Mountain usually shuts down in January for an annual rehab that lasts well into February, timed to the coolest weather, when the fewest guests would miss a wet ride. When the attraction went down in early 2002 for an anticipated ten-week update, Legal did not want the ride reopening until new boats were installed with no lap seating. The logs were retrofitted with five individual seatbacks. Operationally, the change was a nightmare ride operators would have to make the best of. It reduced capacity to, at most, five from the six to eight of the old configuration. And, five made an awkward number for grouping, since most parties were made up of an even numbers of guests, forcing them to dispatch vehicles with empty seats, as they had on the Tomorrowland's short-lived five-seat Rocket Rods ride. (After seventeen months, they eased that problem on Rocket Rods by adding an express line for solo riders to backfill empty seats, but it would take nearly three years to add a single-rider line on Splash Mountain.)

Three weeks after Splash Mountain closed, Disney cut a record-sized check to the family of a boy who fell from Roger Rabbit's Car Toon Spin. Legal then pointed out that, six weeks after that accident, a passenger had been killed at Walt Disney World's Splash Mountain when, panic-stricken, he tried climbing out of his log right before the big drop. Disneyland's new log design terrified them. The flip side of gaining better back support with individual backrests was losing the better oversight of small children that lap seating provided. Now, parents would be in a separate seat from their small child. Park lawyers insisted the ride not reopen until precautions were in place to prevent small children from climbing out of the log. Seatbelts would slow down loading time and might not restrain wiggling children. Coaster-style over-the-shoulder restraints would have held kids securely in place, but blocked their view of the sets. The minimum height limit could be raised from 40 inches to 46 inches and at least seven years old. But adolescents — a target audience for the *Song of the South*-themed attraction — could no longer ride. And, that poor guest who jumped from his boat at Disney World? He was 37. Instead, Splash Mountain instituted a new safety position, wherein an attendant would be seated in the dark at the base of the big lift, to make sure no one stood up. The ride finally reopened, 20 weeks later, with new logs, more safety signs posted throughout the queue and loading area, and recorded safety spiels in English and Spanish blaring even after the logs left the station.

Disney continued to tweak the ride. Three years later, they changed the logs again, adding another seat for a sixth rider and widening the back seat, so a parent could sit side-by-side with a child, restoring theoretical capacity to seven per vehicle. In 2008, they noticed kids increasingly bonking their heads on the front of the log to avoid getting wet and they temporarily prevented anyone under five feet tall from riding in the front seat. And in 2011, new logs were introduced with a higher headrest for the back seat.

Meanwhile, visitor demographics and ridership habits had been changing. With the move in the early 1980s from A through E ticket books to an unlimited ride passport, guests were no longer restricted to riding a set number of E ticket rides and wasting the rest of their day on A's and B's. The old ticket system distributed the crowds among the rides. Now, there was nothing stopping someone from riding Space Mountain over and over and over again. In addition, instead of the typical guest visiting the park once a year or once every few years, the burgeoning popularity of annual passes in the early 1990s was creating a massive group of customers who returned monthly, weekly or even more frequently. Within a few short years, Disneyland would find itself with a roll of roughly one million annual passholders. Consequently, these were visitors who preferred rides with high repeatability, such as thrill rides, as opposed to movie-based or animatronic-based attractions that offered an always-predictable experience.

The pressure was on to design a massive E ticket attraction that offered not only the most thrilling of thrills, but presented them in a highly variable manner. Out of that environment was born the Indiana Jones Adventure. Guests riding in computer-controlled troop transports veered, skidded and suddenly accelerated through *Raiders of the Lost Ark*-inspired special effects in any of 160,000 possible combinations, so that every trip would seem different.

Consequently, riders had no idea which way or at what speed their vehicle would go next and were mercilessly whipped back and forth, from side to side, with no idea when to brace themselves. Even before the ride opened to the public in March 1995, Disney knew the ride would test the limits of what guests could handle. During pre-opening testing, cast members were used as guinea pigs, and exited with an assortment of bumps, bruises and strains. Imagineers toned the ride down twice before opening it to the public. Nonetheless, hundreds of riders would log injury complaints during the attraction's first two years of operation.

Most didn't file suit. The ride was instantly popular and drawing records crowds, so Disney didn't want to spoil the good buzz with news of injuries getting into the press. Instead, its guest claims personnel would consistently, compassionately follow up with the guests, explaining that they hadn't had any other complaints with the ride and their injury was a fluke. They'd then offer to cover any medical costs. It was the opposite of the often-confrontational attitude they were known for taking, and only a handful of victims ended up hiring a lawyer, including a fourteen-year-old who was thrown against the inside of the jeep, striking her mouth (*Katic, 1995*); a man who required back surgery after being whipped around in his seat (*Vasquez, 1995*); and a one-armed woman who suffered a torn rotator cuff because she didn't have two hands to hold on with (*Lerner, 1995*).

As the ride continued to rack up the injuries, Disney continued experimenting, eliminating "ride profiles" that were deemed too extreme. They pored over the injury reports, searching for patterns that would help track down specific causes of injuries that they could address. Riders knocking into each other? Slightly contour the seats and add foot rests. Guests cutting their mouths or cracking teeth when their faces smashed into the bar or seat in front of them? Add more padding on the grab bars.

At the ride entrance and near the boarding area, there were a total of three signs advising guests who were pregnant or who had bad backs not to ride. They added many more, through every expanse of the queue. The problem was that most riders didn't fall into those categories, but still many were getting hurt. They didn't have neck or back problems before they boarded the ride, but did when they staggered off.

On July 17, 1995, the park's fortieth anniversary, a celebration billed as "Forty Years of Adventure," 42-year-old genetics research assistant Zipora Jacob visited the park to celebrate her nephew's bar mitzvah with her two children and sister. Near the end of the evening, they headed for the new Indiana Jones attraction. The ride was so turbulent, it violently rattled her brain within her skull and reportedly tore a blood vessel in her brain, similar to "shaken baby syndrome." She staggered out of the vehicle, vomited and collapsed. Hours later, she slipped into a coma. She required four surgeries to treat a subarachnoid hemorrhage, or "brain bleed," and a permanent shunt was implanted in her head. Left a shell of her former self, she retained attorney Barry Novack. His initial plan of attack was to discover if others had been injured on the ride. Disney stonewalled. The park claimed no injury logs or complaint letters existed. After two years of stalling, the judge fined park lawyers $7,050 and ordered them to turn over the records.

Records revealed the hundreds of unpublicized injuries, plus numerous letters from guests begging the park to tone down the ride. In April 1995, Chris Neynaber wrote to park president Paul Pressler, to alert him of "a potential safety hazard—your newest attraction, the Indiana Jones Adventure... I realize the random nature of the attraction allows for varying the 'potency' of the experience. However, the attraction, at its most violent, still should not hurt your guests. The fun of attractions like the Indiana Jones Adventure is the appearance of danger without the actual threat of danger. Until safety precautions are programmed into the ride system to prevent such harsh and potentially harmful movements, I am convinced that it is unsafe. Guests should not have to board this attraction hoping to be spared from the random program that injures them. Mr. Pressler, I would appreciate it if you would look further into this matter. I hope that you will have the Indiana Jones Adventure more thoroughly tested and, more importantly, correct it so that all of Disneyland's guests may safely enjoy this elaborate attraction. Nevertheless, until it is corrected, I must discourage my family and friends from riding the Indiana Jones Adventure."

"A ride like this one could permanently injure someone," Robbie Harris wrote in 1996. "Take it from one that has found out, for I am still suffering from that ride and did not find Disneyland the Happiest Place on Earth that night! I have always enjoyed going to Disneyland and still would have had a wonderful time had I known that this ride was so forceful and fierce!! Believe I would have just simply skipped over that ride, like I do some of the others that are well posted, and gone on my merry way."

Deposing cast members also revealed that several had themselves been injured during the pre-opening testing, including the ride's operations manager and the resort's claims manager. All the while, Novack kept up the pressure in the press, hitting Disney where it hurt the most: right in the publicity department. No matter what, Disney didn't want the message to get out that its most marketable new ride was dangerous. The notoriety also helped Novack quickly become one of the country's most prolific representatives of theme park injury victims. As of 2015, he had filed twelve suits against Disney, plus actions against Six Flags, Hershey Park, and other amusement parks.

Novack also attempted the familiar trick of avoiding Disney-friendly

Orange County jurors by naming the Burbank-based parent Walt Disney Company so he could file suit in Los Angeles County. What he quickly learned is that one week after his client's accident, Disney had gone through a complex series of machinations to make it appear as if its theme parks were owned and operated separately from itself. On July 25, 1995, the Walt Disney Company incorporated the holding company, DC Holdco. Six months later, the Walt Disney Company changed its name to Disney Enterprises, Inc., and DC Holdco changed its name to the Walt Disney Company. Technically, the new Walt Disney Company merely held stock in various subsidiaries, such as the Florida-based Walt Disney World Company, which controlled the theme parks, including Disneyland. Anyone who tried to sue the Walt Disney Company over an accident at Disneyland would get a response from Disney that the Walt Disney Company did not develop, design, create, assemble, test, build, market or operate Disneyland or any attraction within it. They'd either have to sue in Orange County, where the incident occurred, or in Florida, where the Walt Disney World Company was based.

Novack didn't buy it. He was able to recreate the parent company's tangled history, despite its claims that the current Walt Disney Company had no predecessors, and to prove through excerpts from Walt Disney Company publications and quotes to the press that the Walt Disney Company does have sole ownership of both Disneyland and Imagineering, which designed the attractions, and is actively involved in both divisions' activities and financing. "All of my cases have been filed in and remained in Los Angeles County through creative lawyering, and knowing who and what to name," he said.

One week before the Jacob trial was set to begin, the parties settled. Soon after, Novack would file two more suits on behalf of women who suffered similar injuries on the Indiana Jones ride (*Bynum, 1998; Patino, 1999*). Disney took a year to settle the first case, two years to settle the second.

On June 25, 2000, 23-year-old Cristina Moreno and her husband traveled to Southern California for their honeymoon. They spent an enjoyable day at Disneyland, until they rode the Indiana Jones ride. She was jostled so fiercely, she stepped off feeling as if her "head was rolling around." She was unaware that she'd suffered a brain hemorrhage, only that she suddenly had an intense headache, so she didn't report an injury. As soon as the couple returned to their Hollywood hotel, she passed out. She was rushed to the hospital and later taken by air ambulance to Spain, but she never regained consciousness. On September 1, 2000, after multiple brain surgeries and $1.3 million in transportation and medical bills, Moreno died.

Because Disney had continued to operate the ride at such high turbulence, despite five years of mounting injuries, to the point that it had now taken a guest's life, Novack amped up the rhetoric in his filing. Disney was far worse than negligent, he wrote. "The conduct of the defendants was so vile, base, contemptible, miserable, wretched and loathsome that it would be looked down upon and despised by ordinary decent people."

Disney, however, said the victim made no report of any trouble or injury during or after her visit. The first they learned about the injury was when they were contacted by Novack—after the woman had died. Disney suggested that, like the Sherrill Anne Hoffman case on Space Mountain it had battled two decades earlier, the victim likely had a pre-existing condition that made her extra-susceptible to the dangers and traumatic forces of the Indiana Jones ride. Novack countered that this was no excuse. Disney should protect all classes of visitors, even the most fragile, even if they were unaware that they were a member of such a fragile class. "There is a subset of visitors who have a pre-existing condition that even they're not aware of," Novack said. "They've never been involved in an activity or in an environment that has significant force for it to manifest itself. Then they go on a strenuous attraction, which raises their blood pressure or subjects their body to certain forces or motion. Perhaps they have a weakness in their immunity system. Or suffer an aneurysm. I suggested that (Disney) put up a warning that people should ride at their own risk."

Novack demanded updated injury logs and copies of any additional correspondence, such as this 1999 letter from Marcia Sage to Disneyland's Legal Department: "I exited the Indiana Jones ride at Disneyland thanking God I survived it. Within seconds after the ride began, my body was whipped violently back and forth, side to side. It was not fun. It was not entertainment. It was torture. I immediately felt pain in my lower back and the base of my neck. Terrified, I braced myself in hopes that holding my body rigid would protect me. I remember wondering at the time if I would be safer were I to allow my body to go limp, Raggedy Ann style. Too frightened of possible injury, I stiffened, like a corpse, counting down the time remaining until I could disembark... I did not notify Disney of the incident. I wish I had. Maybe they would have taken action to modify the ride... but maybe my voice, in chorus with those of others, would have motivated Disney to undertake a reevaluation."

Novack accused Disney of not shutting down the ride to make repairs, in part, because, due to the ride's immense popularity, they didn't want to operate for a single day without it. In fact, weeks after the ride opened, mechanics noticed that severe rattling had begun cracking the undercarriage of several of the jeeps. Crews worked feverishly to make repairs so the closure wouldn't extend past a weekend. In fact, while other thrill rides might close for a month-long rehab every year or two for extensive improvements and corrections, the Indiana Jones Adventure ran for more than seven years before its first extensive overhaul, in May 2002. Coming shortly after he filed the Moreno suit, Novack accused Disney of using the rehab to make the ride smoother and safer, in reaction to his lawsuit. Disney insisted the changes were made to make the ride more reliable, so it would run longer.

To strengthen his case, Novack tried to argue that in operating the Indiana Jones ride, Disney was acting as a "common carrier," as earlier cases had proven with the surrey on Main Street (*Kohl*) and boats in the Pirates of the Caribbean (*Neubauer*). Other courts had consistently rebuffed the argument over the years, reasoning that thrill ride operators weren't common carriers because they didn't provide comfortable, uneventful transportation from point A to point B, as would a taxi, bus or elevator. The primary purpose of a thrill ride is to entertain, not to transport passengers to a destination. The superior court judged agreed, but the court of appeals reversed the decision, arguing that the passenger's motive, whether travel or entertainment, was irrelevant. A tourist in San Francisco who took a round-trip ride on a cable car strictly for entertainment was nonetheless transported. Roller coaster passengers, likewise, were deserving of the highest degree of care. The state supreme court upheld the decision.

It took another eighteen months to reach a settlement, so Novack is not sure how the ruling affected the final amount. "I can't go into the minds or heads of their attorneys, but it made our job easier," he said. "Disney would be held to the highest degree of care."

The Game Changers

The 1990s signaled a changing of the guard at Disneyland. For nearly a decade, new corporate leadership in Burbank had permitted the old theme park ways to continue, as an increased emphasis on marketing, adding new attractions, and making Disneyland fun and hip again reinvigorated attendance. But visitorship slowed when a recession hit in the early 1990s. Corporate sent new overlords to Anaheim who weren't steeped in Disney traditions or averse to making drastic changes. Nothing was off limits. They began hyping cheap annual passes to pad the attendance numbers, particularly during slower times. They cut back on staffing and on attractions' operating hours, figuring guests could wait a little longer in lines. They cut back on maintenance, considering prevention an unnecessary luxury. They accepted more frequent attraction breakdowns as a fair trade-off for lower maintenance budgets. What they overlooked— inadvertently or intentionally—was that breakdowns don't just inconvenience guests; they sometimes hurt them.

Certainly, new management presumed, a basic attraction like the Sailing Ship Columbia wouldn't suffer. Like the Mark Twain, the Columbia had been taking guests on placid, twelve-minute cruises around the Rivers of America since the 1950s, with mishaps a rarity. The only recurring legal problem was its cannon, which cast members fired twice each trip with twelve-gauge shotgun blanks/four-ounce black powder charges as the ship passed Fort Wilderness. The blasts were so loud that at least four visitors claimed they seriously injured their eardrums. The first three—an eight-year-old girl *(Wright, 1958)* and two women *(Mosher, 1961; Gzaiel, 1989)*—were passengers on the ship who claimed the cannon was fired too close to their heads. The child's suit made it to trial, but midway through, the judge granted McCray's request that it be dismissed as a non-suit due to lack of evidence. The other two didn't make it that far.

Nonetheless, ride operators were trained to keep passengers a safe distance from the cannon when it was being fired. "We motioned for the guests to step back away from the cannon, gave verbal instructions to cover their ears, and made very large gestures to get them to cover their ears," reported shipmate Larry Kaml.

Such precautions didn't help the fourth plaintiff, 34-year-old Elizabeth Venema, because she wasn't a passenger. She was on the mainland watching a preview of the new Fantasmic show in 1992 when the Columbia, dressed as Captain Hook's pirate ship, passed by and fired. The extra-loud discharge shook her body and caused permanent hearing damage. She was left with constant ringing in her ears and hyper-sensitivity to sound, forcing her to constantly wear ear plugs and leaving her unable to listen to music.

When Venema refused a small settlement offer, Disney sent private investigators to spy on her. They videotaped her around town and playing with her toddler, in attempt to show that the alleged hearing problems had no effect on her day-to-day life. Disney lawyers subpoenaed the records of a counselor she visited following her brother's death, so in court they could argue that her emotional distress really stemmed from family problems tracing back to her childhood. They deposed every client and employee of her daycare center, and tracked down former clients, Venema thinks, in an attempt to "break" her.

But what Venema did have was hard evidence. Two UCLA doctors—hired by Disney—confirmed damage to her auditory nerves. More importantly, her lawyer got his hands on test results showing that the cannon produced noise levels loud enough to cause hearing damage, levels greater than the 140 decibels permitted by Cal/OSHA. In fact, the dates of past sound pressure level meter readings showed that Disney was aware that the cannon was too loud well before the incident, but failed to correct the problem. At trial, Disney's attorney sought to have Venema's lawyer disqualified because he had obtained confidential information. It didn't work. Midway through the trial, the parties settled for $180,000.

By 1998, however, the Columbia—like the rest of the park—was beginning to show the stress of the new way of running things. Spots of peeling paint and dry rot were visible. A metal cleat on its bow, used to tether the boat to the dock, appeared loose—but no operators reported it, figuring their requests for repairs would be ignored. The boat rides previously used natural fiber rope, but if the boat was moving after the line was attached, the rope might break. To save a few pennies, all boat rides switched to stronger, three-strand nylon ropes—far less likely to break, but instead placing increased strain on the cleats.

All rides were staffed to the bare minimums, which meant if any worker became unavailable, the entire ride had to be closed. Attractions also operated less efficiently, because there were no more leads, who were usually old-timers who knew their ride backwards and forwards and could step in and lend a hand wherever needed.

Such was the case with the Columbia on Christmas Eve, which despite being one of the busiest days of the year, was scheduled with the bare minimum of three operators. One of them was running late to work that morning. But with the rest of the boats on the river either closed for emergency repairs or just not scheduled to operate that day, the Rivers of

America desperately needed something open. So an assistant manager, who had never been trained on the Columbia, volunteered to work the dock until the late worker arrived. That meant she was unaware that the ship needed to be practically idle before throwing the rope. So when the Columbia approached the dock moving a little too quickly after its first trip of the morning, she hooked the cleat. The nylon rope stretched until it yanked the cleat out of the ship and shot it back toward the dock. The nine-pound cast iron cleat first tore through her foot and ankle on its way into the crowd, where it struck 33-year-old tourist Luan Phi Dawson in the head and neck, and his 43-year-old wife, Lieu Thuy Vuong, in the face.

Disney went into bunker mode. The three victims were rushed to the hospital. Management had cast members block off the scene of the accident and scrub the dock clean. They never called the police. Instead, Disney gathered and sorted all the evidence itself, then selected and briefed potential witnesses. Police finally did arrive five hours later, after learning of the accident from paramedics at the hospital. But instead of conducting an investigation, police first spent two hours in the Team Disney Anaheim offices, where park management walked them through what happened and interviewed its hand-picked witnesses. The police chief later excused the process by explaining, "In all my years as a police officer, I found going immediately to the scene of a crime is rarely productive."

With his skull fractured and brain hemorrhaged, Dawson never regained consciousness. Two days later, he was disconnected from life support and died. His wife, Vuong, had been permanently disfigured and would require mulitple facial surgeries. If ever there were a can't-lose case for a victim, this was it. And Disney knew it.

"Disney begged that a lawsuit not be filed," shared Vuong's attorney, Wylie Aitken. "They promised full and complete access without us having to sue. We got everything we wanted. When we got right up against the deadline to file, they agreed to extend the statute of limitations. They wanted to control the story. (If a suit were filed) every court hearing would create a new story."

Nonetheless, Aitken continued to build his case, as if he would ultimately end up in front of a jury. The company's culpability was glaring, but—like Walt himself—Aitken was a storyteller. His job was presenting plaintiffs as highly sympathetic victims and turning their misfortune into a compelling narrative and the defendants into ruthless villains, using creative animated exhibits and videotape reconstructions. One presentation

COLUMBIA VICTIM'S attorney created detailed, animated exhibits to demonstrate what went wrong should the case come before a jury.

(Image by Aitken, Aitken & Cohn, 1999)

recounted the heroic story of his client interspersed with a timeline of cutbacks Disneyland was making at the same time.

"Mrs. Vuong is a wonderful woman, who was living the incredible American dream," Aitken recounted. "She was born and raised in South Vietnam. Her first husband was in the South Vietnamese Army. When Saigon fell, he was not killed because he was protected by his cousin, who was with the Viet Cong. He kept trying to escape Vietnam, but would be caught and brought back. He finally escaped into the U.S. through the Red Cross. Later, she and their two kids followed, taking a boat to Malaysia.

They ultimately reunited in Seattle. Shortly thereafter, her husband died of a heart attack. She put herself through school, learned some English, and got a job as a pharmacy assistant. There, she met a man who also had escaped Vietnam, working in the laundry room. He had an engineering background. They married, and she encouraged him to pursue a career. He was hired by Microsoft. For Christmas vacation, they took their younger son and a grandchild to Disneyland, where she lost her second husband and had half her face ripped off. Disney did not want Lieu Vuong's story in front of a jury."

Whereas for decades Disneyland had benefited in court from a halo effect, Aitken was intent on using the company's legacy as a weapon. "Early on, I took the theme: Eisner doesn't represent Disney; we do," he explained. "We symbolized the legacy of Walt. Eisner represented modern corporate America."

Although Disneyland was desperate to settle quickly and buy the plaintiff's silence, its insurer, AIG, was not nearly as motivated. Aitken had made clear that in addition to actual damages, he would also be seeking punitive damages, which in California can be up to ten times the amount of compensatory damages and, to deter future negligence, must be paid entirely by the defendant, not its insurer. AIG must have suspected that Disney was using its money not only to protect the park's reputation, but also to avoid paying punitive damages. It took nearly two years before Disney came to terms both with Vuong, for an estimated $25 million, and with AIG, over what share each party would pay.

Disney also vowed to reexamine and rewrite its Standard Operating Procedures on every attraction to improve the guest experience. Their goal, though, wasn't to make the rules stricter; it was to water them down. A team of hand-picked training managers who were well versed in every aspect of operating every attraction was encouraged to scrap the old SOP's and start from scratch. They started with the Columbia. Their suggestions went to Disney's lawyers, who massaged them into a new set of instructions, renamed "Location Operating Guidelines." These LOG's were similar to the old SOP's, but a bit more vague. Procedures were hard and fast rules. Guidelines sounded a bit more interpretive, presumably providing the company with a little wiggle room on the stand.

Cast members recognized the change as an effort to shift the legal liability for any accidents onto them, as Disney was doing in continuing to blame the untrained dockhand for the Columbia accident. And it also made it easier for management to make up rules and exceptions on the spot. New recruits might be trained to seat small children away from vehicle doorways, but there nothing was written in the LOG's. If preventing a guest from sitting where he wanted to might adversely affect his visit, let him sit where he wanted. If the guest was rebuffed and got upset, the operator would get dressed down by his supervisor. If the guest got hurt, the operator would be held responsible. The new guidelines seemed more to protect the company, than the guests.

Because it was the first land designed from scratch since New Orleans Square in the Sixties, Mickey's Toontown was the first in which company lawyers would be intimately involved in its creation—and its destruction. Disneyland had desperately been searching for a way to entertain children too small to ride all the Mountains added over the last 20 years. The solution came when the Magic Kingdom in Florida added a temporary Mickey's Birthdayland in 1988, to promote Mickey Mouse's sixtieth birthday. It wasn't supposed to be much—a collection of character meet-and-greets, a stage, shops, and a wee play area with a slide. But toddlers, thrilled to be able to meet Mickey in his own house and oblivious to immersive theming, loved it.

Disneyland decided to build its own version and knew just how to upsize the concept, with the release of the hit movie *Who Framed Roger Rabbit?* and its wacky Toontown. The westside could be the kiddie-oriented Mickey's neighborhood, the eastside the slightly edgier Roger Rabbit-centric Toontown, which would more appeal to teens and childless adults. And the areas would be connected by a bouncing Jolly Trolley.

Disney basically designed the place as a control-heavy Tom Sawyer Island, one in which kids would think they're running free, but their every movement would actually be monitored and regulated, like a heavily patrolled McDonald's Playland. As soon as Mickey's Toontown opened in 1993, Disney discovered that playgrounds can be a magnet for accidents and lawsuits.

The seemingly innocuous Acorn Pit, a trough filled with plastic balls, became the first casualty. Children would slip while running around the edge of the pit. Other children apparently mistook it for the restroom, forcing cast members to quickly evacuate and clean the pit, then fill it with a new set of acorns. In addition, the roof above the pit leaked, so every time it rained, the attraction's sponge-like floor swelled up with moisture and had to be shut down until it could dry out. Disney quickly decided it wasn't worth the hassle and began closing the pit for all but the busiest days. It was finally locked up for good.

The companion Chip and Dale tree slide was equally simplistic—and hazardous. The slide curved in a half circle, so to act as a bumper, a thick rubber rail, decorated with plastic acorns, was affixed to the sides. "I remember about nine broken legs," said operator Chris Perley. "People's legs would hit the protective rubber moulding on the sides and stop, but the rest of their body would keep going down." Worse were the parents who insisted on sliding down with their kids between their legs, only to see their limbs become entangled with their child's. Disney quickly began stationing an attendant at the top of the slide and posted a sign reading "No Double Riders."

In 1995, a 41-year-old woman struck her knee against a protrusion on the side of the slide and had to have her kneecap replaced *(Head)*. Her attorney demanded to see reports of all injuries on the slide, but Disney evidently was not forthcoming with the goods. A deposed cast member testified that there should be a record of all serious injuries. "Normally there is a report," the cast member admitted, "but bumps and bruises, you would hear about from cast members that worked on the attraction."

The victim's attorney then got the employee to recall specific incidents of kids who suffered broken bones from sliding down in their parents' laps. Disney settled right before the case was supposed to go to trial. But by that time, they'd already dismantled the slide. The company's excuse was that the slide was so popular, kids were wearing through the fiberglass, so after three years it had to be replaced. But they never replaced it. The real reasons it was pulled were the labor required to watch over it and the liability for the frequent mishaps. So, they just yanked the slide out. And, worse, they left in the treehouse-themed stairway that led to the top of the slide—so guests continue to this day to climb up the stairs, thinking there's a ride at the top, only to have to disappointingly make their way back down again.

Donald's Boat had a few more amusements to enjoy—"boiler pipe" slides, a cargo net, a spiral stairwell—but more amusements just meant more opportunities for injury. In short order, Disney removed the constricted tube slides, then the fall-inviting climbing net, and finally the circular stairs, stripping the boat bare. Ironically, the boat's most severe injury would involve not one of the amusements, but merely the elevated

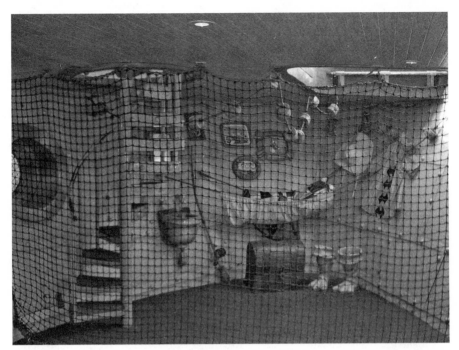

DONALD'S BOAT is still afloat in Mickey's Toontown... barely. Its activities were all either removed or disabled, including a climbing net converted into a barricade to keep kids away from the spiral staircase.

platform for the ship's helm. In 1995, a two-year-old "completely unaware and unable to comprehend the danger of the 'step,' lost his balance and fell, striking his head against a metal object" *(Radke)*. The boy suffered severe head trauma, a concussion, basilar skull fracture, nerve damage, and hearing loss to his left ear. His family waited nine years, until they were sure that their son had developed a speech impediment and a learning disability, before filing suit. They argued the park should have placed warnings and a railing around the four-inch step, and should have gotten medical assistance to the scene in less than 40 minutes. They sought $15,000 for past medical bills, $140,000 for future medical, and $1 million in general damages.

The adjacent Goofy's Bounce House generated a similar volume of bumps and bruises, but lasted thirteen years before it was gutted and replaced with a toddler play zone.

The one "thrill" ride on the westside was a kiddie roller coaster, Gadget's Go Coaster, themed to a Disney television character who would be off the air a few months after the ride opened. But it wasn't all that thrilling, because it operated just a single coaster, sent out at 52-second intervals, and never reached tremendous speeds, gliding along modest heights, drops and turns. One of the few lawsuits to involve the attraction concerned a 38-year-old woman who in exiting the pint-sized cars, caught her foot and fell back into the vehicle, fracturing her arm *(Petrick, 2006)*. She would drop her case.

The Jolly Trolley didn't generate many injuries, but it stopped so gradually and because the area was usually packed with guests, Legal was terrified that sooner or later it was going to run someone down. After a decade of off-and-on operation, the trolley was chained to the station to serve as a photo backdrop and eventually converted into a Disney Vacation Club sales kiosk.

Roger Rabbit's Car Toon Spin combined a blacklight dark ride with taxicab vehicles the guests could spin like the teacups. The ride operated safely for years, apart from the minor scrapes and slips associated with other dark rides. The one Car Toon Spin case that made it to trial concerned a woman who claimed that she was propelled into the ride without being "given enough time to adjust herself in the car" *(Holland, 1994)*. The jury sided with Disneyland.

The ride's reputation — and the park's entire approach to safety — changed on September 22, 2000. That day, the Zucker family visited Disneyland to celebrate mom's fortieth birthday. At about 10 p.m., they decided to ride Roger Rabbit before calling it a night. Mom entered the car first, followed by six-year-old Nicholas and four-year-old Brandon. Dad and grandma got in the next cab. But as they entered the first scene and the car began to spin, Brandon went flying out the open doorway. He was swept under his father's cab and dragged about ten feet underneath, until his crumpled body was wedged in so tightly, the vehicle couldn't go on any farther and shut down the ride.

His parents jumped out of their cars and frantically, unsuccessfully tried to pull Brandon out. Desperate, his father began running through the ride, pleading hysterically for help. He found the ride operator still at his station, wondering why the ride had shut down. But instead of calling 911 directly, the cast member — as he had been instructed — called a central communications center, where another employee pushed an emergency button that dialed the Anaheim Fire Department.

By the time park firemen arrived to remove his crumpled body, Brandon had been folded in half, without breath or pulse, for close to ten minutes. He suffered a broken pelvis and tailbone, ruptured diaphragm, lacerated spleen, internal bleeding, and massive brain damage. He would never walk, talk or eat solid food again.

Fellow guests were upset at the delayed response. One man said he was forced to shove cast members aside to provide help to the panicking father. Ten guests in the queue had to leap the chain fence, against the wishes of the ride operators, to run to the scene to try to free Brandon. Another visitor was so angry, he lodged a complaint at City Hall.

To the press, Disney officials deflected all culpability. They insisted the ride was perfectly safe. Twenty million guests had ridden Roger Rabbit in its seven years and only one other person had been reported to have left a vehicle while it was moving—a teenager who five months earlier jumped out to retrieve a stuffed animal and hurt her foot. Disney intimated that Brandon, too, must have wriggled out of the car on his own accord and that maybe his mother should have been watching him more closely. The family's lawyer, Amy Fisch Solomon, was dumbfounded. "Early on in the litigation, before I even filed the action, an article appeared in *The Register*, and (Disney) blamed the mother. I could not believe that," Solomon said. "As mom was standing in the ICU, looking at her mangled son, with more than half of the doctors and experts telling her to pull the plug, can you imagine hearing that?"

State regulators, citing a new theme park safety law, demanded the ride be shut down immediately, until they could determine what caused the accident and if changes were necessary. Although Disneyland insisted there was no delay in its response time, two weeks after the accident, a memo was distributed throughout the resort directing employees to dial 911 direct, unless they were using a radio. The memo, a park spokesman insisted with a straight face, was entirely unrelated to the Roger Rabbit accident. Seven months after the accident, Disneyland began stationing four full-time paramedics throughout the resort, along with ambulances and emergency equipment. Again, Disney denied that the move had anything to do with the Roger Rabbit lawsuit; it's just that with the opening of a second theme park, another hotel, and a dining/shopping district, the resort had gotten more difficult to navigate and Disney wanted to make sure emergency personnel arrived on scene quicker.

A three-month investigation by the state determined that Disneyland's emergency response was acceptable, but that the ride was inherently dangerous, because of the open doorways, the gap underneath the vehicles, and insufficient training. Days after the release of the report, the Zuckers filed suit, claiming Disney did about everything wrong: The family was loaded improperly, since the smallest in the group was seated closest to the open doorway. Their lap bar wasn't lowered all the way down. The cars had no doors. Employees should have called 911 directly, but had been told to instead call their supervisors, to keep any bad news off the radio. Employees were not adequately trained what to do in case of an emergency. The company failed to make safety changes after a previous accident and in recent years had cut funding for park safety.

Lawyer Amy Fisch Solomon said Disney, which had been warm, caring and generous, putting the parents up in a hotel near the hospital, became markedly less compassionate once they were served papers. The company tried multiple times to have the case moved from Los Angeles to Orange County. "The patent for the Roger Rabbit ride was held by the Walt Disney Company and the design team was based in Los Angeles," she said. "I had to ask the (designers), who signed your paycheck? 'I don't know.' It was like pulling teeth."

Solomon had to go to court three times to compel Disney to hand over the documents she requested. They finally dumped 30 bankers' boxes filled with forms at her office, hoping to bury her in paperwork. She sifted through them all, finally turning up an early design plan showing the Roger Rabbit taxicab—with a door. "A door had been designed, and it was ultimately decided to omit the door because of the precious seconds it would save during loading," Solomon said.

Instead of dragging the case out like the typical slip-and-fall, Disney settled less than thirteen months after the filing. The $43-million deal did not require Disney to assume blame, but did allow the Zuckers to take care of Brandon at home with 24-hour nursing care, instead of at a pediatric facility. Brandon passed away seven years later, at the age of thirteen.

Roger Rabbit's Car Toon Spin remained closed for ten months, while Disney piled on the safety precautions. The cars received thick latching doors. Their sides were raised, as were the backs by adding what was supposed to look like a convertible top. Black, pressure-sensitive skirts were added around the base, closing the gap and, if they made contact with anything weighing more than eight pounds, would shut down the ride within two seconds. Sensors were also installed along the track so that if so much as a cap fell out of a vehicle, it would register on the control panel, so the operator would know exactly where the problem was and could send someone out to remedy it. Warning signs were posted throughout the queue, and an audio recording played instructing how to ride safely. Employee manuals were rewritten with additional safety measures, including how to properly load guests and what to do if the ride stopped. All operators were retrained.

But the changes didn't stop in Toontown. The accident made Disney proactive, committed to anticipating every possible accident that could happen parkwide. They began adding extra safety features and warning signs on every attraction, including diagrams to illustrate proper seating configurations and safety recordings in multiple languages. They made sure every loading and unloading platform had yellow-and-black warning stripes to highlight the edges of platforms. They named a corporate chief safety officer. And, most surprisingly, they released a 30-page report detailing their heretofore secretly guarded safety procedures, including how they designed rides with safety in mind and how they would report accidents going forward, then posted the document online, for the world to see.

Safety, in fact even just the notion that someone could possibly get hurt, had always been something too real-worldly, something Disneyland never wanted to talk about. They basically hoped upon hope that guests would behave as expected, rides would run as expected, operators would run them properly, and everything would come out well in the end. But they finally realized that for absolute safety, they were going to have to petition for the guests' help in protecting themselves. And that they could no longer do everything in their power to get guests to forget about reality. They had to remain vigilant, for their own good.

"As soon as people walk into Disneyland and see the flowers shaped like Mickey, they're in Fantasyland," Solomon said. Consequently, there's a greater need to let guests in on the secret, to tell them exactly what they need to do to stay safe, particularly on attractions that cater to small children. "I was very adamant that employees needed to pay particular attention in Toontown. (The case) changed a culture. Lines are going to get a little longer, but it's worth it to improve safety."

In theory, Big Thunder Mountain Railroad should have been the safest roller coaster Disney ever built. It was the first to use computer-aided design, to ensure a smoother ride. The vehicles don't spend an inordinate amount of time racing through the dark, where it's difficult for riders to brace themselves, or veering through narrow tunnels. There are no loops, overbanked turns, or high-speed launches.

Consequently, Big Thunder never generated the volume or the recurring types of lawsuits that Space Mountain and the Matterhorn did. Big Thunder lawsuits arose once every couple of years and were, for the most part, unique circumstances. The ride's first suit and its most recent were the two that made it to trial. During Big Thunder's opening weeks in 1979, 52-year-old Joyce Corey claimed she suffered whiplash due to the severeness and abruptness of the ride. Had she been warned of the high speed, jostling and turns, she never would have ridden. Disney countered that the woman admitted not noticing any pain until the morning after the alleged accident, and did not report it until nine days later. McCray insisted the ride was not dangerous in design or operation; however, the plaintiff should have known what she was getting into if she chose to board a contraption billed as the "wildest ride in the wilderness." The jury took a half-hour to absolve Disney.

Thirty years later, a 31-year-old woman boarded Big Thunder and, as her train began ascending the second incline, it came to a stop *(Shouse, 2009)*. Operators determined that there were too many coasters on the track at one time and decided to evacuate hers halfway up the hill. As she began lowering herself to the track below, she twisted her ankle, severely spraining it and requiring surgery to repair a tendon. Again, the jury blame the plaintiff for her own injury.

Other suits have involved a guest who was struck by a lap bar *(Satterberg, 1981)*, three friends who said their car tipped over *(Dogra, 1985)*, and a 40-year-old Romanian who in 1991 said he was thrown from the coaster, but couldn't recall how. Grigore Grigorean was found unconscious, lying on a catwalk adjacent to the track, a gash to his leg. The victim would only say, through a translator, that he remembered feeling faint during the ride and may have passed out. Disney, however, was immediately suspicious. The man couldn't have raised the lap bar by himself and never before had a Big Thunder lap bar failed. They rounded up every possible witness, and no one saw him fall off the ride. In fact, no one could remember ever seeing him get on the ride. Disney became convinced that the man had ridden earlier and dropped something, then sneaked into the back area of the ride to retrieve it, when he was struck by a train. Grigorean had a fundamental flawed in his accusation: he claimed he didn't remember a thing. He eventually dropped his case.

In March 1998, the Fackler family from La Jolla, California, made their first visit to Disneyland with five-year-old David tall enough to ride all the roller coasters. Nearing the end of a long day, David wanted one last ride on his favorite: Big Thunder. His seven-year-old brother entered first, followed by his mother. David sat down next to the open doorway. As the trip came to an end, their train stopped about 20 feet shy of the platform. David innocently stuck his left foot out the side of the car, the way he'd slow down his bike. When the train restarted, his foot became wedged between the edge of the platform and the car's running board. The lap bar kept him in the vehicle, but his foot was practically torn in two, connected only by two tendons. The operator hit the E-stop button, but it took workers a half-hour to pry off the running board to free him. After multiple vein, muscle and skin grafts, his foot was saved, but his toes had to be amputated.

David's mother, Kathy, had no intention of taking Disney to court. She realized it was an accident. Disney didn't believe her. The company immediately began stonewalling. Kathy asked to be put in touch with the other guests who had been so helpful, to thank them. Disney said it couldn't; they had to protect their confidentiality. She later learned that when those guests asked to be put in touch with her, to see how David was doing, Disney gave them the same line. Disney conducted its entire investigation of the incident without interviewing the Facklers or other visitors. When Kathy asked if she could see the safety changes being implemented in response to David's accident, she was told she'd have to buy a ticket, stand in line, and see for herself.

Weeks after the Columbia tragedy, the Facklers settled with the company, but refused to sign away their right to speak about David's accident. Kathy, in particular, was uneasy with how secretive Disney had been. Then she read a newspaper article about the Columbia in which Disney claimed the Columbia incident marked "the first serious injuries of visitors in four years." She was incredulous. David's accident had occurred just nine months prior—with dozens of witnesses. She quickly discovered that Disney was able to hide information about most accidents from the public because California was one of ten states that did not regulate fixed-site amusement parks. She began speaking out to the press and lobbying lawmakers for a bill forcing the state's amusement parks to undergo annual state inspections, report any serious accidents, and make that information available to the public. Privately, Disney fought the efforts tooth and nail. Increased oversight by another state agency would be burdensome. Worse, publicizing every accident might make the public fearful of its rides and doubtful of its commitment to safety. It also could diminish its advantages with juries and arm plaintiff's lawyers with extra ammunition.

The bill passed and went into effect January 1, 2000. Months later, Legal demanded that Disneyland install its first safety gates in a ride's loading zone—at Big Thunder. The ride also got its share of new training, additional safety signs, warning spiels, and recordings, like all the attractions did in the wake of the Roger Rabbit accident. On stage, it appeared as if Disney was consumed with safety. Behind the scenes, the company was still cutting corners.

Yet, statistically, Big Thunder still appeared to be one of the safest rides in the park. Mechanics in charge of caring for it knew better. Big Thunder, because of its weight and unorthodox design—with a lighter weight fake locomotive being pushed by a series of passenger cars—placed severe stressors on the ride.

As the summer of 2003 drew to a close, ride operators began noticing recurring problems with train number two, I.M. Brave. It was pulled offline after a clicking noise was reported. Mechanics replaced a guide wheel, but a few days later, the clicking resumed. The train was pulled off again and maintenance replaced an up-stop wheel, but failed to tighten the bolts and place a safety wire around them. They did yellow-tag the train, indicating the train was not ready to be returned to service. Three days later, on September 5, the Friday to start the busy Labor Day weekend, ride operators placed I.M. Brave into service, even though it was yellow-tagged, and without sending it out for a test run. After just a few trips around, cast members detected the clicking. Yet they knew if they pulled the train immediately, they'd have to answer to management for it. So they sent it off for thirteen trips before finally conceding to pull it. But about a third of the way through the ride, as the train was entering the fastest part of the attraction, a floating axle on the locomotive in front of the passenger cars shifted and derailed. Quickly, the train started to deteriorate, just as it entered the final turn before the tunnel. As I.M. Brave barreled through the tunnel, its derailed wheels slammed into the brakes between the rails. The impact yanked the front of the locomotive down and flipped its rear up, tearing away from the cars and smashing into the roof of the tunnel before crashing down on top of the first passenger car. The underside of the locomotive crushed the car's fiberglass and metal frame—and the two 22-year-old men inside. Vicente Gutierrez suffered facial fractures, cuts and bruises, broken ribs, and cracked teeth. His best friend and business partner, Marcelo Torres, was pinned beneath the locomotive—his chest crushed, his ribs, shoulders, collarbone and nose fractured. He died soon after from internal bleeding due to severe blunt trauma.

Guests in the cars behind them suffered neck, back, head and knee injuries, a crushed foot, chest pain, and psychological trauma. In all, eighteen of I.M. Brave's 24 passengers filed suit, most of them represented by the Columbia attorney, Wylie Aitken. Compared to the previous accident five years earlier, the investigation was night and day. "Because of the new law, OSHA went flying into Disneyland, sealed up the place, put up yellow tape, and shut down the ride," Aitken said. "There was no quick clean-up, no sanitation. No one was allowed in there except the OSHA people. The Disneyland people toured the scene when I did."

Aitken was shocked to discover that, despite all the hoopla about safety, little had improved in training, operation or maintenance procedures, as confirmed by OSHA's investigation. The agency pinned the blame on operator and maintenance worker error, exacerbated by poor procedures and vague guidelines. OSHA demanded everyone involved in the ride— operators, managers and maintenance workers—be retrained, particularly regarding the green-tag/yellow-tag system. Any new trains were to be given a test run before being placed into service. Operators were to be given precise instructions on what to do if they detected an unusual noise or smell. And maintenance workers were no longer allowed to sign off that tasks were completed unless they performed those tasks themselves.

Disney jockeyed with the injured passengers for a full year, hoping to reach "fair and just" settlements without having to have them actually file the paperwork. It didn't work. The Torres family, in particular, wanted more than cash. They wanted an apology. "The family," Aitken explained, "wanted someone to say, 'I'm sorry.'" When Disney settles, however, the company rarely if ever acknowledges any wrongdoing. In fact, publicly dodging blame was usually one of its chief reasons for settling in the first place. After another fourteen months of negotiations, three days before the jury selection was to begin, Disney finally agreed to Aitken's price and condition: the company publicly admitted regret and took full responsibility for the accident.

Disney ended up settling every single suit, including with several riders who didn't suffer any injuries, but who claimed they were "subjected to extreme fright and shock, severe and permanent mental pain and anguish,

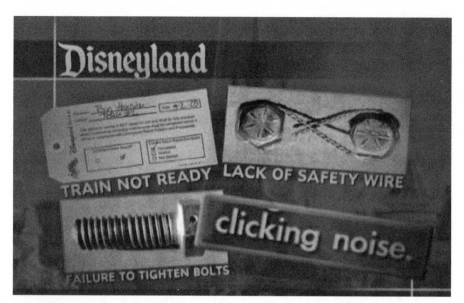

MULTIMEDIA PRESENTATION by the Big Thunder victims' attorney spelled out the multiple failures that contributed to the crash.

(Image by Aitken, Aitken & Cohn, 2004)

and will continue to be deprived of his emotional tranquility, and live in a constant state of emotional tension."

Big Thunder was closed for six months. A few weeks after it reopened, an operator tried to clear the empty vehicles from the tracks after an E-stop and accidentally plowed one empty train into the back of another. DOSH immediately shut down the ride. Big Thunder was back open a day later, but three months after that, on July 8, 2004, the Cope family of Colorado visited the park and decided to brave Big Thunder. Their three-minute ride appeared to transpire without incident, but at its conclusion, the ride operators decided to take their train out of service. But, instead of switching their train to the spur track to be unloaded and removed from service, the operator accidentally sent their train into the main station, where another train was being loaded. As the Copes' train smashed into the back of the other vehicle, the father was thrown backward and then forward. He immediately felt pain in his back. He said the injury led to back surgery and would likely require a future back fusion. His wife and two children were thrown about in their seats, and suffered bruising and emotional distress.

The Copes quickly contacted Wylie Aitken. They filed suit, blaming

Disney for reopening the ride too quickly, before it was safe for the public, "in order to advance their economic interests and detract from the tragic events of September 5 and the root causes thereof." In addition to poor training and maintenance, the suit charged, "Disney knew, or should have known, that the design of Big Thunder Mountain was unsafe from its inception, causing numerous unreported derailments, near misses, and component part failures repeatedly over its 25-year history."

Disney responded that the father already had a bad back and was attempting to make the company pay for surgery he would have required anyway. Nonetheless, when it could make the numbers work, Disney settled.

Big Thunder continued chugging along without major incident until 2013, before Disney decided to tear up the track, replace all the cars, strip down much of the scenery, and basically rebuild the ride over the next fourteen months. Big Thunder, as with Space Mountain a decade earlier, needed a fresh start.

IV

Beyond the Berm

WHEN DISNEYLAND FIRST OPENED in 1955, the company had its hands full trying to maintain safety and tranquility inside its gates; fortunately, it didn't oversee much acreage beyond the berm that it had to worry about. Its primary other holding was the 100-acre parking lot out front. Even then, when the park first opened, only the two closest sections of the lot were paved; the rest started out as dirt parking for the rare days of overflow crowds. Disney figured most visitors would opt to excitedly walk—or run—to the front gate from their cars. But for those who wanted or required assistance, particularly from the outer edges of the lot, Disneyland operated a small fleet of makeshift trams.

Its original blue-and-yellow trams were comprised of aircraft tow tractors pulling cars with long back-to-back seating that faced out to the sides. The configuration forced passengers to board and exit from both sides of the vehicle, often resulting in guests crossing in front of the tram or between the cars. The trams' slick aluminum seats and lack of seatbelts, restraints or doors added an extra hint of adventure.

Less than three months after the park opened, the Wrather Company unveiled the Disneyland Hotel across the street. Disneyland not only licensed its name to the hotel, but also contracted to provided tram service to the park, meaning the vehicles would travel longer distances, across a public street, and often at greater speeds.

At least 35 parking lot tram-related lawsuits have been filed. Eight made it to trial. Disney has won them all. In the first, an elderly woman stepped off a tram while it was still moving, suffering bruises and a dislocated shoulder *(Goodman, 1956)*. She said the fog was so heavy, she couldn't tell the vehicle was still in motion.

One lady tried to walk between the cars and tripped over the coupling, breaking her knee *(Schramm, 1967)*. The jury agreed that she shouldn't have tried to take the shortcut.

Cases that were undeniably driver error were quickly settled. A seventeen-year-old who was hurt when her tram ran into a cement planter was awarded $1,100 *(McCreary, 1967)*. A married couple from Korea were injured when their tram collided with a station wagon *(Choi, 1976)*. Seven other passengers collected settlements ranging from $200 to more than $15,000 when their tram plowed into a cement pylon *(Santos, 1995)*. A motorist settled confidentially after being rear-ended by a tram *(Geher, 1973)*.

Fully half of all tram cases involved guests who claimed to be ejected from the tram. After a few riders slid out, skid guards were applied along the original aluminum seats. Yet, because the seats faced outward, back to back, they could still act as launching pads if trams took sharp corners a little too quickly. Disney was convinced the arrangement was safe if guests remained fully seated, weight back for the entire trip. So, to avoid admitting that its design was inherently dangerous, Disney vigorously fought all suits by riders who were thrown off a tram. The trick was to get plaintiffs to admit they were voluntarily moving or leaning toward the outside of the vehicle. Disney's argument was weaker when victims insisted they were remaining back in their seat, such as 59-year-old Lucille Logdson—who filed suit, following a 1965 incident in which the "tram jerked and swayed violently, throwing her to the pavement." She landed on her head and was knocked unconscious. She awoke to discover she had suffered a bruised temple, black eye, and scratches on her face, knees, hands and arms. Disney handled her case out of court.

When work began designing new, larger capacity trams, Disney knew it needed a new, safer configuration. The new 1969 trams featured six rows of seats per car. The seats were made of less slippery fiberglass instead of metal with a curved lip at the corners, to make it harder for someone to slide out still-doorless doorway. The ejections continued. In 1971, 58-year-old Lillian Kennedy boarded a tram and sat in the back row, but her eleven-year-old grandson was straggling behind and the vehicle took off without him. So, the boy began running after it, for about 100 to 150 yards, before finally catching up with grandma. But when he grabbed her outstretched hand, he was pulled underneath the wheels of the tram and yanked grandma out of the tram. She landed on her head and was knocked unconscious for several minutes.

In 1980, a 42-year-old housewife from New York boarded a tram back to the Disneyland Hotel, when she realized she had left her sweater on a bench near the Main Gate *(Sussman)*. She stood, just as the tram started up. The woman tumbled onto the pavement and fractured her skull. The injury cost her her sense of smell, which she claimed placed her in great peril because she could no longer smell smoke or other signs of danger. She demanded $150,000. She pointed out that, unlike the parking lot trams, the shorter hotel trams often had no attendants riding at the rear, whom guests could notify of an emergency. As well, there were no buzzers or bells to alert the driver. McCray's defense was simpler and irrefutable: the woman intentionally stepped off a moving tram.

In 1984, a 30-year-old unemployed cable installer tumbled off a tram and broke his wrist *(Haminger)*. He claimed the tram was traveling too fast and turned too sharply. An arbitrator awarded him $2,250, but he wanted $25,000. Disney refused to pay a nickel. At trial, witnesses testified they saw the man stand up before falling. The plaintiff responded that he stood up in an attempt to cross his legs because he had to urinate. McCain then got the victim to admit that, while he fell off the tram to the hotel, he had intended on returning to his car in the parking lot, and he didn't report the accident until a week later. Witnesses said after he fell, he quickly stood up and ran to his car. Obviously, the man jumped off when he realized he was on the wrong tram.

Another woman said she had no choice but to step off a moving tram *(Barillas, 1997)*. The tram took a turn so fast, her bag flew out the side. She screamed for the driver to stop, but he nodded no, with a "stupid smirk on his face." So she took matters into her own feet, stepped out, landed on her head, and suffered a concussion. The judge agreed that, smirk or no smirk, the woman was entirely at fault.

Disneyland unveiled a third, red-and-white fleet of heartier parking lot trams in 2000, after much of the parking lot was closed for resort expansion and replaced with a remote parking structure. While the new trams didn't feature any noticeable safety improvements, they did turn more tightly. The back of the old five-car trams would swing out up to five feet. The new seven-car trams had steerable wheels on every car, so the back would swing out no more than two feet. Yet the trams still had no doors, despite having to travel even greater distance and at higher speeds.

Thereafter, about one passenger a year would file suit for flying out the open doorway. Disney continued to play hardball. In 2006, one victim was able to procure a small settlement to cover a broken arm *(Martinez)*. A year later, three Chinese sisters were riding the tram parallel to Harbor Boulevard, when one stood up as the tram turned toward the Lion King parking lot *(Zhao)*. She fell out the doorway. Both sisters tried to grab her, and both fell out. The first women suffered only minor injuries. One of her sisters, though, hit her head on the pavement, cracked her skull, and suffered severe brain damage. At trial, her attorney argued that the driver was traveling dangerously fast. Disney insisted he was traveling closer to five miles per hour. In fact, the trams' speed is governed so drivers can't exceed eleven mph. Yet, shortly after closing arguments, the parties settled.

A month after the deal, Julia Gillin, a private security guard, visited Disneyland with her boyfriend and five family members, and she purchased an annual pass. After a long, crowded day at the park, they headed for the tram at about 1 a.m. The group had to wait about 20 minutes before they reached the front of the line and finally crammed onto a tram. Gillin was the last one to board, barely squeezing on. "The first turn, people started to lean against me, and I thought, whoa," Gillin recalled. "There were no poles to hold on to, like on a bus. I grabbed onto this woman's stroller. She told me not to touch her stuff."

As the tram began taking the wide final turn toward the station, Gillin flew out the open doorway. Her head struck the curb, bounced back against the side of the tram, hit the curb again, and then rolled under the tram. Fellow passengers screamed in terror. The driver hit the brakes, one wheel skidding to a stop so close to Gillin's head, emergency personnel would later have to cut her hair to free her. "I heard that I was the seventh person to fall at this spot, including two girls who, on that corner, stood up too soon. One's a paraplegic," she said. "The next thing I know, I'm under the tram. A woman—maybe a nurse—said, 'Julia? Julia? Can you hear me? Can you feel me touching your hand?' 'I can feel you touching me, but I don't know what you're touching.' My body was so twisted up. I recall them cutting my hair, pulling me out from under the tram, placing me in a collar and on a board. I was in and out of consciousness. It felt like a red poker was stabbing me in the head."

She was transported to the hospital, where several hours later she was visited not by a park representative—but by two Anaheim police officers. The officers were responding to a claim by one witness—the crabby woman with the stroller—that Gillin had jumped, trying to commit suicide. In her purse, they had found Prozac, which she used to treat panic attacks. "I realized they were trying to set me up," she recalled. "Why would I buy annual passes that day? I started getting angry, then I passed out. My boyfriend gave (the hospital) my purse, they went in, took my insurance card, billed it to my insurance."

Injuries forced her to miss a year-and-a-half of work and move in with her parents. Severe headaches continued. And the more she learned about how Disney handled the aftermath of the accident, the more nervous she became. Cast members reportedly told witnesses to put away their phones, because 911 had already been contacted, emergency personnel were en route, and "we don't want to tie up the lines." Fellow riders on the tram were rounded up for two hours of questioning, punctuated by happy talk about Hidden Mickeys and visits from Disney characters. Despite one passenger who admitted to feeling guilty that she may have leaned against Gillin and accidentally pushed her out, Disney said they didn't retain any of the witnesses' phone numbers—except for stroller lady, who supposedly made up the jumping story at 3 a.m. to end the grilling.

Yet for the first several weeks, a friendly Disney representative would regularly check in on Gillin. "He was calling me every day to see how I was doing, until I mentioned that I thought I was being set up and perhaps I'd better contact an attorney. As soon as he heard I might lawyer up, he said he couldn't call me anymore. The only thing they offered me was a $5,000 nuisance fee. I'd already spent $25,000 on medical bills."

After she retained a lawyer, Disney investigators visited her at a firing range, where she practiced for work, to intimidate her, accusing her of being a dangerous threat and threatening that she could lose her license. Her lawyer tried to get a copy of the videotape from a surveillance camera thought to have captured the accident. But, she said, Disney claimed it retained recordings for only three days and then deleted them. But why would they erase the tape if it showed Gillin jumping? When the stonewalling continued, her lawyer quit. She tried to represent herself for a short while, but eventually "they wore me down" and she withdrew.

Unbeknownst to Gillin, Disney had already begun work designing doors for the trams. In 2010, before she even formally filed suit, an outside contractor began retrofitting the new 3.0 trams with locking doors. The installation took about a week per tram and, during the three-month-long changeover, Disney continued operating trams with and without doors. When they were down to just two trams left to fix, Jasmine Esquivel boarded one of the remaining doorless trams at the Mickey & Friends station. During the ride, her camera fell to her feet. As she leaned over to retrieve it, the tram was traveling at such an "unsafe speed," she flew out the open doorway. Her head slammed against the pavement with such force, she suffered a fractured skull, bruised brain, damage to her sense of smell, and temporary amnesia. Her accusation was simple: Disney invested hundreds of thousands of dollars adding doors to its parking lot trams to correct a dangerous flaw—yet continued to force some unsuspecting visitors to ride dangerous, doorless trams. The park settled.

In the meantime, no doorless trams would be allowed to transport guests ever again. And since that time the only passenger to fall out of a tram has been a boy who was injured after unlocking his own door and jumping out.

Even if the automobile accidents inside the Disneyland parking lot didn't involve a company vehicle, Disney would often get sucked into resulting lawsuits because they owned and maintained the scene of the accident. Motorists claimed that their visibility was impaired by Monorail pylons *(Sanders, 1964)*, power lines *(Zamini, 1980)*, bushes and trees, or that the area lacked sufficient stop signs and oversight *(Ginnings, 2011)*.

In 1985, seven-year-old Jennifer Faith Reid was heading back to her car, about fifteen feet ahead of her uncle, when a tour bus drove through a stop sign and made a wide right turn toward her. The girl was knocked down by the right front side of the bus, and then run over by its rear tires, killing her. Her family sued the bus service and the driver. The defendants settled for $1.5 million, but figured Disney's defectively designed parking lot was partially to blame, so they turned around and sued Disneyland for $500,000. The driver insisted that he operated his vehicle "in a completely normal manner," following Disney's instructions and accepted procedures. Disney was the one that set up the bus route, the orange traffic cones, the barricades, the signs, the road markings, the speed limits, the pedestrian waiting areas and walkways, and the size and positioning of the parking lot crew. Disney had agreed to pay $170,000, but at trial the jury cleared them of paying anything.

The construction of Disney's California Adventure (DCA) on

Disneyland's old parking lot required moving the parking across the street and constructing a massive, six-story parking structure holding 10,250 cars. Disney had never been a big fan of escalators, preferring stroller-friendly moving ramps instead. But the descent from the structure was too steep; they had no choice but to build a series of forever-long escalators. Trip and falls seemed inevitable. One woman fell forward onto the "faulty escalator with uneven steps" and landed on the side of her face, cracking two teeth and injuring her knee, back, neck and shoulders *(Nguyen, 2010)*. It was Disney's fault, she charged, because "at no time were there signs warning her of the danger of the escalator."

In 2012, one guest claimed that while his family was riding down, their escalator suddenly increased in speed *(Morales)*. Patrons were sent to the bottom so quickly, they didn't have adequate time to walk out of the way and began piling up at the base of the escalator. Within seconds, riders were being "flung and crushed into the pile of people which had formed at the bottom of the escalator."

Extra care is required when it rains, due to the slick red tile walkways leading to the escalators. A doctor slipped on wet tile as he was exiting the escalator to the fourth level *(Turner, 2011)*. As he reached for his phone to call security, a fellow guest slipped in the same spot. By the time security arrived, two more visitors had wiped out.

One morning, a 65-year-old woman was cautiously making her way through the structure across the soaked tile, when she slipped, injuring her left knee and both wrists *(Judkins, 2004)*. She removed her sandals and resumed her walk, now only on the adjoining concrete, until she arrived at the escalator where she had no choice but to again cross the tile. She took one step and slipped again, injuring her ankles and reinjuring her wrists.

For more than 30 years, the outskirts of its parking lot was where the magic ended, the farthest boundary Disney had to maintain. In 1988, the company acquired the Disneyland Hotel—and all the liabilities that came with it. Certainly, Disney was well versed in hotel operations by this time, as it had owned and run hotels at Walt Disney World in Florida since 1971. For the most part, it just meant more bathrooms, restaurants and swimming pool decks to slip on. Disney purchased a second hotel, now the Paradise Pier Hotel, in 1995 and opened the Grand Californian in 2001.

There have been a few suits, however, that Disney could never have anticipated. In 2000, a Disneyland Hotel guest claimed he was injured by noxious fumes coming through the building's ventilation system *(McCormick, 2000)*.

A Paradise Pier Hotel guest broke her ankle when she put her foot on a couch bed in an attempt to open it, and the bed closed down on her foot *(Gonzalez, 2004)*. A family of four received a combined $2,984 in small claims court, after they contracted scabies from a hotel bed *(Wayne, 2012)*. Disney settled with a man who suffered a knee injury when an elevator at the Disneyland Hotel Convention Center's parking garage stalled, suddenly dropped several feet, and then abruptly stopped *(McFarlin, 2004)*.

A hotel guest claimed she was roughed up by a masseuse at the Grand Californian's Mandara Spa *(Bruno, 2011)*. She said the employee had made an oral promise to deliver a "relaxing" massage, but instead, "through neglect, carelessness and unlawfulness, (she) received a careless and much more forceful deep tissue massage." Her injuries required the use of ambulances, hospitals, nurses, X-rays, medicines, physicians and surgeries, and prevented her from returning to work. She sued for negligence, battery and breach of contract. Disney settled.

Food issues that arose from incidents at its hotel restaurants and from room service have been comparable to the occasional troubles Disney has endured with its in-park restaurants. They usually win cases concerning purported food poisoning and more often settle claims that diners found foreign objects in their food, such as a man who broke a tooth on a rock in his chicken fucilli *(Rosales, 1999)*. But one restaurant at the Disneyland Hotel, Goofy's Kitchen, introduced something the company never had to deal with inside the park: an all-you-can-eat buffet. For the first time, Disney was ceding control of food service—and the mess that came with it—to the guest. Several diners filed suit after falling in the buffet line. One who slipped on spilled eggs settled for a small amount *(Santana, 2008)*. Two other middle-aged women went to trial. The first tripped at the dessert table, fracturing her ankle and cutting her finger when the plate she was carrying shattered *(Sokolow, 2002)*. The second slipped on an unknown "liquidy food substance" on the floor, fell forward, and her face smashed against a wrought-iron handrail, breaking her nose and knocking her unconscious *(Gonzalez, 2009)*. She claimed that when she was revived, a Disney nurse kept insisting she was "just fine," before ultimately relenting and calling an ambulance. The nurse's notes, however, showed that the women initially confessed that she tripped because, while walking briskly, she suddenly changed direction and her foot came out of her shoe. Both ladies went home with nothing.

The opening of DCA also introduced a casual dining trend to the resort that had been uncommon inside Disneyland: food courts and their accompanying self-serve beverage stations. Like with buffets and food, allowing guests to pour their own drinks created constant messes and required cast members to be ever vigilant.

During DCA's first summer, self-employed swimming pool cleaner Darwin Holmes visited the resort for his honeymoon. While pouring himself a drink at Hollywood & Dine's beverage station, he slipped on the wet concrete floor and fell on his tailbone. Allegedly, his tailbone jammed straight up and bruised the base of his spinal cord. He struggled to his feet and had difficulty walking for the rest of the day. When he woke up the following morning, he discovered he had lost control of his bodily functions from the waist down, including movement of his legs. Disney offered him a sweatshirt and a lifetime pass to the park. Holmes was convinced the area was poorly maintained and should have had non-skid flooring. Unable to find a lawyer, he decided to represent himself and, four years later, made it to trial. Disney argued that Holmes should have exercised better care in such an area. More pointedly, they accused Holmes of having a history of faking paralysis. The jury sided with Disney. Holmes, in the meantime, found a new vocation: as a world-class "extreme wheelchair skater."

The Second Gate

The greater challenge was opening an entire new theme park next door to Disneyland. Instead of unveiling and breaking in a single attraction, Disney would be opening nearly two dozen attractions on the same day. But working in its favor, Disney's California Adventure relied on a lot of attractions known for high reliability and predictability, and few incidents of problems. There were more shops and restaurants than rides. There were five movie-based theater shows, two stage shows, a collection of walk-through and sit-down exhibits, one dark ride, two kiddie play areas, a rafting ride, and eight time-tested, "off-the-shelf" carnival rides, re-themed as... carnival rides.

The park seemed specifically Imagineered to avoid accidents by eliminating thrills. That said, there were a few exceptions.

The Redwood Creek Challenge Trail was designed as a 21st-century Tom

REDWOOD CREEK Challenge Trail's double-layered, triple-reinforced rope bridge is engineered for safety, if not adventure.

Sawyer Island—a rustic adventure zone where every activity is organized and supervised. Every path is surrounded by fences and netting to make sure no one ever leaves the trail and wanders into the wilderness. All dirt is covered by softer, rubberized mulch. The climbing rope bridges have a second net below and eight-foot-high nets on each side to make sure no one slips through the bottom or over the side. At the miniature rock-climbing wall, arrows direct kids which direction to climb and an attendant stands nearby to make sure climbers don't get too close to each other.

The one feature that has generated multiple lawsuits has been the zipline. Cast members instruct kids—42 inches and up—to hold on tight as they reach the end of the cable, because their seat will pop up and slide back about 20 feet. Such warnings didn't prevent one woman from flipping off and crushing her pelvis *(DePriest, c. 2001)*, and a six-year-old girl from flying off and breaking her arm *(Lydon, 2008)*. Disney broke out the checkbook in both cases.

The company has also paid off victims of rear-endings on and slip-and-falls near the adjacent Grizzly River Run whitewater raft ride.

Even rougher was Mulholland Madness, a "Wild Mouse"-type coaster that featured sharp, unbanked turns and quick, short drops. The sudden braking and jarring changes of direction whipped early riders around like rag dolls. During one preview, a 53-year-old grandmother's car stopped so quickly, she was thrown against the lap bar and cracked a rib. A week later, a rider was injured when her head smacked into a railing. Because of the new theme park safety law, Disney was forced to notify state officials of the accidents. DOSH investigated the ride and found nothing wrong with it. But five days later, a nanny broke her nose and the eleven-year-old girl she was watching suffered a cut to her face. This time, DOSH told Disney to shut down the ride until it could be smoothed out. The stops and turns were eased slightly, with modifications continuing until the ride was entirely rethemed as Goofy's Sky School. In the meantime, most of the injury claims were settled out of court.

By sheer numbers, DCA's high-speed roller coaster—California Screamin'—generates the most accidents and lawsuits of any ride in the park. Early on, most cases centered on the ride's hulking over-the-shoulder restraints—a first for an Anaheim attraction. State investigators suggested Disney modify the restraint after it hit one rider on the head, requiring stitches. DOSH became insistent after the bar cut another guest's face and pinched the hands of two others.

Also during the coaster's first summer, Milwaukee surgeon David Heber claimed that his restraint jammed and would not lower sufficiently to protect him from being "violently shaken, jolted and pummeled against the ride's interior." He exited the car with neck pain, which in time significantly worsened, spread throughout his body, and left him with neuralgia and complex regional pain syndrome. He demanded $10 million. His suit took Disney by complete surprise. They said Heber did not complain to cast members after his ride, never sought First Aid at the park, and never submitted an injury claim. No rider before him or after him reported any problems with the restraint. Disney's investigation revealed Heber had been diagnosed with a degenerative spine and carpal tunnel syndrome before ever visiting DCA.

Yet five months before the case went to trial, Heber's lawyer found his hook. The fatal Big Thunder accident occurred, and fingers quickly pointed at shoddy maintenance. Three months later, DOSH released its official findings, confirming charges of improper maintenance. At a pre-trial hearing, however, Disney convinced the judge that Heber should not be allowed to introduce the report as evidence or to even mention the Big Thunder crash, since the accidents happened in different years, in different parks, and the rides were maintained by different workers. The plaintiff's attorney instead alluded to a culture of faulty maintenance, hoping jurors would connect the dots on their own. Specifically, he accused the mechanics of not properly lubricating the lap bar according to the specifications set by the ride's manufacturer, Intamin. Disney's attorney replied that workers didn't oil the restraints because they weren't meant to be oiled; they were self-lubricating. Disney even tried to recreate the restraint failure by intentionally sabotaging the ride, but the restraint wouldn't stick. The trial lasted six weeks. The jury deliberated two hours before ruling for Disney.

Days before Christmas of 2002, about five minutes after riding California Screamin', Claudia Napiorkowski complained to her husband and daughter that she was getting a headache. She sat down as her daughter rode about three more attractions, but her headache continued. The family left the park and soon after returned home to Cancun, where her condition deteriorated. She was later diagnosed with a brain bleed and underwent surgery. About this time, two months after visiting DCA, her husband asked the doctor if a roller coaster could have caused the injury. His suspicions confirmed, Napiorkowski contacted Barry Novack, the lawyer who had successfully represented brain bleed victims on the Indiana Jones ride and other Disneyland attractions. Whereas Novack typically had to jump through hoops to prevent his cases from being relocated out of Los Angeles, this time he could name the ride's manufacturer as a co-defendant. Intamin was based in Switzerland.

Novack suspected the injury was caused by the coaster's high-speed launch, which propelled riders from 0 to 55 mph in four seconds. In spring 2004, a few months after the suit was filed, Disney softened California Screamin's "launch profile," so there was less of a jerk at the start. They blamed it on guests complaining they were hitting the backs of their heads against the headrest.

Although he lacked proof of any other brain bleed cases on California

Screamin', Novack did cite eight other brain hemorrhage cases caused by Disney thrill rides to that point, including a woman on the Maliboomer drop ride months prior *(Kowaleski, 2002)*. He considered it proof that Disney knew full well that its thrill rides were causing serious brain injuries, yet refused to warn the public of the risks.

Disney's position was that there was no evidence tying the woman's condition to her ride on the roller coaster. She never notified anyone of a problem during her trip. In fact, no one even linked the coaster ride to her injury until two months later, when her husband asked her doctor if they could be related. But by that time the list of similar victims was growing, Disney had settled before, and the park's 50th anniversary was fast approaching, when news media—and millions of guests from around the world—would be descending upon Anaheim.

A few months before the case was settled, on July 17, 2005, Disneyland celebrated its 50th anniversary. There were speeches, special events, new shows, parades and attractions. The only thing missing was much mention of its struggling sister park, DCA. Twelve days later, DCA and California Screamin' found themselves back in the headlines. One train was stopped before the station, waiting for its turn to enter and unload its passengers, when a second train approached. Recently replaced valves in that brake zone failed, the train blew through the brake zone, and crashed into the back of the first train. The moving vehicle was slowing down, so the 48 passengers between the two trains appeared to have suffered, at worst, minor injuries. Yet fifteen riders did ask to be taken to the hospital, most of them complaining of neck or back pain. Paramedics administered a neck brace to one guest, a back brace to another. Sure enough, several riders filed suit, claiming soft-tissue injuries and emotional distress for witnessing their children undergo the ordeal *(Garcia, Valerio)*. DOSH shut down California Screamin' for three months, during which Disney replaced every valve in the ride with a different brand, which they used in their other coasters.

Disney continued to tinker with the rest of the park, as well, hoping progressively larger additions would miraculously change the public's perception of DCA as an underwhelming theme park. In 2007, after spending hundreds of millions of dollars building new attractions, shows, parades and entire lands—none of which significantly improved park attendance—Disney finally decided to bite the bullet and spend over $1 billion remaking the entire park to mimic the nostalgic and cartoonish elements of its sister park.

Through it all, legal liability would remain an overriding consideration with every new project. In fact, for DCA's first largescale addition, Imagineers acheived defendant nirvana. They designed an entirely lawsuit-proof land. In 2002, A Bug's Land featuring Flik's Fun Fair opened, offering four new rides designed to be almost impossible to hurt someone — at least physically.

Flik's Flyers is a Dumbo-type spinner ride, but passengers have no control over the altitude of their vehicles, which are themed as giant discarded food containers with sides so high that small children can't see over them. Francis' Ladybug Boogie mimics the Mad Tea Party, but spins the vehicles for you — only slower and on a predetermined figure-eight path. Heimlich's Chew Chew Train is a shopping mall train disguised as a caterpillar with an eating disorder that slowly winds its way through massive half-eaten fruit and treats. Tuck and Roll's Drive 'Em Buggies is advertised as bumper cars, but they crawl along so slowly that when they bump into each other, there's no bump; they just stop. That might make some sense if the ride was aimed at toddlers, but anyone under four-feet-tall must ride with an adult and anyone under three-feet-tall can't ride at all.

The land is a complete delight — for Disney's lawyers.

V
Unequal Access

W HEN DISNEYLAND FIRST OPENED, the idea was to welcome all guests to all attractions, no matter how young or old. Walt wanted the whole family to be able to enjoy everything the park had to offer, together. There were no height limits or age restrictions. No attractions were directed at just toddlers or just teens or just adults. Even grandparents were welcome; the baby stroller concession in Town Square also rented wheelchairs for folks with limited endurance.

That said, there was a lot that couldn't be enjoyed by guests who were confined to a wheelchair. The Americans with Disabilities Act wouldn't pass until 1990. Curbs, steps or porches barred entry to most shops and restaurants. People operating their own wheelchairs who wanted to eat at the old Hills Brothers Coffee Shop in Town Square, for instance, would have to travel halfway down Main Street and around the corner past the Market House, to get around the curb and then have to double back. Only a few attractions—the Mark Twain, the Main Street Cinema, the shooting galleries—accommodated wheelchairs. Some rides did allow guests to transfer out of their chairs, if they could walk a short distance. Even if they couldn't, cast members were typically willing to help however they could.

"I really enjoyed helping our handicapped guests onto the rides because I knew their time and activities were so limited compared to our regular guests," recalled longtime attractions host Earl Archer. "A lot of them didn't come with helpers or, if they did, there were usually one or two helpers for about five or six handicapped guests. So we jumped at the chance to help them all we could. We used to carry children aboard the Jungle Cruise or team up with another captain to assist an adult in, swinging across from dock to boat and seating him properly for comfort. We really looked forward to doing this little extra for all our handicapped guests. Then the insurance companies began to look at things in a different light and told the supervisors that we could be sued if anything happened while we were helping them. Some people sure know how to take the fun out of things."

Indeed, in 1973, cast members helped a 21-year-old paraplegic into a Matterhorn bobsled, but the ride was so rough and the rider so physically unable to steady himself, he reportedly was thrown out of the vehicle and onto the ground *(Mason Jr.)*. He filed suit, but before it could be resolved, the young man passed away.

To allow wheelchair-bound guests to enjoy the Haunted Mansion, the entire ride has to be momentarily stopped twice, so the guest can be assisted into and later out of a Doom Buggy. Originally, guests would be assisted into the vehicle in the loading station, and then a cast member would run their wheelchair downstairs so it would be waiting for them as they disembarked and they would sit in their chairs to ride the escalating ramp to the building's exit. In 1980, Catherine Levesque helped her 81-year-old father back into his rented wheelchair and was instructed to lock both wheels as soon as she pushed him to the ramp. But she locked only one wheel, causing the wheelchair and dad to tip back on top of her, and they were dragged in a heap to the top of the ramp. She suffered cuts, bruises and a sprain to her ankle, and her father suffered bruises to his neck and back.

At trial, Levesque testified that the ramp was unsafe for wheelchairs. It moved too fast and was dimly lit. McCain argued the ramp was safe and well lit. The fault was Levesque's alone for not following instructions. The locks were in perfect working order. She just didn't lock both wheels. Before trial, Disney offered them $5,000. They insisted on no less than $25,000. The jury awarded them nothing. Disney, meanwhile, began having disabled guests remain in their Doom Buggies past unload and disembark upstairs, at the loading station.

A 22-year-old quadriplegic accused a longtime cast member of terrorizing instead of assisting him *(Vierra-Lambert, 1994)*. The attendant at load allegedly grabbed the guest under his arms, yanked him out of his electric wheelchair, and "threw him headfirst into the ride." The man's head hit the seat and his back and shoulders struck the back of the Doom Buggy.

The cast member then refused to let the victim's friends move his wheelchair off the ramp, yelling at them to leave it alone. The operator pushed the controls himself and sent the chair crashing into a pole. At this point, the disabled rider yelled for his friends to help him off the ride, but the attendant first pulled him out and threw him back into his wheelchair. The rider demanded $25 million for general negligence, assault and battery, and mental distress.

By the time the ADA passed in 1990, Disney knew it would have to begin making concessions. The new law mandated that by July 1994, Disneyland had to make reasonable modifications to provide equal access, including removing architectural and communication barriers where readily achievable, providing alternative measures where barriers couldn't be reasonably removed, and designing and constructing new facilities and altering existing facilities in accordance with ADA guidelines. That meant, at minimum, cutting curbs to provide ramps and widening extra-narrow doorways.

Older rides were allowed to continue as is, assuming they were as compliant as they could be without undertaking drastic measures and they didn't undergo significant changes in the future. Originally, rides at risk of being closed were selected on the basis of if they were out of fashion and if they were too expensive to operate in relation to their capacity. Now there was an additional criteria: were they or could they reasonably become ADA-compliant? The Motor Boats? No. The Skyway? Never.

When the Submarine Voyage and later the Sleeping Beauty Castle walk-through closed temporarily, temporarily almost turned into foreverarily, in part because complete makeovers might force the riders to be made handicapped-accessible—an impossibility for a submarine and a cramped staircase past a series a display cases. So Imagineering got the idea to present a "like experience." They built small rooms near the exits of the two attractions where mobility-impaired guests could view the shows' scenes on a monitor.

Attractions that couldn't accommodate wheelchairs were forced to make it easier for impaired guests to transfer out of their chairs. Cars on Pinocchio's Daring Journey, Big Thunder Railroad, and other rides got "flip-up" sides, to provide a larger area of access to slide onto the seat. Most attractions, however, would require custom-made vehicles or severely retrofitted modifications to allow passengers to ride with their wheelchairs.

Disney built its first vehicles specifically dedicated to accommodating wheelchairs because it had no choice. Disneyland had previously directed handicapped visitors to park in the Donald section, seconds away from the Main Gate. But when the parking lot was displaced to make way for Disney's California Adventure, Disney knew wheelchair guests would now be forced to ride on trams. A new generation of high-powered, red-and-white trams that could better accommodate the longer transport distance were introduced in 2000, with attachable ramps for wheelchairs to roll right on.

One day in 2001, 63-year-old double amputee Paul Garner rolled his wheelchair onto the tram, but the cast member assisting him had trouble tying down his chair. As the employee grew increasingly frustrated and embarrassed, and the other passengers grew impatient waiting to depart, the legless guest finally offered to be moved onto a regular bench. But as soon as the tram "lunged forward," Garner slid off the seat and smacked onto the floor of the tram. Disney handled his suit out of court.

The company next turned its focus to figuring out ways to get wheelchairs on more rides. In 2003, a bench and a special-assistance entrance were added to the King Arthur Carrousel. A ramp folded down so wheelchairs could roll right onto the turntable platform. They could then sit on the bench or its seat could be flipped up so wheelchairs could be secured to it. Security cameras were also added to watch the ride from all angles.

But taking a wheelchair on a ride actually presented added danger. In 2012, 80-year-old Frances Hernandez, wheelchair-bound since suffering a stroke, was rolled against the carousel bench. Cast members placed blocks in front of her wheels and attempted to strap her in place, but—according to her subsequent lawsuit—did so inadequately. Once the carousel began to move, so did her wheelchair. Hernandez and her chair went flying right off the carousel. She lost one tooth, chipped another, broke her collarbone, and suffered swelling and bruising to her shoulder, neck and hip. The park settled.

When The Many Adventures of Winnie the Pooh opened in 2003, two of the beehive vehicles had ramps and no front seat, so wheelchairs could roll right on. At the same time, the Jungle Cruise began after-hours testing of a modified, wheelchair-accessible boat. It featured a metal platform that lifted up, rotated 90 degrees, and extended to the dock, for chairs to roll onto. But Disney waited over a year, tinkering with the device, before finally introducing it to the public, over concerns that guests wouldn't be able to safely cross the platform on their own and that the ride's capacity would take a hit, since the boat accommodated far fewer guests and loaded so slowly.

When the boat was finally unveiled, it was well received, because it allowed guests who had never before had the opportunity to enjoy one of Walt's original, signature attractions for the first time. Consequently, when It's a Small World was being remodeled in 2008, and its flume and boats had to be replaced, Disney took the opportunity to introduce a similarly accessible Small World boat and a canal deep enough to accommodate its weight. One unforeseen problem, however, was that passengers confined to a wheelchair that was strapped to a boat were trapped in the event of an evacuation. In 2009, Jose Martinez, a 49-year-old paralyzed filmmaker, was halfway out of the final scene, the "Goodbye Room," when the ride broke down. The boats were backed up far from the loading station, so all passengers had to be helped from their boats where they were—all except Martinez. He couldn't move until his boat did. As mechanics worked furiously to get the boats moving again, Martinez sat there stranded for 40 minutes, unable to urinate, on the verge of a panic attack. Worst of all, he claimed, the "It's a Small World" song played incessantly the entire time, causing dysreflexia, an emergency medical condition sparked by nervous system overstimulation that elevated his blood pressure and could have led to a stroke or death. When he was finally rescued, it took him three hours to medically stabilize.

He sued in federal court in Los Angeles, citing violations of state and federal discrimination laws, including the ADA. No matter that Disney went out of its way to accommodate disabled people on the ride. It discriminated by making it harder for them to get off. Disabled riders should have been warned that they might be stranded if the ride broke down. As well, Disney should have called firefighters to rescue them. Legal was not going to let this one slide, however. Martinez was a serial litigant who had sued at least 41 other businesses for disability discrimination, many with remarkably similar charges. As well, much of his story didn't jive with cast member reports—records showed the ride began taking passengers again in 33 minutes, meaning Martinez was stranded less than that. "It's a Small World" wasn't played over and over again. It was Christmas music, and was eventually shut off. Cast members checked on him regularly to make sure he was okay. He never appeared panicked and declined help reaching his backpack, which contained his anxiety medication and urinary supplies. In fact, after he was freed, Martinez told the nurse on scene that he didn't require paramedics and, instead of heading to the nearby Princess Fantasy Faire restrooms, he was fine traveling halfway across the park to First Aid. There, after noting his elevated blood pressure, the nurse insisted on calling paramedics, but again Martinez declined and eventually his blood pressure came down.

Nonetheless, Disney admittedly had stranded Martinez with no procedure for immediately extricating him mid-trip. The judge awarded him $8,000.

Six months after Martinez filed suit, a 74-year-old man who suffered from kidney problems and Parkinson's disease rolled onto the Small World wheelchair platform *(Delgado, 2011)*. But evidently he wasn't properly secured to the platform, because as the ride started up, he rolled off the edge of the platform and his chair flipped backwards. Disney quickly pulled the boat and spent two months modifying it and implementing the use of anchors for extra stability, before returning it to service.

The advent of motorized wheelchairs and scooters concerned park management, for fear a driver would terrorize the other guests. Sure enough, out-of-control Electric Convenience Vehicles (ECVs) have clipped the corners of buildings and the ankles of pedestrians, been driven off curbs, and one went flying off a dock and into the Rivers of America.

Amanda van Deusen, 35, had been confined to wheelchair since childhood due to spinal muscular atrophy. Her greatest love was Disneyland. She belonged to several fan clubs and, as a longtime annual passholder, visited the park frequently in her motorized wheelchair. For an after-hours Mickey's Halloween Party in 2011, the park had set up several trick-or-treat stations, including one in Tomorrowland on a ramp that ended with a two-step descent. Because of the low lighting, Van Duesen drove her chair off the staircase, tumbled out, and—unable to break her fall because of her disability—smashed face-first into the pavement. Her mouth and jaw were shattered, both legs and her right wrist and thumb broken. Despite multiple surgeries, she was left in constant pain and so weakened she could no longer operate her own wheelchair. She filed suit, claiming the station was a hazard she had no way of identifying because of inadequate lighting. The park settled.

A guest staying at Disney's Paradise Pier Hotel attempted to drive her scooter into an elevator in the lobby, when the doors began sliding closed *(Weathers, 2010)*. Her daughter blocked them, but when mom tried to reenter the elevator, the doors again began closing prematurely, this time with such force that they starting tipping over her scooter. Afraid she was going fall, mom lifted up her leg to stop the door, but the door crushed her foot against the scooter, breaking her ankle. Disney settled.

More dangerous were rented scooters, operated by folks often inexperienced in operating such devices. One visitor was walking through the park when she was run down from behind by another guest on a Disneyland scooter *(Freyer, 2012)*. The front of the scooter struck and ruptured her right Achilles tendon. The victim claimed Disney failed to properly maintain the scooter, train and supervise guests using their scooters, and assess the capacity of the driver, such that he should not have been allowed to operate the scooter in the park.

In 2007, a visitor from West Virginia was riding a rented ECV through the park with a child on her lap, when the scooter suddenly accelerated *(Fisher)*. She lost control of the vehicle as it zipped down Main Street, unable to bring it to a stop until it ran into a queue rope that tipped it over backwards, throwing the passengers to the ground. The woman complained of injuries to her neck, back, leg, arm and nervous system, in addition to mental anguish.

In 2002, a woman who was two-and-a-half months pregnant rented an electric wheelchair and was trying to maneuver it through the buffet line at the Plaza Inn restaurant when she was plowed into by a second diner in an electric wheelchair *(Giourgos)*. The second guest then rammed into a pedestal, knocking off a marble urn that tumbled on top of the first guest. The first guest sued the park, claiming the urn and pedestal should have been secured. Her case was transferred to small claims court.

Another woman rode her scooter around to the side of the Haunted Mansion, so she could enter the back-door handicapped-accessible entrance *(Morales, 2011)*. While she was waiting, a cast member attempted to move an unoccupied scooter out of her way and accidentally drove the 150-pound ECV into her, injuring her neck.

Some visitors who require mobility assistance have trouble in a wheelchair or ECV. Tina Baughman suffers from muscular dystrophy, which makes it difficult for her to walk long distances or to stand up from a seated position. So she prefers to travel by Segway. In 2006, she called Disneyland in advance of a visit to ask if they would allow her Segway in and was told no. She would have to use a wheelchair or ECV instead. Baughman filed suit under the ADA, claiming disability discrimination. Internally, Disney knew it had its hands full working around ECVs; the park was simply too congested to accommodate Segways. And, initially, the court ruled in the company's favor, reasoning that Baughman could not

DISNEY custom-designed a stand-up scooter, with a backrest in place of a seat, as an alternative to a Segway.

present evidence that the use of a Segway was essential, Disneyland did not commit any statutory violations, and she was not denied access to the park or afforded unequal treatment. The park's policy banned all two-wheeled vehicles, including bicycles, and applied to all guests.

The appellate court, however, ordered Disneyland to reconsider its decision. The park had argued that use of a wheelchair or scooter would have made Baughman's trip possible, even if it were "uncomfortable or difficult." But, the court pointed out, if the ADA required only changes that were absolutely essential, it wouldn't require much of anything. After all, the courthouse wouldn't have to install a ramp out front, since a paraplegic conceivably could drag himself up the steps.

The ruling was not an order to change its practice, just to think about it. In fact, Disneyland already had. As part of a class action settlement of a similar Segway suit against Walt Disney World *(Ault, 2007)*, Disney had recently agreed to develop "electric standing vehicles"—four-wheeled scooters with backrests and platforms instead of seats, as substitutes for Segway users at all U.S. Disney parks. The ESVs would provide better stability and control than a Segway, be governed to a slower speed, and Disney could hide them in the back of the stroller and wheelchair concession, to offer them only by request. Based on the terms of the class action settlement, Baughman's federal lawsuit was dismissed.

Disney then asked the state court to dismiss her state suit on safety grounds. In 2013, the court agreed and a California appeals court affirmed the ruling, explaining that Disney had "demonstrated a Segway is an unstable two-wheeled device that could accelerate quickly, either forward or backward, and injure the rider and/or others if the rider is bumped." After seven years of fighting to ride through Disneyland, Baughman claimed she had racked up $124,000 in legal bills. She asked for the court to have Disney reimburse her costs. It declined. Baughman never went to visit Disneyland, either. And, the half-dozen ESVs sit in the back of the stroller rental building, rarely used and accumulating dust.

Disney's furious drive to become disabled friendly has had its downside, in at least three ways. First, the park's willingness to go out of its way to provide equal—and even preferential—treatment to disabled visitors has enticed able-bodied guests to fake disabilities to cash in on the treats. In 1977, Disneyland started a Happy Hearts program, which allowed disabled guests to purchase discounted admission on twelve select days during the year. Since Disney required no proof of disability to purchase the cheaper tickets, thousands of non-disabled people also bought them, overcrowding the park on Happy Hearts days. So, in 1997, the park decided to quietly end the discounts. The moment word got out that Disney was killing the program because, obviously, it no longer cared about handicapped children, hysteria broke loose. Two weeks later, Disney not only reinstated the program, it expanded it from twelve days to 24.

Disneyland also traditionally allowed guests in wheelchairs other special privileges, such as special viewing areas for shows or back-door access to attractions with inhospitable queues. As the practice caught on, the non-disabled began renting wheelchairs to get front-of-the-line privileges. It wasn't unusual to spot groups of wild teenagers pushing each other in wheelchairs crazily across the park, then later in the day notice that the pushers had changed places with the pushees. So many visitors began seeking back-door access that both the regular lines would slow to a standstill and the disabled guests who truly required the shortcut had to wait even longer. One afternoon, the supervisor at Star Tours grew so frustrated, he began repossessing wheelchairs from teenagers who appeared to be faking it.

Disney eventually began requiring visitors to present a Guest Assistance Card (GAC) to gain back-door privileges. Since the ADA prevented cast members from inquiring about an individual's disabilities, visitors had to bring in a doctor's note to be issued a GAC. That didn't stop some fakers from illicitly gaining GACs or borrowing them second-hand. Even worse, some wheelchair-bound GAC-holders started renting their services as "tour guides" to help guests cut the lines. With abuse of the system out of control, in 2013 Disneyland replaced the GAC with a Disability Access Service card (DAS). Visitors would have to show proof of need to receive a DAS, be photographed to ensure the card wasn't transferred to someone else, and then present it at an attraction where, instead of being quickly back-doored, they'd be assigned a time to return, based on the length of the regular stand-by line. They wouldn't have to travel through the regular queue, but they would be delayed a more or less equivalent period of time.

The switch showed Disney a second drawback to its increasing disability-friendliness. The attitudes of many visitors toward Disney's accommodations policies changed from one of appreciation to one of expecting and even demanding special treatment. Among those most affected by the switch from GACs to DASs were autistic children. Unlike the wheelchair-bound who were back-doored because they physically could not maneuver through the queues, the autistic were back-doored because they mentally had trouble waiting in lines.

The first day the DAS was introduced in October 2013, families were shocked to discover they would no longer be able to walk up to an attraction, flash their card, and be boarded within minutes. The line of disgruntled families snaked down the steps of City Hall, as Guest Relations clerks firmly tried to explain the new system. There was no need to show any medical proof, since the new DAS didn't promise any special treatment (although many families insisted their paperwork be examined, to prove their child required special treatment). Before, hosts and hostesses would decline looking at it and courteously inform guests that it was unnecessary, because the ADA prevented further inquiry into the nature of a disability; now, they admitted they were "instructed not to review" the information. Cast members avoided all discussion of guests' particular circumstances. Everyone was to be treated the same; procedures could not be modified to accommodate an individual's special needs.

Families begged, pleaded and screamed. Mentally and physically, their kids could not handle walking across the park to an attraction only to be told to come back later. In response, Disney added scattered kiosks for families to procure ride times without having to walk up to—and be temporarily turned away from—each ride. But, the families complained, this concession wouldn't work for kids "incapable of making and changing spur-of-the-moment plans."

Over the ensuing weeks, Disney tried to secretly tweak the program to grease the squeakiest wheels. Cast members were trained to tolerate as much resistance as they could and, when they couldn't take any more, they were to consult a supervisor, who would give families up to three no-appointment ride entry passes. Some complainers would get several, others none. After three months, they stopped handing them out all together. Instead, they allegedly began compiling a "Magic List" of persons who would be granted five no-appointment ride entry passes, without need for a DAS or getting their photo taken. Still, many families wanted their GACs back.

Their cries caught the attention of disability discrimination attorney Eugene Feldman in Southern California and Dogali Law Group in Central Florida, which months before had collected $1.55 million in attorney's fees and costs from Disney to settle a class action suit by visually impaired visitors. Disneyland also conceded to add Braille menus at certain restaurants, Braille park maps, special keyed lockers, and more animal service areas. The attorneys filed a new federal suit claiming that because the elimination of the GACs made it more difficult for autistic children to visit the park, Disney apparently was motivated by a desire to drive autistic visitors away from their parks. They claimed that Guest Relations staff, which for years, had "exhibited only the highest care and attention overnight turned into terrible new versions of themselves. (They) uniformly reversed all of their prior characteristics; courtesy was replaced with rudeness, acceptance with suspicion, understanding with impatience, consideration with discourtesy." And, to rub it in, the new program featured the "stigma-emphasizing title of *Disability* Access Service card."

Fourteen families initially filed suit in 2014. They were soon joined by another 74 families of developmentally disabled children with a range of cognitive impairments, including autism, ADHD and Down syndrome. But the court noted that each plaintiff had symptoms that manifested in different ways and in response to different stimuli. Some were annual passholders or

Disney Vacation Club timeshare members who visited frequently and spent thousands of dollars on Disney vacations; others were single-day visitors, who sustained far lower economic damages. Some visited Disneyland, others Disney World. So the court ruled that the vastly differing claims should never have been filed together in the first place. That said, the families, if they chose, could continue their suits, if they filed separately.

The third downside to Disney's increasing accommodations is that, for some folks, no matter how many changes the resort makes, they will never be enough. They will always find some barrier that's too high, or large, or low. It's because they're not looking for fun; they're looking for problems. In 2006, quadriplegic attorney Scott Johnson spent two nights at the Paradise Pier Hotel. Confined to a wheelchair since being hit-and-run by a drunk driver in 1981, he later started a crusade not against drunk drivers, but against businesses, large and small, that violate the ADA. He filed more than 2,000 lawsuits demanding companies correct violations and pay him several thousand dollars for his trouble. Disney was no exception. During his two-night visit, he noted the hotel lacked properly configured, van-accessible parking, an accessible check-in counter, and accessible elevator buttons, since trash cans were placed immediately beneath them, blocking wheelchair access.

According to his suit, he "naturally was frustrated, angry and/or vexed." Although the conditions didn't cause him any economic loss or physical injury, they did continue to violate his civil rights, cause him "highly unpleasant emotional distress," and deter him from returning.

The suit was followed up in 2012 by wheelchair-bound spina bifida sufferer Nicole Rosenbloom, who charged that not only was the Disneyland Hotel unlawfully inhospitable to "mobility disabled individuals," so was most of Disneyland. The hotel lacked accessible guest rooms, roll-in showers, sufficient room between the beds, and beds low enough for a guest to climb onto from a wheelchair. The park had too many inaccessible attractions, with Pirates of the Caribbean and the Finding Nemo Submarine Voyage among the worst. Rosenbloom demanded full and equal access to all attractions and all hotel rooms. Instead, Disney paid her off.

Year by year, Disneyland does get a little more accessible. Unfortunately, the logistics of efficiently processing and entertaining tens of thousands of guests a day are diametrically opposed to meeting every need of hundreds of guests a day who each require constant, individualized concessions. It's a tug of war Disney has come to accept.

Schemes & Scams

Disabled visitors aren't the only ones who have accused Disneyland of unfair treatment. Over the years, a number of guests have claimed the company was trying to swindle them through trickery with their ticket books, contests and promotions. The first instance occurred in 1976 when attorney Brian J. Campbell took issue with Disneyland's pricing system. After handing a C coupon over to the attendant at the Frontierland Shooting Gallery, he noticed that he alternately could have paid 25 cents cash. But the C he'd just used was clearly marked as having a value of 40 cents. He—and millions of sharpshooters before him—were being robbed of 15 cents! He filed suit for $1,000,000.15 ($1 million in punitive damages plus the fifteen cents he was cheated out).

Disneyland had always listed the Shooting Gallery as a higher ticket level because the majority of the tickets it sold were as part of a discounted ticket book, and it wanted to make sure it collected the equivalent of about 25 cents from every gallery patron. McCray argued that Campbell was given the option to use his C coupon for the Shooting Gallery, and he did so, so he suffered no damages. After all, the coupons in his ticket book had a combined face value of $5.80, and he paid $3.50, so each C coupon cost him less than a quarter.

Campbell argued, however, that Disneyland was actually making *more* than face value for every ticket it sold as part of a ticket book. Citing *Blue Chip Stamp v. Superior Court of Los Angeles County*, he noted that the ticket books provided the park with added benefits: guests paid up front for a quantity of tickets that they might lose or never use. And by predetermining how many of each level ticket was in each book, Disney could spread the crowds over a wide range of attractions. Campbell did not seek to have the suit certified as a class action, because, as in Blue Chip, the loss suffered per guest was too insignificant. He would pocket all damages.

In the end, Disney did make one concession. For the first time since it produced ticket books in 1955, it immediately stopped printing the price on each individual ticket.

In 1982, Disneyland discontinued the A through E ticket books in favor of an unlimited use pass. Most other theme parks had already switched to the one-ticket-rides-all system. More importantly, Disney needed to use such a ticket for its new EPCOT Center, since EPCOT had so many international pavilions with nothing to collect tickets for and a number of corporate mega-pavilions whose sponsor might be offended if they were told another company's ride was worth an E ticket, but theirs merited only a C. Plus, a single price made it easier for Disney to raise its rates more frequently, without hiking the charge for each individual ride by a nickel or a dime.

Attendance at Disneyland, nonetheless, remained in the doldrums through the early 1980s, until corporate happened upon a special promotion to celebrate the park's 30th anniversary in 1985. Every thirtieth guest would receive some sort of prize and every 30,000th guest would receive a brand-new GM car. Occasionally, to accommodate the press, as they neared the 30,000 mark, all the turnstiles except one would temporarily stop admitting guests, so photographers and reporters could converge around the lucky winner.

On the third day of the promotion, an African American visitor from Michigan said his nine-year-old daughter, Jennifer Wright, was held back from her entering for four minutes, so a white teenager could pass through another turnstile after her and win a Pontiac. He filed suit, accusing Disney of discriminating against his daughter because she was black. Wright wanted the car, plus damages. To strengthen his case, Wright's lawyer demanded to know how many of the 391 guests who won cars during 1985 were black. Disney responded that the percentage was immaterial. The winners were determined randomly by computerized counters.

For the promotion, Disney had also calculated that its 250 millionth guest would be passing through the turnstiles during the summer, so it set up a twelve-foot-high digital scoreboard in front of the Main Gate to count up to the magical mark. What the counter also allowed some sly guests to do was to anticipate when the prizes would be given away, and they could jump into line at just the right time to be a winner.

Through trial and error, frequent visitors Henry and Elizabeth Killackey figured out when the cars would be given away and began camping out in front of the main entrance, waiting for their chance to win. According to the Killackeys, when security caught on, they began to harass them and instruct them "when they could enter, and at other times holding them back from entering and singling them out so they couldn't win the grand prize." One afternoon, while "standing peaceably near the entrance," security ran them off the property. The Killackeys filed suit, seeking $30 million for loss of prizes, being denied access to the park, and for rigging a contest that was supposed to be random.

Disneyland repeated the promotion in 1986, but this time every guest won a prize (usually a pin), only one guest per day won a car, and the digital scoreboard was hidden behind a giant banner.

All the while, Disney continued hiking admission prices, sometimes several times a year. The public seemed unfazed. Attendance continued to grow. Internal research showed that local residents were significantly more price sensitive than tourists. If someone who lived nearby thought admission was too expensive, they could choose to do something else and delay a visit to the Magic Kingdom. But if someone flew in from out of state, they weren't going to walk up to the ticket booth, look at the price, and walk away. They were still going to pay.

As well, the park continued to draw a hugely disproportionate number of visitors during weekends and peak seasons. So, to increase visitorship year-round, Disneyland began marketing to local residents with off-season discounts cut-rate annual passes. Locals were required to show proof of residency (that their zip code was between 90000 and 93599) to qualify.

In 1997, Texas high school football coach Burnis Simon was visiting his friend, attorney Greg Hafif, in Southern California, a vacation that included an obligatory trip to Disneyland. As he waited in line at the ticket booth, Simon overheard the patron ahead of him being charged $26 for a one-day ticket. Simon walked up to the ticket booth and was asked for $36, solely because he lived outside of the favored zip codes. He was incredulous and later shared his travails with Hafif.

Hafif had heard of the recent ruling in the Neubauer Pirates suit and of other cases snaking their way through the court system attempting to try Disney and other theme park operators as common carriers. And he knew that common carriers were not only held to a higher standard in regards to safety. According to state law, "A common carrier must not give preference, in time, price, or otherwise, to one person or another." Hafif filed a pricing discrimination suit, seeking class action status for anyone who lived outside the eligible area and had paid full-price for admission during Disneyland's Resident Salute promotions.

Initially, the trial court denied class certification. There were no precedents for such a case, making its chances of success slim. Class members individually would have to prove which common-carrier-classified rides they had ridden. The payoff wouldn't be worth it. Hafif appealed. In the interim, the California Supreme Court ruled in *Linder v. Thrifty Oil Co.* (2000) that certification of a proposed class should not be conditioned upon a showing that class claims for relief are likely to prevail—eliminating much of the reason the trial court denied certification.

The appellate court remanded the trial court's decision, and Hafif renewed his efforts for class certification. The court subsequently certified a class of all persons who visited Disneyland during the promotion, lived outside the applicable zip codes at the time of their visit,and paid the non-discounted price for a one-day ticket. The class would total more than 4.95 million people.

At trial, Disney's attorneys argued that the park could only be viewed as a common carrier within the context of certain attractions, but not as a whole. However, Hafif argued, "The whole purpose of Disneyland is all the rides. It's basically what they do. I got hold of an internal survey, which showed that 93 to 94 percent of guests go on a ride. The defense argued that they do more. There are shows, and arcades, and Mickey walking down the street."

Once the judge sided with Disney, that Disneyland was not a common carrier to all customers who merely pay for admission, Hafif's entire case collapsed. The appellate court backed it up, explaining that the issue of whether or not Disney is a common carrier in regards to admission is a "yes or no" proposition. Whether or not someone elected to be a passenger on a particular ride was irrelevant. People enter into a carrier-passenger relationship when they board the vehicle and end the relationship when they safely exit. For example, a railroad wasn't considered a common carrier in regards to a passenger who tripped in the station, because the carriage relationship would not exist until he had boarded the train (*Falls v. San Francisco R.R. Co., 1893*). During a visit to Disneyland, some guests will enter many carrier-passenger relationships, others none.

The appellate court concluded that Disney was not a common carrier to everyone who pays admission, no more than a ballpark or a movie theater could be considered a common carrier, even though they also contained elevators, escalators or other people-moving devices.

As the price of Disneyland tickets continued to climb through the 1990s and beyond, into the hundreds of dollars for multi-day passes, so did the number of small-time brokerages trying to cut in on a piece of the action. Discount ticket brokers would buy multi-day passes either new or second-hand with unused days left on them, then "rent" the remaining days to new guests. At 2010 prices, a one-day park-hopper pass cost $101, the broker would pay $256 for a six-day pass and rent it to six different people for, say, $80 a day. The renter saved $21 a day and the broker nearly doubled his money.

Disneyland had been printing on the tickets that they were non-transferrable since it introduced multi-day passes in the 1980s, but had never done much to enforce the policy. Disney appeared content to let the ten or so local brokers live on in the shadows, until employees started noticing brokers brazenly walking down Harbor Boulevard with giant signs hawking their sale-price tickets. By 2011, management finally began analyzing just who was using six-day passes. They discovered that the vast majority were being redeemed by a different person every single day. So, ticket sellers began requiring those who purchased multi-day passes to print their names on the ticket. Brokers responded by applying Wite-Out to the old name and writing in the customer du jour's name. Soon after, the turnstiles at the Main Gate were computerized, providing ticket takers with instant access to when a pass had been used before. So, the brokers had to begin arming customers with a use history of each pass.

Ultimately, in May 2012, Disneyland just stopped selling six-day passes. The brokers just bought more three-, four-, and five-day passes. Disney responded by requiring anyone using a multi-day pass to show ID before being allowed in. The lines out front soon grew so long that the park set up separate turnstiles for four- and five-day ticket holders. New training was instituted to help ticket spot reused tickets—by asking the right questions, requesting to see ID, or checking to see if the passes were altered.

A few months later, in January 2013, cast members began photographing anyone using a multi-day pass, so their image could be stored inside the ticket takers' computer system, in the same way they tracked annual pass holders. The next time the pass was used, if the user's face didn't match the face that popped up on the computer screen, the guest wasn't allowed in and their ticket was confiscated.

One by one, the discount brokers began closing up shop. One reseller, Ryan Swan, found himself with hundreds of partly used park hoppers. He'd shelled out $30,000 for them and they had an estimated $120,000 worth of visits left on them, visits Disney now had a system set up to prevent ever taking place. So, Swan filed suit.

Up front, he admitted that his business violated Disney's terms of sale. The passes were clearly marked: "Not for resale... revocable... nontransferable; must be used by the same person on any and all days. May

not be sold, bartered, nor exchanged for goods, services or benefits." Yet
what he was doing wasn't illegal, even if Disney didn't like it. He paid
Disney for authentic tickets worth x number of days. He just wanted to be
able to rent out what he'd paid for. Disney's ability to void out the terms of
its contract, according to Swan, prevented him from conducting his lawful
business. He claimed the park's terms of sale consequently violated
California Code section 16600 ("Except as provided in this chapter, every
contract by which anyone is restrained from engaging in a lawful
profession, trade or business of any kind is to that extent void.") and
themselves should be voided.

To make matters worse, Swan said that until Disney began
photographing everyone who used a multi-day pass, cast members had been
racially profiling his customers. For the most part, his customers who were
white, looked affluent, or spoke English well were permitted to use their
tickets, without hassle. But his customers who looked poor, had difficulty
speaking English, or were foreigners—particularly Mexican—were singled
out.

"Multi-day tickets are fairly expensive," Swan charged. "If an employee
saw a Mexican family with such tickets, Disney would hassle the family,
interrogate them as to where they obtained the tickets, make them feel like
they committed a crime, and ultimately take the tickets away from the
family and kick them out of the parks. In addition, when Disney suspected
that any of (my) customers had rented their tickets from (me), they would
harass that person, interrogate them, lead them to a separate area, and try
and determine where that person or person obtained the tickets. (Disney)
treated them like a criminal, and told lies to that person about the tickets
(such as they were fake tickets, when they were not; that they were
purchased with stolen credit cards, when they were not; that the person who
sold them the tickets was engaging in a criminal act). Then they would take
away the tickets."

Swan asked that he be immediately granted a temporary restraining
order, particularly with a holiday weekend fast approaching. Disney
responded that the California Supreme Court refused to ban non-
transferrable tickets more than a century ago. A "public place of
amusement... can make them non-transferable and place in the contract of
sale any conditions necessary for the protection of himself or his patrons,
and by printing such conditions on the tickets he can prevent their resale to
innocent buyers. He can restrict or limit the number of tickets sold to one

person, and, in general, manage his own business according to his own will..."

Swan admitted his entire business was based on reselling multi-day hoppers, and he was aware that Disney forbade the practice when he set his business. And he should have known that Section 16600 doesn't apply to contractual conditions on the disposition or use of property. It is concerned with restrictions that prevent individuals from working, such as non-compete clauses. His case was quickly dismissed.

VI
Security Alarms

WALT'S GRAND ILLUSION—his "show"—depended on an absolutely secure environment. Nothing could take a guest out of thematic hypnotism quicker than the sight of criminal activity, police, accidents or ambulances. Yet the very nature of the clientele ensured Disneyland would be a target for illicit behavior—whether by guests chafing at all the rules to see what they could get away with, or by hoodlums targeting the large masses of tourists, pockets stuffed with wads of cash, their attention constantly diverted by the surrounding magic.

When the park first opened, Walt hired a private agency to patrol the grounds, but he quickly reversed course and hired his own staff, whom he could train to provide security with a smile. They were ideally to remain in the background, making their presence felt only when necessary. He quickly built up a close-knit group of several hundred officers. Disney, noted former security manager Garry Wood, "wanted Security to be as big as could be, both the size of the force and the size of the officers. You had to be at least six foot, 200 pounds, and 21 years of age. It was for show, for the intimidation factor."

Potential trouble was to be diffused quickly. If there was any chance a situation might escalate, suspects would be swiftly escorted backstage, so as not to interfere with the show. "The way we got them backstage," Wood added, "was we'd ask, 'Can I see your ID, sir?' and then when we got their drivers license or military ID, we'd start walking and then they'd follow, because they didn't want to lose their ID. Teenagers especially didn't want to lose their drivers license. Get them offstage. Don't make a scene."

Due to park security's non-confrontational approach and its inability to be everywhere at all times, there have been a number of guest-on-guest assaults, after which the victims have sued the park, blaming Disney for not protecting them. Usually, guest fighting results from tempers boiling over in hot, crowded lines or along a congested parade route. The long-awaited opening of the Haunted Mansion in 1969 led to waits the likes Disney had never seen before. "The crowds were so thick," recalled Steve Odgaard. "They came out the front of the Haunted Mansion, up to the railroad station, back down to Pirates, and doubled back to the Indian Village. It was a good three-hour wait." During the attraction's first week, one woman said two other patrons attacked her—and she expected Disney to compensate her for the abuse (*Phillips*).

In 1989, Nga Tran claimed she and her young daughter were the victims of a road rage attack on Autopia. A father and son in the next car kept ramming into her back bumper and, when she protested, he "verbally threatened to cause bodily harm." Frightened, Tran stopped driving and called for a cast member to complain that she was being bumped. The employee reportedly refused to intervene and ordered her to continue driving. When Tran finally reached the loading zone, the guy in the next car slammed into her one last time, at full force. The impact terrified the Trans, injured mom's back and her child's head, and left both with trouble sleeping.

In 2006, Christopher Marler, 37, was waiting with his girlfriend in the Autopia line, within earshot of six ruffians who were impatiently yelling and cursing at everyone, including the ride operators. Marler asked the gang to calm down. Words were exchanged, including threats by the men. As the confrontation escalated, ride operators called security, who instructed the hooligans to get out of the line and leave the area. Marler suspected the men would lie in wait for him near the ride exit, so he asked security to escort him and his girlfriend out of the area. The officers refused. Marler nervously exited the ride and began heading toward Main Street, where he was ambushed by the gang. One member punched him in the side of the face, causing multiple fractures. "That's what you get," another retorted. Marler insisted that once he haad told cast members he'd been threatened, they had a responsibility to provide reasonable security. He eventually dropped his case.

Sometimes the perpetrators aren't necessarily malicious; there are just too many of them in too small an area. About a dozen guests have sued over the years, claiming that they were knocked down and trampled by unruly crowds and that Disney should have done more to keep the masses under control. One visitor was stomped so severely, he suffered a broken leg that allegedly led to him contracting Paget's disease (*Nutlie, 1965*). He was dead within five weeks. His estate sued Disneyland, until realizing that the bone deformation he suffered took years to develop.

Tempers and confrontations intensify right before parades, when large crowds jostle to squeeze onto limited curb space, often pushing and shoving for a better view or arguing over who was there first. A 39-year-old man was trying to cross Matterhorn Way right before the Christmas parade, when the crowd reportedly turned on him (*Rataezyk, 1961*). In a desperate attempt "to protect his wife and three children from the dangerous crowd," he climbed over a guardrail, was bumped by the crowd, and fell over the rail. He lost in court. So would a fifteen-year-old boy who was exiting a crowded Monorail at the Disneyland Hotel station when he took off sprinting—right into the short stucco wall (*Paotello, 1994*). He flipped end over end and fell nearly 20 feet to the asphalt below. In court, he tried to blame a Monorail operator for suggesting he run to beat the crowd.

Other attacks were unprovoked. In 1979, a woman sued for insufficient security during her ride on Pirates of the Caribbean (*Gibson*). An unknown assailant jumped into her boat and dragged her into the next row of seats. Lacking proof or physical injuries, she eventually let the case lapse.

In 1996, a guest returned several times to ride the Haunted Mansion, so he could sidle up next to pretty females inside the elevator and, as soon as the lights dimmed, grab their breasts. One 38-year-old victim said the man grabbed her so hard, she couldn't breathe and was left with bruises (*Rogers*). As soon as the lights came back on, she pointed him out and threatened to turn him in. The molester fled, pushing other guests out of the way to quickly reach a Doom Buggy. At the end of the ride, he sprinted up the exit ramp, with the woman in hot pursuit. When she saw him duck into another attraction, she called security, who nabbed the man and took him to the security office. Under questioning, he became nervous and began shaking, sweating, sobbing and couldn't stop talking. He apologized, explaining that he had been having trouble with his ex-wife and was sexually frustrated. Before the police arrived to arrest him, he confessed to fondling other women that day and on another recent trip to the park. Security, in fact, had already received a complaint that morning from another accosted Mansion visitor. The latest victim was incredulous. Security had a known problem and had done nothing to prevent it from happening again. Her case was handled out of court.

From the mid-1970s to the mid-1980s, security was forced to deal with gang activity in and around the park. Usually, security would track large groups thought to be gangs and disperse them at the first sign of trouble. The parking lot was harder to patrol. In 1987, a man sued after he said he was attacked in the parking lot and suffered a broken nose (*Camacho*). But instead of helping him or trying to apprehend the criminals, security began grilling him, searching his car, and demanding he leave the premises. Less than two months later, a fight broke out between rival South Pacific gangs that resulted in fifteen-year-old Salesi Tai being fatally shot. His parents sued the park for its security being so lax a gang fight could break out on its premises (*Amanaki*). But the case went nowhere, since Tai had helped instigate the fight and the gun he was shot with was his own.

In 1995, 52-year-old Billie Jean Matay, who in 1955 had been a second-tier Mouseketeer, claimed she was mugged at gunpoint in the farthest corner of the parking lot. It was bad enough that insufficient security allowed a gunman to steal $1,650 in cash, jewelry, checks, credit cards, and drivers licenses from her and her daughter. Worse, Disney security interrogated her mercilessly for over an hour, refused to release her, and subjected her three young grandchildren to the backstage sight of parade characters removing their heads. Two days into her trial, before Disney's attorneys had called any witnesses, the judge dismissed the case, saying Matay and her lawyer had provided zero evidence of any wrongdoing on Disney's part.

In 1990, another guest filed suit after being shot inside Disneyland—by someone who fired a gun into the air from outside the park. Eight-year-old Nayeli Plascencia was riding with her family in the last row of the last car of the Disneyland Railroad. As the train pulled into the Videopolis Station, she felt a sudden, sharp pain in her back. No one knew why. She was rushed to the hospital, where doctors discovered a medium-caliber bullet in her lower back. Meanwhile, Disney momentarily closed the train. Their only clue was a bullet hole in its red-and-white canvas roof. The girl recovered, and the park offered to pay for her medical bills. The family wanted more. Her mother sued, saying Disney should have known of the "dangerous, defective unsafe condition of the premises" and taken "proper actions and precautions to prevent patrons of Disneyland from being injured by persons using firearms at or near the business premises."

Obviously, there was nothing security could have done to prevent a bullet from falling from the sky. Another plaintiff's attorney took a different approach—security erred not so much in what it did before the accident, but in what it did *after* the accident. On March 7, 1981, eighteen-year-old Mel Yorba of Riverside was attending a private party at the park with a group of buddies. While walking past the Matterhorn, he pinched another patron's girlfriend. The boyfriend turned on him, they struggled, and Yorba was stabbed twice. Another guest, a vocational nurse, rushed to the wounded teen. Four security guards arrived soon after, but allegedly provided little assistance. It took 20 minutes for a park nurse to show up. The park's written procedures stated that employees were to call paramedics and have seriously injured visitors rushed by ambulance to a trauma center. But no one ever did. They didn't want sirens blaring in Tomorrowland or an ambulance tearing down Main Street. The unwritten rule was to move victims backstage, then transport them by white, unmarked company van to the low-profile Palm Harbor Hospital. By the time Yorba's van arrived at Palm Harbor, he was dead.

On behalf of Yorba's parents, attorney John Luetto filed a wrongful death suit against the park. Part of his argument was Disney's failure to adopt and implement proper security measures; after all, a guest was allowed into the park packing an eight-and-a-half-inch hunting knife in his belt. But Luetto's greater focus was that security and First Aid personnel ignored the company's written SOPs, which would have given Yorba a 50 to 60 percent chance of survival. Disney, conversely, believed all employees acted reasonably and, because the boy was stabbed in the heart, he would have died regardless of the level of medical care.

"With Disney, you had to over-prove your case," Luetto realized. "You had to demonstrate that what they did was so egregious or they went against their SOP. In my case, my whole theory was failure to deliver a standard of care. There used to be the Grand Hotel across the street from Disneyland. It was a base station for paramedics. Disneyland chose to have a part-time nurse, put the kid in a van, and take him to Palm Harbor Hospital. The kid's best friend, who was in the van with him, testified he died in the parking lot of Palm Harbor Hospital. Think about the biggest days of summer, there are 50,000 people inside Disneyland. That's the population of an average town. Would not a town that size have a hospital? A team of medical professionals? Even a doctor? How can you not have a plan for that?"

Publicly, Yorba's family demanded $60 million. Privately, Luetto told Disney they would settle for $100,000. "Disneyland's only offer, made through an insurance adjustor, was that they would donate $1,500 worth of athletic equipment to the kid's high school," Luetto recalled. "I don't think (Disney) ever got it. It didn't matter how the accident happened. I focused on what Disney did after the accident. But Disney couldn't look past the fact that they didn't cause the accident."

At trial, Luetto didn't ask for a particular amount in damages. "I don't know what the value of a teenage boy is to his mother," he told the jury. Again and again, he stressed that Disney set the standard and failed to follow it.

The trial lasted nine days. The jury took two-and-a-half hours to unanimously find Disney liable and awarded the family $600,000. To avoid Disney appealing, the family settled confidentially for somewhat less.

The hysteria surrounding the killing and lawsuit convinced Disney to hire an ambulance service with 24-hour access to a full-time driver and fully-equipped emergency vehicle. Company vans also added sirens and other Code 3 equipment. The suits also inspired several copycats. Four days after Disney was served the Yorba papers, the company was hit by another suit, this one by the widow of a man who had suffered a fatal heart attack at the park a year earlier *(Brandt, 1980)*. After riding the canoes with his family, the 40-year-old sheet metal worker was walking through New Orleans Square and became dizzy. He sat down on a brick planter for a few minutes, then remarked, "If I didn't know better, I think I'm having a mild heart attack." He started to sweat profusely and was in pain. His wife sent their daughter to get a cold drink, while she sought help. Meanwhile, a sweeper saw the man lying down on the planter and reported to a security officer that a guest was ill. The guard called First Aid. A nurse arrived with a gurney, but the man didn't want to leave without his wife. He finally was taken to the hospital in an unmarked van. An hour later, he was dead.

His family sued for $1.7 million, claiming paramedics should have been called immediately and rushed him by ambulance to the nearest medical facility. McCain argued no one knew how serious the man's condition was, considering his wife left him and he refused to leave without her. Plus, there was no medicine paramedics could have given him that would have prevented his death. Still, the park offered $10,000 to make the case go away.

Three months later, an Israeli visitor collapsed while walking through the park (*Holzer, 1981*). He, too, was transported to the hospital by Disneyland van and died of heart failure. His widow's contention—that he could have been saved if Disneyland had promptly summoned for medical assistance— was even weaker than the previous case, considering the man was 68 and had a history of heart disease. So, after a jury cleared Disney in the sheet metal worker trial, the Israeli widow dropped her case.

Other suits have arisen because Disney supposedly didn't do enough to protect guests from themselves. In 1983, Phillip Straughan from Albuquerque, New Mexico, was celebrating his eighteenth birthday and his high school graduation by heading to California with his class to enjoy Grad Nite. But, right before the bus picked him up at his motel room to take the class to the park, Straughan and a buddy got drunk. Once inside the park, they snuck into an off-limits area and stole a ten-foot motorized inflatable raft. Their joy ride on the backside of the Rivers of America was cut short when they ran it into some rocks and were thrown overboard. Straughan struck his head on the rocks and drowned.

An autopsy revealed his blood alcohol level to be .19 percent—nearly twice the legal limit for adults. His mother quickly hired the Yorba lawyer, John Luetto, to pursue similar charges. She contended Disneyland and chaperones for tour organizer Academy Travel Bureau should not have let the obviously intoxicated teen into the park. Although Main Gate attendants didn't point out his drunkenness, they did note his clothing didn't meet the dress code and sent him off to wardrobe to get a jacket and tie, giving them every opportunity to properly assess his condition and bar him from the park. The judge reasoned that ultimately chaperoning rambunctious teens wasn't the park's responsibility and dismissed Disney from the case. Three days before the co-defendants' trial was to begin, the chaperones and travel bureau settled.

But inadequate security is a less common claim. In three-quarters of the 50-plus security-related cases filed against the park over the years, officers were instead accused of being overzealous. Indeed, particularly in the early years, security was encouraged to approach over anything deemed inappropriate—whether behavior or cosmetic.

"We helped enforce the grooming policy," confirmed Garry Wood. "We'd screen people at the Main Gate, to make sure their hair wasn't too long or they weren't wearing something that would draw attention to themselves. If they appeared offensive, we'd talk to them at the side. (Disney) wanted it to be a family park, to keep guests from detracting from the show or from becoming the show."

Disneyland has always had strict grooming standards for cast members. In the 1960s, security used the same standards for guests. If men's hair went past their collar, security might direct them to the nearest haircutter before they'd let them in. (The requirement made a fortune for the barber shop down Harbor Boulevard and the salon at the Disneyland Hotel.) If clothing was deemed offensive, too revealing, or even too flamboyant, the guest was required to change or cover up. Unlike the restrictions on employees, which were recorded in minute detail, the rules for guests were unwritten and subjective.

The trickiest place to patrol was the dance floor, where couples were prohibited from dancing too suggestively or behaving too amorously. Anything untoward — including same-sex dancing — was strictly forbidden. Figuring "where the girls go, the guys go," security heavily over-staffed during weekend dances, scheduling fifteen or more officers for "the intimidation factor." Officer Bill Fields explained, "Most guys in security started on dance crews — a horrible job, with all the unwritten rules for dancing (designed) to minimize physical contact."

Although grooming requirements were eased as fashions changed through the 1970s, the dance rules remained intact. It was only a matter of time before someone challenged them. In 1980, nineteen-year-old gay activist Andrew Exler learned that his lesbian roommate was fast-dancing with another woman at Disneyland, when security guards asked them to stop. They complied and left the dance floor. Exler was incensed and vowed to force a change. He contacted civil rights attorney Ron Talmo, for help in suing the park to change their policy. Talmo explained that, to have legal standing, Exler himself would have to have been prevented from dancing. Soon after, Exler heard a radio ad promoting Date Nite at Disneyland. He thought it would be the perfect event to test the dance policy. He contacted several local media outlets, but none showed. Undeterred, Exler and a male friend, Shawn Elliott, visited the park that night. They walked down Main Street holding hands, enjoyed several attractions, and then headed for the Tomorrowland Terrace. Multiple officers were stationed at each entrance to the dance floor, and they were only allowing guests to enter between sets. Exler waited for one set to end, then for one guard to leave his post, so he and his date could rush past the remaining female officer and dash to the center of the dance floor. After several minutes of disco dancing, the couple was approached by several officers, who requested they stop dancing. The pair ignored them. Finally, according to Exler, the guards grabbed hold of Exler and forcibly escorted him to the backstage security office.

"I knew what would happen," Exler recounted. "It was like a movie script. I had called earlier that day and told (Disney) what I wanted to do and basically asked, 'What are you going to do about it?' We were stopped and escorted from the dance floor. The security person said, after they interrogated us and took down our information, 'If you agree not to dance together, we will kindly let you back into the park.' We said, 'No way. We're going back to the dance floor.' That's the whole reason we were there. So we were ejected from the park."

One week after the incident, Exler and Elliott filed suit, seeking a preliminary injunction preventing Disneyland from discriminating based on sexual preference. The judge denied the request, reasoning there was no constitutional right to dance. Exler appealed, but the appellate court also refused to strike down the dance ban. Exler remembers the ruling stated, "Disneyland is not a gay bar or bawdy house." There were plenty of other places where men could dance with each other, he was lectured. They didn't have to do it at Disneyland.

Nonetheless, he and Talmo stayed the course, and in 1984 the case finally made it to trial. Right before the proceedings began, Talmo advised Exler to drop all financial demands because that made it more likely to forego a jury trial. Disney, however, requested a full jury, and the judge agreed: "This is too important of a decision for one man to make." During the trial, several Disney executives shared why the policy was instituted for the first Date Nite at Disneyland in 1957 and how it helped maintain the family-friendly atmosphere patrons expected, rhapsodizing on the wishes of Uncle Walt. Talmo objected. Witnesses could not invoke the ghost of someone who'd been dead nearly 20 years. Security chief Ike Isaacson tried to make the policy a safety issue, saying that the park attracted a large number of military and foreign visitors who might be set off by two men dancing together and attack.

The jury voted eleven to one that the policy did illegally discriminate based on sex. Disney had to pay Talmo court costs of $25,000. But the park, going by the letter of the ruling, was convinced their ban was still intact; an exception was being permitted only for Exler and Elliott. It was business as usual back at the park. But four months after the trial, new corporate leadership took over in Burbank, executives who weren't beholden to Walt's philosophies and were willing to consider that there might be better ways than those that had been clung to, frozen in time, for 30 years. Within months, they began construction of their first new attraction at Disneyland—Videopolis, a teenage dance club. Halfway through construction, cast members quietly received word that same-sex dancing would now be allowed.

Some officers, however, took the revision to apply only to fast dancing and continued to break up same-sex slow dancing. In 1987, three students from UCLA were prevented from touch-dancing at Videopolis (*Hubert*). They contacted a lawyer. Park management responded by repeatedly assuring them that they never, ever discriminate. The students knew better and filed suit. They eventually dropped the action, after the park demonstrated that it had adopted a *written* policy that prohibited discrimination based on sexual preference.

For Exler, though, his fight with Disney was just the beginning. He began filing a litany of other discrimination suits—against Chippendale's for barring men from watching the male dance revues, against a Hollywood nightclub that staged a "ladies night free" event, against a chain of salons that only served women, and even against a mobile home park that only permitted senior citizens. The quests so consumed him, he legally changed his name to Crusader.

His work also inspired other Disneyland visitors. Days before Exler's trial began in May 1984, lawyer-in-the-making Victoria Penley, her husband, and their fourteen-year-old daughter were entertaining their visiting niece. Although hers was a "conservative family," Penley had a short, punkish haircut with a rat's tail-style ponytail. Her daughter had an even wilder hairdo, dyed red. "My niece's father had just passed away, and I brought her out here from Vermont to get away," Penley recalled. "She wanted to go to Disneyland. We purchased tickets by the hotel and tried to enter (at the Monorail station). I was denied entrance. I was told I 'didn't represent the American woman.' But the attendant suggested that maybe they might let me in at the main entrance."

As the Penleys turned to walk away, the attendant phoned the Main Gate, so a half-dozen security officers would be waiting to welcome them. "At the main entrance," Penley recalled, "I was told I would distract from their rides, and that they had a lot of visitors from other countries who wouldn't understand. I was a school principal. I've worn my hair quite short for many, many years. It's naturally bright red. I was dressed nicely, in designer slacks and a silk blouse. My husband, daughter and niece could go in, but they stopped me." After quarreling, Disney refunded the Penleys for their tickets, and the family headed to Knott's Berry Farm.

Days later, Exler won his case. The Penleys returned to the park later that summer and were allowed in this time, after being briefly questioned by security. Evidently, they were allowed to pass through, because they were "expensively dressed." Nonetheless, the interrogation coupled with the earlier banishment didn't sit well with Penley. She began attending law school and then sued the park for $10,000 in damages for violating her civil rights and causing humiliation and severe mental anguish. Disney admitted that, as a private facility it reserved the right to maintain a "certain atmosphere" and that it did turn away visitors whose appearance could be deemed "offensive to others at the park." They likened their dress code to a restaurant that requires diners to wear a coat and tie.

Several years later, just after Penley graduated from law school in 1988, her case was thrown out, after her attorney failed to submit paperwork in a timely fashion. She ended up having to reimburse Disney's costs.

But Disney wasn't out of the woods. No sooner had the Penley case been resolved than a fourteen-year-old filed suit for being prevented from entering Disneyland because her pink and purple hair would detract from the show (*Slobod, 1986*). A cast member said she could come in if she wore a hat. She declined. At trial, Disney's attorney argued that the park had no record of the girl's visit, but that if cast members did bar her from entering, they must have had a legal reason to do so. The judge ruled that since the only thing unusual about the girl was her hair color, Disney failed to prove that her appearance violated any park standards. It rather sounded like "arbitrary discrimination." The judge awarded the girl $250 plus costs, but denied punitive damages because there was no proof of more widespread discrimination.

More often, plaintiffs in security cases accused officers of roughing them up or otherwise treating them too harshly after they were caught doing something illegal. But unlike the run-of-the-mill accident suits, Disney rarely settled security-related cases. They were fights to the death. Disney was often facing an unsympathetic plaintiff, possessed security and police reports detailing blow-by-blow accounts of what happened, and were preaching in front of Orange County jurists, reliably partial to authority figures. About half of such plaintiffs ended up dropping their suits. Almost all of those who made it to trial fared even worse.

The cases began in the 1970s, when security was comprised of a self-described "rough and tumble" bunch. Protecting the show and the "good" guests was paramount. They were considerably less concerned with hurting the feelings of lawbreakers. In 1970, security apprehended two men for hawking copies of their fledgling underground newspaper, the *Long Beach Free Press*, in the Disneyland parking lot (*Dodson*). Incensed that they were detained by security and then arrested by police—and hoping for a little publicity, they filed suit for wrongful detainment. They lost their trial and, before the year was up, shut down their newspaper.

In 1974, a juvenile was apprehended for jumping from car to car on the PeopleMover *(Reese)*. Since he was underage, rather than just kick him out of the park, security called his parents to pick him up, resulting in a two-hour wait in the security office. The teen sued for wrongful detainment. He lost his trial—and was lectured that he was lucky he didn't lose his life.

On New Year's Eve of 1975, security called Anaheim police for assistance in forcibly bringing under control a belligerent sixteen-year-old who had been drinking (*Trejo*). The teen claimed he was assaulted, had his wrists and ankles handcuffed, was threatened with force repeatedly, falsely arrested, and unlawfully imprisoned. Disney conceded cast members had no choice but to get physical with him, because the teen had become a danger to himself and others, and he struck the guards first. Witnesses reported he was indeed creating a disturbance, did use abusive language, and was clearly drunk in public. So as soon as the teen and his father filed suit against Disneyland, the park filed a counter-complaint, which scared the plaintiffs into dropping theirs.

A year later, a 21-year-old was hauled into the security office, suspected of being high (*Winters, 1976*). He was held for two hours, until Anaheim police arrived and arrested him for being under the influence of narcotics. Criminal charges against him were later dropped, but the damage had been done. The arrest had cost him his job. So, he sued Disneyland and the police for false imprisonment, intentional infliction of emotional distress, and malicious prosecution. At trial, McCray argued that security had probable cause and the right to detain, confirmed by the fact that he was arrested by police. Jurors sided with Disney, ten to two.

In 1977, two men were smoking cigarettes while riding on the Skyway, only to have security waiting for them at the end of the line (*Covas*). The men were escorted to the security office, where they were berated for ignoring the ride's no-smoking signs, then kicked out of the park. They sued for false arrest. The only problem was, they were never arrested. Their suit died.

The same year, a 24-year-old woman was seen leaving the Crystal Arcade with three pairs of sunglasses she hadn't paid for (*Lewis*). Guards met her on Main Street, where they asked her to accompany them to the security office. Along the way, they noticed her speech was slurred and her walk unsteady. In the office, she attempted to ingest an unknown substance—she said it was a "prescribed drug"—but the officers didn't know what it was, so they attempted to restrain her, and the woman became violent. When she was finally brought under control, security said they were going to have to call the police to arrest her for shoplifting, at which point she again flipped out. Security thought their only recourse was to restrain her on the floor, but during the struggle she hit her head on a desk and bruised her eye. She later claimed she was thrown to the floor and, when she tried to get backup, an officer grabbed her hair and pulled her back down. Officers cuffed her hands and feet, and held her against the floor until police arrived. The police report noted she had a black eye and bruises on her throat. She sued the park for $25,000, alleging assault, battery and emotional distress. In court, officers testified that they had to restrain her in whatever way necessary, because she was obviously under the influence and could have overdosed or been attempting suicide. The jury ruled for Disney, ten to two.

In 1987, two undercover officers saw three children, aged from seven to thirteen, taking merchandise from a souvenir stand without paying for it (*Giroux*). They followed the kids—straight to a woman, who opened up a shopping bag for the kids to dump their loot into. The guards escorted the family to the security office, where they discovered close to 30 items in the bag from various shops throughout the park, but no receipts. The woman was arrested, and all four sued for wrongful detainment. Their case fizzled.

Another guest who was suspected of being on drugs didn't want to join the approaching officer backstage, so he took a swing at him (*Lee, 1979*). The guard wrestled him to the ground, until backup arrived. After a night in jail, the man sued the park and the officer, who supposedly didn't fight fair. He hit him with his fists and his walkie-talkie. The officer said any blows were strictly self-defense. The man dropped the case.

In 1979, two housewives in their 20s were observed taking two plastic figures from the Character Shop without paying for them (*Garcia*). An officer detained them and, when the ladies couldn't produce receipts, called the police. They were cited for petty theft and kicked out of the park. At their criminal trial, the women suddenly came up with the receipts and the charges were dropped. Emboldened, they filed suit against the park and the guard for $1.5 million, alleging false arrest, emotional distress due to malicious prosecution, and loss of personal property (since security impounded their figurines). At trial, their lawyer argued that the ladies' husbands had actually paid for the souvenirs and that if the officers would have performed even a rudimentary investigation, they would have discovered the husbands had the receipts the whole time. McCain responded that the officers exercised a lawful "shopkeeper's privilege" to stop and detain the ladies, who were unable to produce receipts. Their husbands joined them in the security office and never presented any proof of purchase. Disney won.

Security stopped another woman who placed red visors on her two kids' heads and had them exit the Character Shop in Tomorrowland without paying for them (*Fernandez, 1982*). In court, the parents admitted the kids inadvertently walked off with the hats because they were distracted by a parade. That sent off an alarm. McCain asked the mother what characters distracted the children. Snow White and the Seven Dwarfs, she responded. To lighten the mood, he asked her if she could name all seven dwarfs. He then called to the stand a representative from the character department, who testified that not only do parades not run through Tomorrowland, but neither do Snow White and the Seven Dwarfs. And, according to park records, at the time of the arrest, the dwarfs were backstage with their heads off, on a 30-minute break. Disney prevailed.

Another guest claimed that officers thought he was drunk so they prevented him from boarding the Monorail at the Disneyland Hotel station (*Sardina, 1982*). He was then handcuffed, dragged through the crowd, and detained for three hours. He lost his case.

In 1982, a visitor from out of the country was accused of stealing a Mickey Mouse T-shirt from the Crystal Arcade (*Ravindran, 1982*). She later produced a receipt, then sued over how poorly she was treated in the security office. Supervision refused to let her contact her husband, her son, her attorney, or even the clerk who sold her the T-shirt. Her rights were demonstrably violated. Disney quietly settled.

The same year, two families were stopped in Bear Country, on suspicion that their three-year-old swiped a bag of candy from a merchandise stand (*Fittro, 1982*). The entire group was hauled off to the security office, where up to eleven guards at a time pressured them, hoping for a confession. After the case dragged on for seven years, Disney finally conceded to give the families $1,200 each.

In 1983, the two intoxicated buddies of James Higgins, the teenager paralyzed after he was thrown from a Space Mountain rocket, sued the park for emotional anguish—not over the accident, but for being "falsely imprisoned" in the security office for more than five hours. Security officers testified that they were forced to detain sixteen-year-old Robert Doss and seventeen-year-old Michael Garrett for so long because the boys refused to cooperate and were visibly intoxicated. They also had to wait for police to arrive to question the boys about the accident. Doss and Garrett demanded $360,000. Like Higgins, they won zero.

By the mid-1980s, with Disney's gang troubles a thing of the past and the gay dancing and grooming cases convincing them to take a more hands-off approach, security claims against the park began to drop. A couple of cases were filed by shoplifting suspects who insisted they had their receipts the whole time (*Sanchez, 1988; Boozer, 1989*). Disney settled.

In 1986, California enacted a "civil recovery" law, enabling shoplifting victims to recoup a civil demand of between $50 and $500 to cover their expenses, plus the cost of lost merchandise. Instead of just booting shoplifters out of the park or calling the police, Disney could literally force them to pay for their crimes. When the park's head of security, Ike Isaacson, heard of the new law, the old-timer sloughed it off. "You know, we're not in the collections business," he reasoned. "We're here to protect and serve. It muddies the water."

In 1992, Karl Andrews was named the new head of security. A transfer from Walt Disney Travel, he had a background in business and finance, as well as in law enforcement. He saw no problem with making civil demands. Hopefully, it would help dissuade shoplifters from further crime or from returning to the park. And, the civil demands would come in handy for funding new projects and equipment for the department. At first, they mailed letters to shoplifting suspects demanding they pay damages "in order to minimize further time and expense to you." In time, officers began making the civil demands in person, while the suspect was still in the office. The payments were easier to procure that way—and they could be used as a confession of guilt in any legal proceedings. Most suspects gladly forked over $250 to $500 (based on what officers thought they could get away with). They figured that either they had no choice or that if they paid, security wouldn't notify the police. Sometimes they did, sometimes they didn't—as suspects would discover when they were called in to see a judge and required to pay hundreds more dollars in court fines and fees.

But over the next four years, as the proceeds began piling up, security began encouraging its officers to get more aggressive. More aggressive in trapping shoplifters, more aggressive in shaming them into a confession, and more aggressive in threatening the ill that would come their way if they didn't pay the civil demand.

The aggression first began to be leaked to the public at the end of 1995, with news of the claims by the mugged Mouseketeer that security didn't believe. In short order, four more lawsuits were filed by visitors who alleged they had been physically abused by Disney security. But since the plaintiffs were somewhat unsympathetic witnesses and they didn't make a point of publicizing the civil demand, they slipped under the radar. The first was brought about by a family that had their annual passes revoked for stalking two cast members, but were able to get back into the park using fake ID (*Paulson, 1995*). When five officers approached them on the back trail behind Big Thunder Mountain, the family resisted. Strenuously. They began shouting and flailing their arms and fists about uncontrollably, striking the officers as they tried to rein them in. They were removed from the park for trespassing, and the two teenage daughters were convicted of criminal assault and battery. So, the family filed suit against Disney, claiming the guards had attacked, sexually molested, and falsely imprisoned them. Interestingly, their primary intent wasn't money; they said their family had been visiting the park about twice a month since it opened in 1955 and they just wanted their annual passes back.

Another couple began hassling an outdoor vendor whom they claimed had positioned his popcorn cart to purposely block their view of Fantasmic (*Sowards, 1995*). The vendor called security and when the officer arrived, the couple decided to beat it. When the officer caught up with them, the man spilled his coffee on him. Seconds later, the couple found their escape route blocked by seven "hostile" security guards. They claimed they were "imprisoned" for three hours, searched, touched and assaulted. The couple sued, claiming the entire conflict was a misunderstanding and that the coffee was cold and accidentally spilled on the officer when the man tripped. Their suit was dismissed.

Weeks later, security was tipped off by a visitor that another guest was trying to collect used one-day passports from guests exiting the park (*Mazza, 1995*). He planned to use the non-transferrable tickets to get a discount off renewing his family's annual passes. When confronted by officers, the guest told them three different stories on how he got the passes. Security called the police, who arrested the guest—who was a longtime Irvine police officer himself and ended up losing his job after he was convicted of attempted petty theft. He in turn sued Disney, claiming the officers were too rough on his two children—interrogating them and detaining them in the security office for two hours.

The fourth suit was filed after officers confronted three sixteen-year-olds for knocking over an orange cone in the parking lot (*Roberts, 1995*). Disney accused one of the girls of overreacting and "assaulting" them, for which she would be sentenced to community service. But the girl sued, claiming it was the guards who flipped out and struck, pushed, tripped and dragged her and her friends.

If anything, the suits left security emboldened. They ramped up their civil recovery demands. Yet from the end of 1995 to the end of 1996, a dozen security suits would be filed—twice as many as had been filed over the last decade. First came Denise Winters from Riverside, who was stopped by a plainclothes officer as she walked out of the Star Trader and accused of stealing a $30 Mickey Mouse plush. She tried to explain that she had bought the doll hours before, at a souvenir stand. But when she couldn't come up with a receipt, she was taken to the security office, along with her fiancee and toddler. Winters refused to confess or to pay the civil demand. She worked in retail and suspected that if she was convicted of shoplifting, she would lose her job. During the 90-minute detention, her three-year-old was so upset, he threw up. Disney chalked it up to the fact that "he had spent an exciting day at Disneyland and just eaten an oversized lollipop." As the family was leaving the office, the woman checked her pockets one last time and came up with the receipt. But security refused to look at the receipt or to discuss the matter any further. So she took the receipt to the clerk who sold her the doll. He verified the purchase. Winters thought that was the end of it, but Disney insisted on pressing charges. Three months later, she went to trial for petty theft and was found not guilty. So she promptly sued Disney and won $65,000.

All the while, other plaintiffs kept stepping up, complaining to the press that they too were being blackmailed by the security. A seventeen-year-old girl was stopped as she walked away from the Hatmosphere gift stand wearing a Mickey Mouse hat she had purchased earlier in the day at a different shop *(Cortez)*. She tried showing the officer her proof of purchase, but the receipt listed the sale as "stuffed animal," not hat. Supposedly, the clerk at the souvenir shop confirmed her purchase and told guards that her cash register recorded mouse ear purchases as "stuffed animals." Nonetheless, her father was asked to pay $500 and the teen was kicked out of the park and told she would be prosecuted. Her attorney subpoenaed Disney records, which showed that over the last twelve months, park security had billed 3,938 guests in excess of $1 million for civil demands.

Soon after, another woman was accused of being a "lookout" for a shoplifter at the Star Trader *(Burton)*. She said she was taken against her will to a small room, where for four hours two guards interrogated her in a threatening manner. During the ordeal, another suspect confessed to the crime, was ordered to sign an admission of guilt, forced to pay $200 in restitution, and released. The "lookout" was given the same choice, lest she be sent to jail without notifying her family what happened to her. She ended up spending three nights in custody, although no criminal charges were filed due to insufficient evidence.

A week later, Cecille Menard was walking out of the Emporium when she realized her four-year-old had placed three plush toys in his little sister's stroller. Mom chastised the children and began to return to the store when she was nabbed by security. She said she was held for five hours, accused of other thefts, denied contact with her two other daughters, prevented from changing her toddler's diaper, and subjected to a citizen's arrest. Officers demanded $500 and later reduced their asking price to $275. The arresting officer contended that the woman was halfway to the train station, where she was supposed to meet her other kids, when she discovered the toys—which she placed in a Disneyland shopping bag, before continuing on her way to the train.

Two weeks later, a 43-year-old housewife, Cynthia Taylor Canada, went through a similar ordeal, after spending $460 at various shops and then purportedly slipping a T-shirt into her bag without paying for it. She was held for five hours, while her two kids, ages seven and nine, remained outside.

The ladies would have varying success at trial. Canada lost. Menard won, but settled for $15,000 after Disney appealed upon hearing that a juror had shared her own Disney security horror story with fellow jurors. Yet both women did succeed in getting the media's attention. After an onslaught of bad press, Disney agreed to no longer make civil demands, at least in person. They'd wait until thieves were convicted and pleaded guilty. Even more significantly, management decided that security should basically place no demands on guests whatsoever. The security office was redecorated, with input from a psychologist who selected colors and a floor layout that would create a relaxing atmosphere. TVs around the room would play Disney cartoons. Managers with law enforcement backgrounds, like Karl Andrews, were replaced. Shoplifters caught in the act would be told to return the merchandise to the shelf and start behaving. Teens might first be instructed to write a confession before being released to an adult. Police were called only if the stolen merchandise was worth hundreds of dollars or more. Officers were instructed to tread gently with suspects and, if the criminal complained, the officer would be disciplined. Guards, previously trained to look for mischief, began looking the other way.

In 1996, the park turned over to police 704 shoplifting suspects. In 1998, the number fell to 37. During the same time, lawsuits against security, which had reached a historical high in 1996, became extinct. A handful of suits have been filed in recent years, and Disney quickly settled. In 2009, a Hispanic woman and nine extended family members were stopped by security as soon as they boarded a parking lot tram at Downtown Disney (*Cromwell*). The woman was escorted to the World of Disney store, where a manager accused her of stealing a ring. After a barrage of questions and accusations, the woman produced a receipt for the merchandise and was allowed to leave. Nonetheless, she was mortified by the episode, claiming the cast members' "extreme and outrageous conduct went beyond all possible bounds of decency so as to be regarded as atrocious and utterly intolerable in a civilized society." She wanted $50,000 to remedy the mental pain, suffering, and injury to her psyche and nervous system.

A year later, another Hispanic woman was detained for allegedly trying to sneak into the park after rubbing someone else's ink stamp on to her hand (*Perez, 2010*). She claimed security treated her unfairly, detained her without cause, publicly shamed her, ruined her family's vacation, and caused her emotional distress, economic loss, and bodily injury. Disney handled both cases out of court.

For better or worse, for the first time in park history, Disneyland security is no longer looking for trouble.

VII
Labored Relations

THE OVERWHELMING MAJORITY of lawsuits filed against Disneyland—and for decades the only lawsuits filed against Disneyland—have been filed by guests. Employees, whether prevented by workers' compensation laws or, at least in the early years, deterred by love of company, never thought to sue Disney. Working for Walt, they felt part of a special club or rather part of a family. If injury befell them, it never occurred to them that Disney wasn't doing everything it could to protect them and that Disney wouldn't do everything in its power to take care of them going forward. Litigation, they realized, might harm the company financially and in the press. Filing a lawsuit would have been treasonous. Most victims then were faithful soldiers, willing to keep the park's dirty laundry hidden from the public and trust that the company would make things right.

Construction workers injured on-site, since they were typically employed by a subcontractor, had no such allegiance to Disney and were much more likely to sue if injured. Disney would typically work out a settlement, although litigation sometimes dragged on as the park, the workers' direct employer, and the insurance companies tried to hammer out a fair sum and an equitable distribution of blame. The first known construction worker injured on-site was walking past the Flying Saucers' construction site, when he inhaled noxious fumes from the fresh paint *(Gillibanks, 1961)*.

During the construction of Splash Mountain, two designers were setting up to film a commercial of the almost-finished ride when one of the water cannons went off unexpectedly *(Werle, 1989)*. An electrician rehabbing the PeopleMover slipped on a walkway freshly moistened by sprinklers *(Morgan, 1990)*. Another subcontractor was working on the PeopleMover track for its conversion to the Rocket Rods—at night, in the rain, without proper lighting. He slipped and fell 35 feet to the concrete below *(Cisneros, 1997)*. A welder installing floor drains for the Fantasmic stage suffered scars to his back, shoulder and leg when he was burned by sparks and falling pieces of hot metal *(Barnes, 1991)*.

The Indiana Jones Adventure, like Pirates of the Caribbean and the Haunted Mansion, required constructing a vast show building beyond the berm reached from the park by an underground passageway. Yet, to make Indy's tunnel appear more like an archeological dig, several spots in the ceiling were left open—one of which a carpenter fell through and was seriously injured *(Decenzo, 1995)*. Disney immediately added netting over the highest holes.

Another subcontractor was assured the gas was turned off before he began cutting through a steel pipe with a power saw *(Ortega, 1997)*. It wasn't. Gas leaked out on to his pant legs, and sparks from his saw ignited the gas, burning his legs, as well as a co-worker standing nearby.

A plasterer was injured backstage while leaning against his truck, when his vehicle was rammed by the double-decker Omnibus *(Pionke, 2002)*. A carpenter renovating the Plaza Pavilion injured his ankle when he tripped on a spool of electrical wire *(Tolmachoff, 2008)*.

At least two cases proceeded to trial. An ironworker helping to demolish part of the Adventure Thru Inner Space roof to accommodate the Star Tours simulator fell off a ladder, breaking his back *(San Angelo, 1986)*. He claimed he was provided too short a ladder that had to be tied off at the top—but wasn't. He rejected a combined offer of $70,700 from his employer, his supervisor, and Disney. At trial, the jury was convinced there wasn't time for Disney to have spotted and corrected the dangerous situation. The park was cleared, but its co-defendants had to cough up $191,054.

Two weeks before the opening of the Grand Californian Hotel, two workmen were assigned to paint a large gate *(Palestino, 2000)*. While painting it, the gate collapsed on the men. One man suffered a fractured leg, shoulder, knee and ankle. The other suffered a torn disc. They settled for $450,000.

Disney wasn't named in a suit involving another construction accident at the Grand Californian months earlier—in which two workmen were installing trim along the top of the hotel, when their scaffolding collapsed. They plunged 30 feet and would collect $2.25 million from the various construction firms involved.

Workers' compensation laws all but prohibit cast members injured in the line of duty from suing the park, in exchange for partial replacement of lost wages. There's no compensation for pain and suffering, and no opportunity to seek punitive damages to punish the park. There are only a handful of exceptions, such as if an employee's injuries were caused by a defective product the park manufactured or damages were caused by the employer's intentional or egregious conduct.

The first time Disneyland was sued following a cast member accident was in 1969, after a Fantasyland counterworker tripped over a spike protruding from the canoe dock *(Foote)*. Her suit was allowed to proceed to trial because she wasn't actually working when she was injured; she was participating in the annual employee canoe races before her shift. Nonetheless, she lost.

As for the next employee accident suit, the plaintiffs had absolutely no desire to sue. It's just that the employee was no longer in the club. In 1974, eighteen-year-old Debbie Stone was working the new America Sings rotating theater, when she got too close to where the moving wall of the seating area passed the stationery wall of the stage. She was crushed to death. Disney management went into damage-control mode. They refused to comment on the accident to the press. They wouldn't even share details of what happened with her family. Management knew that when it transformed the theater from the Carousel of Progress to America Sings, changing the seating area from rotating clockwise to counter-clockwise, they'd unwittingly created a death trap. Instead of safely separating, the walls adjacent to the hostess station were now closing in on each other every four minutes. Disney was fearful that everything they told the Stones would be used against them in court. Debbie's parents just wanted to know what happened. Ironically, they were forced to file suit simply to find out what happened. So, after their attorney was able to piece together how the accident occurred, he quickly settled with the park for an insignificant amount.

More typical was the reaction of Bill "W.C." Fields, whose attorney worked with Disney's lawyers to hammer out a fair compensation package. A security officer in the early 1970s, Fields was assigned to patrol the parking lot on Super Bowl Sunday 1976. He was coming off a break at the Inn Between, when he received a call that someone was attempting to steal a CB radio from a Dodge van conversion in Eeyore, the lot's motorhome section. He and a partner raced over, to discover the theft in progress. Fields parked his scooter behind the vehicle, his partner parked in front, behind a light pole.

Fields recounted, "The guy was under the dash, I assumed taking the CB. We made eye contact and suddenly the engine started up. He used one hand to put it in drive, the other hand to press the gas. He lurched forward into the light pole. Then he started backing up. I got picked up by the door. He hit my scooter and crashed into other vehicles. Then he took off forward before I could jump off. He was driving eastbound against traffic, about 50, 60 miles an hour. Now he's got a lot of 'angry bees' coming at him on scooters."

With Fields hanging onto the door for dear life, his head ducked inside the cab, the thief tried to knock off his unwelcome passenger by grazing a Monorail pylon (one that years later would be incorporated into DCA's Golden Gate Bridge). The side of the vehicle smashed into the pylon, shearing off the door, crushing Fields, and chopping the bottom off his feet. He ended up underneath the vehicle, covered in the contamination of the motorhome's burst septic tank. He suffered a concussion, bruised kidneys, a ruptured spleen, a mass of broken bones, his left foot completely severed, and a right foot so badly sheared and infected that ten days later it had to be amputated.

The thief, a notorious gangbanger, faced an attempted murder charge of five years to life. He plea-bargained down to grand theft and was sentenced to two to ten years. He served eighteen months. Asked in prison why he nearly killed Fields, he replied coldly, "He was trying to stop me. Nobody stops me." Seven months after his release from prison, the hoodlum was killed in a shootout with police in Santa Ana.

Disney, however, should have known he wasn't after a radio. They had already had reports of seven motorhomes being stolen from their parking lot, one on each of the last seven Sundays, and should have had police stationed in the lot waiting for the thief's return. Evidently, he was flipping the motorhomes in Mexico to fund his drug habit.

Nonetheless, Fields tried to remain loyal to the park, and his bosses tried to take care of him. A year later, he was able to return to work in security's communications center—but quit after ten months and later became a world-class disabled skier and skiing instructor. When his workman's compensation claim took him to court, his lawyers negotiated an equitable settlement that included a lifetime "silver pass." Disney's top corporate and park executives met personally with Fields' wife after the accident, and top managers showed him respect, gratitude, concern and friendship long after he left the company.

"Disney stood up at every turn and did the right thing," Fields says. "They could have handed it over to Legal and probably would today, but back then, they stood with me and did everything possible to get this past all of us."

Injured cast members who wanted to sue had to prove an exceptional circumstance. In 1978, a security officer cut up his arm when he accidentally put his elbow through the glass window of the back door of the Inn Between cafeteria (*Churchill*). He thought Disney should have used safety glass. The judge ruled for Disney, since the use of regular glass in a window was commonplace, not malicious.

In 2001, as part of a team-building exercise, Disney had five cast members circle the park on a vintage rail handcar. The cart had been on display at the Main Street railroad station ever since the Kalamazoo Manufacturing Company gave it to Walt in the 1950s. Yet it was a vintage reconstruction, never intended to transport passengers on real railroad tracks. During one trip around, as the handcar neared the Toontown station at an estimated 25 miles per hour, an operator hit the brakes. A co-worker was thrown on to the tracks in front of the cart and then run over by it, suffering thirteen broken vertebrae, broken toes, and assorted other injuries (*Zendejas*). The accident happened on her seventeenth birthday. She sued by naming the handcar's manufacturer as a co-defendant (unaware that Kalamazoo Manufacturing had closed its doors a decade earlier). She claimed the vehicle had no safety system to prevent passengers from being ejected, while Disney afforded no training on how to properly operate the vehicle and no warning that it stopped so abruptly. The parties settled.

In point of fact, while Disney focused on guest safety with laser-like intensity, its protections for employees were traditionally less so. After all, guests were outsiders, whose misfortune could end up in the papers, who were typically not paying attention to what they were doing, and who might sue. Employees, on the whole, were better focused, intelligent, alert, and loyal. Yet they occasionally found themselves in precarious situations, particularly maintenance workers and ride operators who had to traverse unguarded catwalks or other dangerous walkways as they evacuated attractions or checked the track before or after a day's operation. In 1985, a 33-year-old mechanic working along the 30-foot-high PeopleMover track fell off *(Attaman)*. He sued, but was forced to accept workers' comp-mandated terms.

Over the years, DOSH intensified its scrutiny of park safety, particularly after the Columbia accident and the enactment of new state legislation that resulted in inspectors visiting Disneyland on a near-daily basis. In particular, investigators had a keen eye for fall prevention, reasoning that falls were a leading cause of workplace injuries and the number one cause of deaths on construction sites. Increasingly, safety representatives began not so subtly hinting that nearly every corner of Disneyland contained some potential falling hazard, even though many were technically allowed due to being grandfathered in before more stringent fall-protection standards were implemented. Ideally, the park would act before citations and fines had to be issued.

The park finally got the message in the summer of 2010, from an OSHA investigator visiting the park on an unrelated matter, who was walking past the Alice in Wonderland attraction. The attraction ended by snaking down a "Vine" only marginally wider than the four-foot-wide vehicles. Reportedly, no one has ever fallen off the Vine. In fact, guests never step foot on it. If there's a breakdown, any vehicles stalled on the Vine would be individually powered down to ground level. Only maintenance workers walk the Vine. Operator Rich Johnson recalled, "There was a breakdown, and one of our maintenance guys was walking by on the Vine. The OSHA guy saw him. Nobody got hurt, but he notified the company. The company shut the ride down."

The ride sat closed for more than a month, as management scrambled for an acceptable solution. Their solution, advertised as temporary, was massive green scaffolding along the entire run of the Vine, with lower portions hidden from passersby by covering them with a green vine-printed vinyl tarp. The thrill of riding the Vine and enjoying its views was obliterated. Worse, visually, the once-charming Wonderland now looked like it was tented for termite fumigation. The set-up also made operation more difficult for employees. Johnson said, "Every morning, they'd have a scaffold guy

ALICE IN WONDERLAND had been Disneyland's only dark ride with an elaborate, drive-through exterior—except for the four years it spent covered in a vine-print tarp to hide safety scaffolding.   *(Photo by Adrienne Vincent Phoenix, MousePlanet, 2010)*

(from the scaffolding contractor) double-check all the supports and sign a book in the breakroom. A few times I had to call to get their butts down there and sign the book because we could not open the ride in the morning if he hadn't signed the book."

The temporary monstrosity lasted four years before Disney got around to widening the Vine to make room for retractable railings.

In the meantime, Disney began mapping out a timeline of gradual safety overhauls to bring each attraction into line with current standards. A slow rollout, starting in 2012, gave Disney time to devise better themed solutions and install them during regularly scheduled rehabs, to minimize attraction downtime. Rustic railings were placed alongside the bobsled track. Indiana Jones' collapsing bridge was widened. The Disneyland Railroad cars were rebuilt with little booths for the conductors to ride in, instead of standing on the authentic, yet unprotected, side-platforms.

But just months into the phased fall protection makeover, Disney was forced to speed up the timeline. A subcontractor was suspended in a boatswain chair to clean the roof of Space Mountain, when the safety line became detached from its anchor. The man slid 30 feet down the roof, crashing into a barrier and breaking his leg, collarbone, and several ribs. After a four-month investigation, OSHA fined Disneyland $234,850 for a variety of infractions, including failing to provide adequate anchor points on the roof and lack of approved ladders, guardrails and other fall-protection devices inside the ride. The figure not only got Legal's attention, they also realized identical problems existed on attractions throughout the resort. They immediately shut down Space Mountain, the Matterhorn, and Soarin' Over California, in the heat of spring break. Quick fixes allowed the latter two to reopen within days. Space Mountain, with its tight, unforgiving catwalks, took three weeks. Other attractions were then gone over with a fine-tooth comb. The narrow stairways and kid-sized railings of Tom and Huck's Treehouse on Tom Sawyer Island were deemed unsalvageable, and the entire structure was boarded up. It's a Small World and Splash Mountain continued to operate, but animatronic figures that were too high to be reached from ground level were allowed to fall into disrepair, until months later when the park could devise legally approved methods for maintenance workers to reach them.

During its first decades, Disneyland employees truly felt like part of a family. It was a sometimes abusive family, but a family nonetheless. They shared a common noble purpose — serving happiness to millions of strangers — and gave everything they had for the company. Managers typically earned less than they could have in most other industries, but relative poverty was a small price to pay for the opportunity to be part of something so special.

But in the early 1970s, as time passed since Walt's passing, cracks in the family began to develop. And, as with so many family problems, they surfaced because money started getting tight. When the 1973 oil crisis slowed attendance at Walt Disney World significantly, management reacted swiftly by slashing staff. Disneyland didn't take an attendance hit, because it was visited by a high percentage of locals, but nonetheless realized that, like Florida, it could also improve its financials by trimming middle management. Savings would be even larger in California, because Disneyland still employed many workers who had been there since the first year and, like the park itself, were now entering their nineteenth year. Once they reached 20 years of service, they would be entitled to retirement benefits.

So a week into 1974, Disneyland reorganized its org chart and terminated 63 managers. Ironically, most of them were model Disney cast members, who loved the company and their co-workers, but were just too loyal. "Most of us started with the park," recalled Bob McDonald Sr., one of the 63. "The way it was set up, (Governor) Reagan had a passed a law that you could retire with a company if you were a certain age and had been there for 20 years. We were getting too close. Management blamed it on the Nixon energy crisis, that not enough people were driving in to visit the park. They had the best year they ever had."

Every one of them was crushed. Although the Age Discrimination in Employment Act had passed in 1967, none of them thought to sue. Many assumed, at least at the time, Disney was doing what it had to do. That it was nothing personal.

But what they had also bred was the feeling that the company would protect them no matter what, and that they had a job for life. But Disneyland was a business first. Starting in the late 1970s, a couple of cast members filed suit after being fired on suspicion of theft. Another was fired after complaints that he was harassing a female co-worker *(Kloris, 1979)*. He claimed he was entrapped and that he was let go despite passing a lie detector test. More importantly, he said that he had made an "oral agreement" with management that he could work at the park as long as he liked and have all his medical bills paid in exchange for not suing a cast member who years before had run into him in the Disneyland parking lot.

The 1970s also brought increasing awareness of race and gender discrimination. In the early years, Disneyland, like many big businesses of the 1950s, was run by a Boy's Club—white males who smoked and drank a lot and often treated women and minorities as their lessers. The park, however, continued to operate by its outmoded customs, no matter what was happening—and what discrimination laws were passed—in the outside world. Among hourlies, they justified it by explaining that they were casting a show; different roles required different genders and different "looks" (usually attractive ones). And all management was promoted from within, by like-minded individuals. Until the 1970s, only a handful of black workers were even hired, always in hourly positions, usually backstage. And their treatment by certain managers and co-workers could be horrible.

Wheeler Kelly, the park's token black maintenance worker during the late 1960s, said he was given less overtime and less desirable shifts than the white carpenters, and was constantly subject to racial comments, epithets and jokes. When he complained to supervision, he was told to rise above it all. When the harassment continued, he filed a discrimination complaint with the state. One month later, he was fired. The state dismissed Kelly's complaint, but ten years later a related filing with the Equal Opportunity Employment Commission confirmed that there was "probable cause" that Kelly and other blacks had been discriminated against. The ruling empowered Kelly to sue Disneyland. After a nine-day trial in 1985, Kelly was awarded more than $100,000 in back pay. He had also wanted his old job back (for long enough to qualify for a pension), but instead agreed to a promise by Disneyland—monitored by the federal court—to recruit and sharply increase hiring of minorities in all trades.

The move did lead Disney to hiring more black tradesman—one of whom would also sue the park *(James, 1988)*. When he was hired, he was told he would receive full carpenter's pay two years after completing a 90-day probation period. Seven weeks before he was to reach that level, he was fired for altering his timecard, even though his changes didn't cheat his employer out of any money. Nonetheless, he did alter the card, so Disney had the legal right to let him go.

Seven Hispanic landscapers were fired after a Caucasian co-worker reported that the group would drink beer and tequila while riding home in their Disney-subsidized van pool *(Pinto, 2009)*. The plaintiffs threw every discrimination claim imaginable at Disney, hoping at least one of their eleven claims would stick. None did. The judge found no racial discrimination because even though the squealer was given preferred treatment (only getting suspended instead of fired), it wasn't because he was white; it was because he reported everyone's drinking, including his own. Plus, another white passenger who did drink was fired and another Hispanic passenger who never drank was spared. There was no disability discrimination because, until they made mention of their alleged alcoholism in their lawsuit, Disney was not even aware of it. And, Disney never allowed them legally mandated medical leave to treat their alcoholism or participation in the company's drug and alcohol rehabilitation program, because, during their entire time working for Disney, they never requested it. The van's alcohol ban didn't invade their privacy rights, because Disneyland operated the van and set the rules for riding it in, even if the California Vehicle Code permitted open containers in certain larger vehicles. And taking the van was voluntary.

Disneyland also took a while to catch up with the outside world regarding treating women more equitably, until sexual harassment lawsuits began being filed more frequently. The last hold-outs were in testosterone-heavy departments, such as Security and Facilities, or in areas that might employ minorities with poor language skills or who were unsaavy regarding their legal rights, such as behind-the-scenes hotel staff.

That didn't sit well with most of the female officers, including Janis Newsome. She was particularly irked at one of her supervisors, who reportedly would kiss, grab and proposition co-workers. Then in 1996 she said she learned from an annual passholder of a male prostitution scandal involving the Main Street Electrical Parade. Evidently, Entertainment staffers were assigning roles and positions in the parades and shows in exchange for sexual favors. And some of the boys who exchanged sex for job preferences and stolen park memorabilia were minors. Newsome notified the investigations department, which interviewed the annual passholder. The head of investigations then admonished her to keep the allegations quiet and to stop observing the alleged activities.

Soon after, she was called to assist a plainclothes officer who was being assaulted by a combative shoplifter. The suspect, she said, might have to be "taken down." Newsome explained, "Disney does in fact have an unofficial policy to 'take down' suspects that are considered dangerous to guests or security officers." As Newsome and a partner tried to physically restrain the shoplifter, she allegedly touched the suspect's face. Newsome was promptly suspended for "slapping a guest." A week later, she was fired. She sued, convinced she was terminated for reporting pedophilia and objecting to sexual harassment by other officers.

Another female officer sued for gender discrimination, after her husband—also in security—was caught reselling Disney merchandise and both of them were fired *(Guerrero, 2007)*. What he would do is purchase pins at a cast member discount and then sell them on eBay at a profit. When confronted by Loss Prevention, he admitted to a small number of sales, but not the quantity he was accused of. Management's report—used as a pretext for his termination—counted customer feedback as separate sales, thereby doubling the number of actual transactions. The report also claimed he made use of a 55-percent employee discount, when the true discount was 35 percent. Disney had a written policy prohibiting the purchase of cast-discounted items with the intent to resell for profit, so he couldn't sue for wrongful termination. Instead, he claimed that he had been defamed and slandered, because "the bulk of the statements made in the investigation report were false, defamatory, slanderous, and made with malicious disregard for the truth." His wife didn't violate the policy, yet was also fired. The only charge Disney had against her was her marital status. She said Disney targeted "her gender by applying a stereotype of a wife and woman who is subservient to her husband and does as he bids." Her firing violated the Fair Employment & Housing Act and damaged her financially, mentally, emotionally and maritally.

Employees have also sued for disability discrimination, usually after suffering a workplace injury. Workers who are injured on the job are, by law, entitled to a certain number of weeks of medical leave. During or after their leave, they can't be fired for having suffered the illness, injury or disability. But they're not exactly guaranteed their old job back. Disney usually justifies such firings by noting that employees were not able to return to work after their protected leave expired or that there was no job available that they were able to perform.

Occasionally, Disney has admitted to screwing up. A longtime "pageant helper" who specialized in playing taller characters, like Goofy, Sulley and the Queen of Hearts, claimed a patron violently attacked and jumped on him in 2005, severely injuring his shoulder *(Polselli)*. His supervisors convinced him not to sue or report the incident to the police, since his injuries would be covered by workers' comp and allegedly the perpetrator was "a UCLA student and UCLA had a large account with Disney." After surgery, he returned to work and for three months was given light office duty, but then was told that the only work available to him was returning to costume—but the only roles he'd be allowed to play were Baloo, Sweetums and Brer Bear, three of the heaviest suits, each of which would exceed the shoulder-weight restrictions mandated by his doctor. Instead, he went back on leave and was eventually fired. This time, the park settled.

Following an unsuccessful three-week strike in 1984, management reworked its contract with employees' primary unions, allowing Disney to avoid paying benefits to new hires. The rancorous 22-day protest not only divided the family, pitting picketers against non-striking workers and management, it also made new employees cheaper than old-timers—and thus more valuable to an increasingly bottom-line-fixated company. One by one, more expensive old-timers were targeted and made to feel less comfortable, to encourage them to quit.

But Disney wanted to speed up the process. In 1986, the entire cast of the Golden Horseshoe show was terminated and told they would have to re-audition. Only one band member over 40 was rehired—a 51-year-old trumpet player who was promoted to replace the even-older conductor. The rest of the band was replaced by 20- and 30-year-olds, with far less experience and training. Two years later, the conductor was demoted and, a year later, forced to re-audition. This time, he wasn't rehired *(Olson, 1990)*. He filed a $750,000 age discrimination suit against the park, but the judge ruled for Disneyland, citing evidence as circumstantial.

The management consultants retained in the mid-1990s confirmed that, according to their spreadsheets, many older employees were a liability. They typically earned more, required more medical leave, were closer to retirement, and were less adaptable to change. The firings started in the Facilities division. Most of the displaced managers signed "voluntary" agreements not to the sue the park in exchange for a certain number of weeks of pay. At least two refused.

Supervisor Don Long did the math. He was 60. The new hire who took over most of his duties was 32. Of the seven other managers fired at the same time, one was 40 and the rest were between 56 and 60. Obviously, Disney was targeting older workers. But Disney argued that all the supervisors fired were 40 and older simply because of the 40 Facilities supervisors, only one was under 40. Supervisors' job duties had been changed, increasing the amount of education, computer skills, and business disciplines required—all of which Long and the other older, terminated managers lacked. The judge ruled for Disney and was backed by the appellate court, which noted, "We are certainly sympathetic to Long's completely justified disappointment and anger at being terminated after 25 years of what by all accounts appears to have been loyal and devoted service to Disneyland. Disneyland's decision may have been unfeeling and disloyal to an employee who has faithfully served the company. And Disneyland may have made an unwise business decision by letting go an experienced employee. But Long has not shown any evidence from which a rational trier of fact could find, more likely than not, Disneyland's proffered legitimate business reason for the termination was untrue or a pretext for discrimination."

Another manager who refused the buyout was Bob Klostereich, who was convinced he was being targeted because he had complained that streamlined maintenance procedures were jeopardizing ride safety, particularly on Big Thunder Railroad. Months after the Columbia incident, he was let go, after a supervisor accused him of insubordination. His problem was he had no hard proof linking his termination to his whistle-blowing or to his age.

After the purge of the Facilities department, the consultants turned their sights on Security, Attractions and other divisions. One by one, old-timers said they were targeted, treated poorly, given unattainable goals, impossible assignments, and ultimately deteriorating evaluations, leading to their placement on "performance plans," filled with vague threats for improvement. Along the way, everything was documented for use in inevitable termination. During the excruciating process, Disney apparently hoped that the cast members would be so traumatized, fed up, frightened, or aware of its inevitable outcome, that they would simply quit before the company got around to firing them—thereby saving it unemployment liability.

Just as in the first management purge 25 years earlier, older "nice guys" in management were disproportionately targeted. They were were usually beloved by their troops, but consequently less trusted by upper management to rule with an iron fist. The problem for Disney was that the unlucky old-timers on their "hit list" were often among their best workers, so dirt might have to be manufactured, failures forced if not outright fabricated. One security manager testified that when it came time to evaluate the assistant managers, his boss instructed him what overall grade he was to give each one, despite it having little relation to their actual performance *(Devitis, 1999)*. Anyone on the hit list was to be given a "Below Expectations," no matter how great they did their job. He'd have to figure out how to fudge different criteria to somehow justify the grade.

Until the late 1990s, one or two cast members a year might sue Disneyland for wrongful termination. This time, the harassed managers didn't take their firings or forced resignations lying down. Individually and in groups, at least a dozen filed suit for age discrimination. They claimed that they were singled out for disciplinary action because they were over 40, issued written warnings to create a paper trail, had their complaints of discriminatory treatment ignored, were given unrealistic goals, worse shifts or arbitrary schedule changes, given fabricated performance reviews, falsely accused of job violations, and denied requests for vacations and days off, all in an attempt to make them quit or to create justification for termination.

Cartoon of the Week

There goes Bobby! He sets a good example for the cast members by not drinking alcohol, not smoking, doing drugs or swearing. He gets guest compliments, has a Bachelors degree, has an Honorable Discharge from the Air Force, is an Eagle Scout, and has an 8 week old baby! He treats cast members with respect which will filter down to the guests! What should we do with him?

Fire him.

UPPER MANAGEMENT'S cockeyed priorities were lampooned in this underground comic by ousted attractions manager Bobby Muleady. In 2001, Disney submitted the drawing as evidence in the *Bury* age discrimination case, after a ride operator posted the picture in several backstage break areas.

A couple of the plaintiffs had legitimate dings on their record that could be used as justifiable reasons for discharge. The majority, though, were fired because they were old-timers. Legally, Disney dodged liability by parading out mounds of documentation and having statisticians demonstrate that those who fired were oftentimes younger than those who stayed behind. But in the end, being an old-timer didn't necessarily mean they were physically older. Being an old-timer was someone who was allegiant to the old way of doing things, the ways of Walt, of putting yourself in the shoes of those who reported to you, of placing people—guests and cast members alike—above the bottom line.

Bob McDonald Jr., cut from the same kindly cloth as his father, lasted 29 years before resigning as a security manager in 1999 after suffering a heart attack due to the harassment. "I loved the place," he said. "But there was a big push to change the whole philosophy, to focus on marketing rather than the park. Sell, sell, sell. In order to achieve this, they had to get rid of the Walt Disney philosophy."

Backed by its mountain of paperwork and statistics, Disney won most of age discrimination suits. But after the barrage, the company had learned its lesson. When a recession began slowing business in 2001, instead of immediately targeting older workers and reviving the harassment routine, Disney announced it was offering a companywide buyout package to targeted employees who elected to quit before the firing began. Although old-timers weren't specifically named, they did get the biggest incentive to leave: they'd receive eight weeks base pay plus one week of pay for every full year of service. The early retirement purge worked so well, that when the economy got even worse eight years later, Disney offered buyout packages to 600 more resort division executives.

The Security department overhaul in the late 1990s changed the force from overly aggressive toward troublemaking guests to overly passive. Ironically, at the same time, new department managers encouraged turning up the heat on potentially troublemaking employees.

In 2000, Loss Prevention suspected that Guest Relations hosts and hostesses, who had authority to print complimentary tickets for guests who complained of bad experiences, may have been handing out passes to their friends. Rather than set up a sting or wait until the employees were witnessed in the act, as was policy for taking action on sticky-fingered guests, security instead locked fifteen employees, one at a time, in a cold, windowless room and harshly interrogated them for up to seven hours apiece. Denied food and bathroom breaks, six of them signed company-manufactured confessions and were terminated. They complained to the state labor board, which ruled that Disney provided zero evidence of wrongdoing, except for the confessions, which were procured under duress. A day later, one ex-worker filed suit *(Madory)*. Disney quickly worked out confidential settlements with all six of them.

All the while, officer Roberta McMillan knew the problems went much deeper. In particular, two new managers had begun directing her to perform clandestine investigations of other Disney managers without revealing why. They even ordered her to download personal information from the computers of several managers without explaining its relevance to any pending investigation. She was also very concerned about how one of the managers conducted investigations, often using profanity, lies and false threats in interrogating cast members suspected of wrongdoing. After the Guest Relations lawsuit was filed, Disney questioned McMillan about the managers, and she confirmed that both had been engaging in a number of illegal practices, including conducting unauthorized background checks of employees, invading the privacy of employees under the pretext of investigating possible misconduct, and advocating physically aggressive and dishonest interrogation sessions.

When she later complained directly to the manager about his conduct, he exploded. Other managers stood by idly, as he berated her, presumably because she was a woman. All the security managers and all but two assistant managers were men. Supposedly, McMillan was paid considerably less, despite having more experience, more education, and better job reviews than some of her male counterparts. She and the other female assistant manager were regularly excluded from important departmental meetings and functions. They weren't even allowed on the Loss Prevention softball team. In fact, one manager instructed her not to discuss anything with upper management unless she cleared it with him first. When she told the other manager that she considered the directive inappropriate, because it would compromise her ability to perform her job and didn't apply to any of the male assistant managers, she was advised that she wasn't hired to investigate crime. He hired her to "look good." McMillan became so distressed by the sexist work environment that she developed severe anxiety and depression. When her doctor faxed a note to management requesting that she be placed on medical leave, she instead was terminated without explanation. She was later told she had been accused of inappropriate conduct—despite receiving a glowing performance review just two weeks earlier. She filed suit for gender and disability discrimination. The park settled.

Usually, whistle-blowers didn't fare as well. A nurse was terminated after informing the Board of Registered Nurses that Disney instructed her not to document all injuries and dispensing of medications, in violation of California law *(Scales, 2003)*. Two maintenance workers on Innoventions were let go after pointing out unsafe working conditions *(Scott, 2012)*. A ride architect lost his job after repeatedly reporting alleged building code violations at the Haunted Mansion that should have caused the ride to be shut down *(Gordon, 2009)*. A pyrotechnician was canned after complaining that his new boss was allowing countless safety violations, mismanaging the fireworks crew, shooting off fireworks past the time permitted by the city, underpaying certain workers, and tolerating sexual harassment by others *(Reinartz, 2006)*.

Yet, in all of their cases, their bosses carefully documented unrelated performance issues that were cited as the real cause of their terminations. For instance, a Club 33 waitress claimed she was let go for complaining of co-workers using cocaine at work—including while they were on the clock *(Slater, 2002)*. Yet she had a special-needs daughter who required extra attention and occasionally caused her to arrive late to work, a fireable offense.

A longtime attractions host claimed he was fired partly in retaliation for embarrassing the park in the press—even though it took over a decade to happen. In 1983, the park refused to lower its flags to half-staff to honor the U.S. troops killed in Lebanon, irking ride operator William Smith, a Vietnam War veteran. His boss reportedly told him that the park didn't want to remind visitors "of what's happening on the outside." He notified the *Orange County Register*. Disney responded that it only lowered its flags when a U.S. president died. When Smith's supervisor saw the article, he vowed, "I will get you for that some way." Two years later, Smith began experiencing a series of work-related accidents, several requiring surgery and extended medical leave, culminating in 1993 when he slipped in the rain, fell, and broke his shoulder and back. Six months later, he was back on the job—and reinjured his shoulder. When he wasn't able to return to work after another twelve months of leave, Disney released him. He claimed the park was discriminating against him because of his disabilities, caused by the endless series of accidents, and belatedly on free speech grounds, for punishing him for having spoken out twelve years earlier.

Class Actions

The expansion of the resort in 2001 created a much bigger resort physically in acreage, but also in the size of its workforce. Employment jumped from 13,000 to nearly 20,000. And the thousands of new hires dumped into the system were not the previous generation's Kens and Barbies, who grew up on *The Wonderful World of Disney* and always wanted to work at the park. They'd be assigned to work farther from Sleeping Beauty Castle, both physically and in spirit. It's would be more difficult to brainwash a laundry worker in a hotel basement that her real job is creating magic than a tour guide on Main Street. As a result, for the first time apart from a handful of ineffective strikes, cast members began plotting to band together for change.

An early, noticeable effect of the expansion on existing employees, like security guard Bobby Overton, was that they'd have to park farther away. Previously, cast members parked in Alice and Bambi, the closest sections of the old parking lot and a two-minute walk from the Harbor House backstage entrance. With bulldozers arriving to raze the lot to make room for DCA in 1998, cast members were forced to park in remote, off-site lots and then take a shuttle to and from the park. They had long received fifteen extra minutes of pay for "dress time" to change into their costumes, but they were still seeing an extra hour of travel time added to their workday.

Overton was assigned to park in the Katella lot, the farthest one, nearly a mile away. He was ticked. A year later, he quit. In the meantime, Disneyland reassured its cast members there was nothing they could do, at least until its contract with the unions expired in early 2002. At that time, Disney increased its dress time allowance to 20 minutes per shift, now attributed to "dress and/or walk time," since cast members recently began taking their costumes home with them and dressing away from work. Overton felt not only that 20 minutes wasn't nearly enough, but that the change was an admission that Disney knew it should have provided appropriate walk time. In addition, a recent California Supreme Court ruling (*Morillion v. Royal Packing Co.*) held that employees must be compensated for travel time when their employer requires them to travel to a worksite on employer-provided buses.

Overton filed a proposed class action suit, to reimburse all inconvenienced cast members for their shuttle time after being forced to park so far away. Cast members were under the company's complete control from the time they entered the lot, through the time they waited for and rode the shuttle, and then walked to their work station, and were compensated for none of it.

Disney didn't dispute that employees were under its control, without pay, for extended periods. It did dispute that cast members were required to park in off-site lots. No one said they had to drive their own cars to work. They could have been dropped off by someone else. They could have traveled by carpool or vanpool, affording them a closer parking spot. They could ride a bike or take a city bus or Metrolink train. Or, they could have parked in the Katella lot, but biked or walked to the entrance instead of riding the shuttle. Overton provided documents that supported his contention that employees assigned to the Katella lot were "required" to park there. But the judge agreed that Disney wasn't requiring anyone to drive to work; they were forced to park at Katella only if they chose to drive. In fact, Disney sponsored van pools and offered other incentives to cast members who opted not to drive themselves. The judge also rejected Overton's "simple solution" of relocating the time clocks to the shuttle departure area in the Katella lot. That would force Disney to compensate employees for their time waiting for the shuttle, as well as any other time they wasted getting to their final work station. Plus, any employees who didn't already park at the Katella lot would now have to.

Disney won—and learned a valuable lesson. In all future references to changes to cast member parking, it would make sure to stress that free parking for work wasn't a right, but a benefit that could be altered or taken away at any time, and there were plenty of other ways to get to work.

For years, Disneyland operated with the same, under-documented shifts that it had always had. Ride operators worked in a "rotations" system, in which, to keep them fresh, they would rotate to a new position every fifteen minutes, such as from ticket taker to loader to unloader to break. Characters would appear on stage in 30 to 40 minute sets. So long as you were where you were needed about the time you were needed, the system ran fine. But in 2001, California passed a law that required all employers to give employees a ten-minute rest for every four hours worked and a meal break to anyone working more than five hours a day. Legal pointed out that the old rotations system provided no proof that employees had received their rest periods.

The park hurriedly began rolling out a new computerized Cast Deployment System (CDS), with terminals spread in every corner of the park that employees had to clock into throughout the day to find out exactly where they were supposed to be next—and how many minutes they had to get there. By constantly checking in with the CDS computers, employees created a paper trail of exactly where they'd been and when, so Disney would be protected from any class action suit accusing it of not providing sufficient breaks.

It wasn't enough. CDS wasn't instituted for every employee, particularly at full-service restaurants where a continuous flow of demanding diners made it more difficult to get to breaks at exact times, and even where it was, CDS would occasionally misfire. Over the next several years, two class action suits were filed—one on behalf of Goofy's Kitchen employees *(Galloway, 2007)*, one on behalf of all other resort hourlies *(Lam, 2004)*— claiming that Disney failed to provide adequate meal and rest periods. Disney agreed to pay more than $2.5 million to employees shorted on their breaks from 2004 to 2008.

No sooner the ink dried on that settlement, than another hotel worker filed another class action for shorting breaks after 2008, and for forcing hotel employees to work overtime at regular pay rates *(Galvez, 2011)*. Again, Disney settled.

In fact, Disney's relationship with its primary union representing hotel workers had been growing increasingly contentious, as union representatives became increasingly bold, loud, provocative in negotiations and in gathering publicity, staging over-the-top press conferences and protests, often with an activist dressed in a strange, homemade Mickey Mouse costume. The union heavily backed a string of harassing lawsuits—a clerk who complained that employees were not provided with suitable seating while on the job *(Rodriguez, 2009)*, a Muslim hostess who was not allowed to wear her headscarf at work *(Boudlal, 2010)*, and hotel clerks afraid that identity thieves could decipher their Social Security numbers from the barcodes on the ID cards *(Richards, 2011)*. The actions were all topics management sounded willing and open to discussing and resolving, but the plaintiffs and the union preferred to argue in the court of law and the court of public opinion.

VIII

Who Wants to Be a Millionaire?

So, YOU'VE SUFFERED a grievous wrong at Disneyland. You've been injured—physically or emotionally—and you're convinced Disney should pay for allowing it. Should you sue?

Probably not. As you've read, a big payday is possible, but the odds are against you. Of the nearly 1,300 cases analyzed, only 265 (or about 20 percent) made it to trial. Disney won 231. That means approximately one out of every 38 plaintiffs has beaten Disney in court.

If your injury is minor, if you're more at fault than they are, if you can't prove their culpability, if you're unwilling to devote several years of your life to high drama and risking thousands of dollars, your best course is probably to suck it up.

However, if the opposite is true—if you have suffered significant, objectively verifiable harm, if Disney or its employees did something that caused (or intentionally didn't do something that allowed) the harm to take place, and you're committed to the long haul—here are a few strategies to increase your odds for a favorable resolution:

(1) Find the right attorney, preferably one experienced with fighting Disney. The company and its legal team will try their best to intimidate you and, by being associated with Mickey Mouse, possesses a raft of inherent advantages. Your representation must be prepared for it.

(**2**) Research similar cases, to establish a pattern of neglect on Disney's part. "The main thing," advises Barry Novack, "is to see if you are the first person to suffer this type of injury or if there have been a slew of people. Previously, Disney had done a good job hiding its (accident) records. Nobody wants their dirty laundry aired."

(**3**) File the case, if possible, anywhere but Orange County. For a slip-and-fall, you may have no other option, but other types of incidents may offer another geographic tie-in. Novack has successfully kept ten cases in L.A., and Disney settled nine of them. Other attorneys argue that Orange County is no longer as uniformly conservative as it was in the Fifties and that love of Disney doesn't stop at the county line. Nonetheless, the statistics don't lie.

(**4**) Make sure you have hard evidence. Juries, noted one attorney, "require a little more proof for Mickey than for other people." If it comes down to "you said, they said," you're in trouble.

(**5**) Track down impartial witnesses and qualified experts, then prepare yourself for a protracted fight. "Before you get into litigation, first analyze whether you can win or not," warns attorney John Luetto. "Most companies will settle. They'll pay something. But your injuries have to warrant signing on for a three-year sojourn. You know immediately you're going to have a strong defense on the other end. Have your experts in place, right away, ideally before you even file a suit. Then gird your loins and go to battle. You're in for a long haul."

(**6**) Assume a trial is inevitable. The vast majority of Disneyland cases never make it that far. And sometimes your case is so rock-solid, you may be certain that Disney will settle. Don't be. "Prepare your case as if you are going to trial," advises Wylie Aitken. "Put in all the time and effort and work, and spend the money to make your best case. Don't cut any corners. If you take the position that they're going to try this case, there's a great likelihood that they will settle."

(**7**) Don't fight Disney's natural advantage; co-opt it. "Don't make the case yourself vs. Disney," Aitken says. "Make it about you *protecting* Disney. We all love the mouse. No one wants to see unfortunate incidents. I always delivered the subtle message: we want to make this place safer for everyone—including Disney."

Meanwhile, inside the Happiest Place on Earth, things have changed drastically from Walt's respite from reality. Nowadays, you can't fall under the spell of the Haunted Mansion for more than a few seconds before being jerked out of the illusion by the jarring green glow of an emergency exit sign. Attraction wait times grow perpetually longer, with the addition of new safety checks and double-checks and triple-checks. Cast members, unlike decades ago, are no longer cast on how well their looks, or gender, or even ethnicity matches their "role in the show."

Certainly, today's Disneyland is safer, more cautious, and more diverse than Walt's wonderland of 1955. And what did it give up in return? Its sense of wonder.

Case Index & Sources

This book and the statistics within it are based on court records in the following cases. Dates listed (below and within the text of the book) are when the central incident took place, not when the case was filed. The vast majority of cases were filed several months to two years after the incident. Other details about a number of these cases can be found in *Mouse Tales* (*MT*) or *More Mouse Tales* (*MMT*).

D = Defendant (Disney)   P = Plaintiff

Any case not noted as settled, dropped or with a verdict was dismissed with prejudice, so it may have been settled or dropped, or is ongoing.

– Slips, Trips & Bumps –
Falls

Mays, Roy (11-8-55) on fruit
  Verdict: P (settled after appeal)
Walker, Lillie Jane (3-6-56) Carnation entryway; dropped
Goodman, Fannie (5-19-56) restroom
Zimpirics, Catherine Mary (9-24-56) tripped over curb as exited Omnibus
Stangenberg, Richard (4-20-57) rain-soaked floor of Plaza Pavilion restaurant
Stein, Betty (7-23-57) sidewalk near House of Future
Mizerak, Marcella (9-3-57) pathway
Golden, Ida (11-11-57) broke wrist after fell on uneven floorboards in 20,000 Leagues
Gaunty, Carlie (12-29-57) Dairy Bar
Krause, Esther (6-4-58) Casey Jr. stairs; dropped
Toft, Nielsine Marie (7-3-58) World Beneath Us
Clausen, Elsie (9-9-58) sidewalk
Wicht, Ida (2-26-59) pathway to House of the Future
Huddeston, Pauline (3-22-59) curb
Poliner, Shirley (4-25-59) debris near City Hall exit; dropped
Duncan, Ronald (5-3-59) fence near train station
  Verdict: P ($1,000)
Boyle, Anna (7-9-59) melted ice cream
Talent, Helen (7-19-59) wet step inside castle walk-through
  Verdict: D

Nease, Elvina (1-30-60) broke arm in fall
  Verdict: D
Hagan, Marilyn (9-1-61) banana peel while watching fireworks
  Verdict: D
Chormicle, Nellie (10-8-61) tripped over cable on Mark Twain
  Verdict: D
Solt, Margaret (8-11-62) tripped over piece of metal protruding from Monorail
  Verdict: D
Krause, Veronika (12-9-62) dropped
Moss, Lloyd (8-29-64) truck crank; dropped
Haynes, Catherine (9-19-64) Frontierland sidewalk; dropped
Swede, Hilda (10-10-64) Tiki Room ramp
Paquin, Beatrice (12-28-64) parking lot; dropped
Perkins, Maria (2-13-65) parking lot
  Verdict: D
Eichner, Samuel (7-14-65) tripped over rope surrounding rock garden; dropped
Daugherty, Margaret (4-6-66)
  Verdict: D
White, Ella (8-13-66)
Lapon, Albert (4-1-67) slipped on wet platform exiting train; dropped
Goldfinch, Annie (4-5-68) New Orleans Square debris; dropped
Kramer, Roberta (8-25-68) New Orleans Square

Waleden, Margaret (5-31-69) pathway to House of Future
Verdict: D
Bullock, Lillian (7-3-69) Opera House rope
Lefler, Helen (1-11-70) Hub
Verdict: D
Gamble, Gladys (3-8-70) cobblestones; dropped
Nemecek, Octavia (3-26-70) cobblestones
Brown, Hazel (6-29-70) curb; dropped
Kenney, Rebecca (9-20-70) Opera House steps
Kimbrough, Willie (11-9-70) sidewalk
Verdict: P ($3,000)
Bentz, Audrey (7-7-71) fell over stroller
Washburn, Marjorie (5-28-72) Crystal Pavilion; settled
Pinney, Herlinda (6-17-72) cobblestones
Martin, Thais (8-21-72) Mile Long Bar porch; *MMT*
Veres, Julius (1973) New Orleans Square
Verdict: D
Jolly, Dorothea (6-6-73) Opera House steps
Wrobel, Betty (8-22-73) dropped
Guerrero, Estella (10-7-73) melted frozen banana
Verdict: D
Domby, Anna (11-18-73) Adventureland bridge
Carlisle, Curtis (12-1-73) Casa de Fritos floor; dropped
Monillo, Teresa (4-11-74) dancing at Coke Terrace
Khalafbeigi, Mahin (10-26-74) wet Pirates steps
Tuller, Betty (2-13-76) cobblestones
Eisermann, Wolfgang (4-17-76) parking lot; dropped
Valgardson, Dorothy (7-20-76) melted frozen banana; settled
Harris, Rita (9-25-76) sprinkler head
Verdict: D
Langley, Mary Lou (10-23-76) Town Square steps
Verdict: D
Fremont, Richard (10-27-76) Candy Palace
Pereria (2-19-77) melted ice cream
Verdict: D
Silex, Maria (7-11-77) curb
Lamb, Ovella (c. 1978) trolley track
Verdict: P ($75,000)
Loesch, Beatrice (9-10-77) curb
Verdict: D
Adkinson (6-28-78) grape juice
Verdict: D
Christie, Ruth (7-4-78)
Peters, India (7-17-78) New Orleans Square
Reif, Florence (7-17-78) Main Street
Dillard, Jewell (8-14-78) Small World mall
Brumbaugh (12-78) curb
Verdict: D
Winhoven, Norma (2-21-79) Fantasyland
Verdict: D
Hughes, Joyce (6-7-79) parking lot
Johnson, Bennve (7-9-79) near Autopia
Rexroth, Kathy (8-17-79)

Oliver, Patricia (11-12-79) New Orleans Square
Verdict: D
Beltramo, Sandra (11-25-79) varying floor levels in Merlin's Magic Shop
Weber, Richard (1-13-80) Frontierland
Ferrington, Erma (6-19-80) cobblestones
Verdict: D
Digerose, Kari (7-12-80) tripped over rope near Small World; settled
Powell, Inez (7-23-80) Plaza Inn
Shtofer, Elza (1-2-81) parking lot
Gard, Mary Jane (3-22-81)
Marlow Jr., Herman (4-4-81) dropped
De Martini, Mildred (4-20-81) dropped
D'Antonio, Ofelia (5-2-81)
Stone, Perlie (5-15-81) parking lot
Verdict: D
Moreno, Yolanda (8-3-81) tripped over post
Baro, Phyllis (8-22-81) food stuffs; dropped
Green, Irene (5-14-82) Fantasyland
Verdict: D
Singh, Shereen (8-4-82) wet, muddy sidewalk
Hirai, Kazuko (3-19-83) Main Street; dropped
Diego, Lydia (6-3-83) outdoor theater
Valdivia, Rosa (9-4-83) liquid
Allen, Marilyn (9-9-83) fell off bench
Hubert, Diane (11-12-83) Frontierland
Verdict: D
Munushian Sr., Vernon (11-13-83) restroom
Rowse, Marie (12-9-83) wet, muddy walkway
Bond, Christine (12-17-83) curb during Candlelight
Bates, Mildred (12-19-83) Small World steps
Verdict: D
McKinney, Barbara (7-4-84)
Hershmann, Lester (1984) bridge
Marinelli, Judith (9-15-84) wheelchair crashed after rolled off Frontierland boardwalk
Hulbert, Darlene (3-31-85) evacuating Matterhorn
Sellars, John (8-15-85) dance floor
Homier, Mae (11-2-85) Main Street curb
Verdict: D
Sorotsky, Rose (7-17-86) fell off curb
Manny, Nora (8-9-86) steps
Mesa, Claudia (1987) fell as entering Country Bear Jamboree when lights suddenly went out
Elvidge, Mark (2-17-87) puddle
Collins (2-24-87) parking lot
Verdict: D
Zaichik, Mark (7-5-87) squashed fruit
Soto, Manuela (7-24-87) near restroom
Cuzzolino, Helen (9-11-87) Main Street
Verdict: D
Staele, Linda (9-25-87) liquid
Gameroz, Leticia (12-29-87) Main Street restroom
Chen, Sun (1988) Monorail ramp
Andes, Jean (2-14-88) gravel

Mufti, Shamin (4-18-01) tripped over bakery rope
Verdict: D
Zamora-Anderson, Linda (4-20-01) steps
Powell, Fern (4-25-01) DCA walkway
Verdict: D
Velasquez, Michelle (4-26-01) wet mat
Verdict: D
Escobar, Nemecia (6-1-01) Innoventions step
Verdict: D
Maldonado, Luis (7-23-01) wrongful death, after gift
shop fall
Verdict: D
Dees, Shannon (7-26-01) DCA walkway; settled
Holmes, Darwin (8-16-01) Hollywood & Dine
Verdict: D
Rafaelli, Charlene (9-2-01) DCA entrance
Verdict: D
Bird, Natalie (9-22-01) Disneyland Hotel restroom
Gentry, Barbara (9-27-01) Who Wants to Be a
Millionaire steps
Martinez, Arturo (12-30-01) Hungry Bear porch
Kenyon, Kathy (1-31-02) stepped off curb
Moreno, Marlene (3-17-02) restroom
Petty, Marion (5-16-02) cobblestones
Smithour (c. 2002) Tarzan's Treehouse
Verdict: P
Lee, Mae (6-9-02) Adventureland planter
Swank, Nema (6-13-02) trolley track
Verdict: D
Nguyen, Thin (7-27-02) pavers
Nelson, Rebecca (8-2-02) hurt knee falling from
hotel shuttle
Verdict: D
Flessati, Gloria (11-9-02) parking structure
Sokolow, Valerie (12-12-02) Goofy's Kitchen
Verdict: D
Frederickson, Elma (12-26-02) Aladdin show
Frizzi Jr., Cono (2-2-03) DCA
Miller, Heidi (2-27-03) wheelchair
Verdict: D
Fragoso Jr., Alfonso (3-25-02) ran into rope
Becker, Deborah (4-3-03) peach skin at Grand
Californian
Fields, Sharyl (4-14-03) DCA restroom; settled
Garcia, Bertha (5-11-03) restroom; settled
Ishmayeva, Lidiya (5-11-03) liquid
Kitt, Kennth (5-21-03) Splash Mountain photo
viewing area
Lymon, Joann (5-30-03) rope; dropped
Yost, Sylvia (6-7-03) DCA walkway
Vazquez, Bernard (6-15-03) curb
Ivey, Sharon (7-22-03) "dangerous and defective
broken curb;" settled
Rogers, Patricia (7-23-03) restroom
Mayes, Stephanie (7-25-03) uneven boards near
California Screamin' launch zone
Verdict: D

Mirabal, Alexandra (8-8-03) tripped over rope;
settled
Lee, Yetta (8-19-03) slipped in spit on castle bridge
Moe, Elvira (9-19-03) curb
Grunnman, Tina (11-19-03) Disneyland Hotel
bathroom
Smith, Molly (11-29-03) pavement
Meyer, Jacinda (12-7-03) restroom
Verdict: D
Pettey, Roxanne (12-7-03) DCA debris; settled
Knight, Terry (12-18-03) parking lot; settled
Barrille, Jean (1-18-04) fell off curb; settled
McFarlin, Jonathan (1-20-04) Disneyland Hotel
parking garage elevator injury; settled
Argretto, Ralph (6-18-04) fell off curb; settled
Miller, Frank (7-28-04) Plaza Inn debris; settled
Cofino, Paige (11-26-04) Tarzan's Treehouse;
dropped
Haag, Dianne (12-19-04) parking structure
Verdict: D
Judkins, Margaret Ann (12-31-04) parking structure
Zaldivar, Carmen (1-02-05) wet restroom mat;
settled
Kelly, Danny (c. 2005)
Breeling, Cynthia (4-2-05) parking structure elevator
injury
Brown, Jeanne (6-17-05) berries; settled
Pleasant, Christina (7-12-05) New Orleans Square
Minton, Denise (7-19-05) DCA walkway
Lugger, Phyllis (8-18-05) pavement; settled
Bonn, Stephen (9-13-05) parking structure escalator
Lavin, Betty (10-30-05) pavement; settled
Silveira, Michael (4-18-06) Disneyland Hotel
sprinkler head; settled
Osuna, Martha (7-22-06)
Reichard, Joyce (8-21-06) steps
Trost, Laura (11-27-06) Space Mountain ramp
Tesfay, Leul (12-26-06)
Rillorta, Renee (1-5-07) curb
Verdict: D
Derone, Marianne (4-6-07) DCA debris
Good, Kathryn (5-20-07) trolley track; transferred to
small claims
Combs, Michael (8-23-07) ticket booth chain
Fry, Tanya (10-13-06) DCA boardwalk
Verdict: D
Garcia, Linda (10-20-07) slipped in vomit in Peter
Pan queue
Tenorio, Juanita (11-30-07) Soarin' queue; settled
Marquez, Antonio (3-8-08) tripped over pallet jack
while making delivery; settled
Weldon, Angela (3-24-08) Indiana Jones rope
Verdict: D
Farrell, Soyla (5-31-08) curb; settled
King, Teri (9-27-08) Village Haus puddle; settled
Krok, Carol (10-21-08) Hub
Leal, Heather (11-8-08) DCA walkway

Narvaez, Alicia (12-31-07) umbrella; settled
Cruz, Markus (6-27-08) cut fingers on nail in Tortilla Factory ceiling
Harrison, Katherine (4-08-09) umbrella
  Verdict: P ($546,000)
Gala, Juan (12-3-09) lightpost
Mays, Michelle (12-12-09) lightpost
Davidson, Chauncey (3-27-10) popcorn cart; settled
Weathers, Grace (11-19-10) elevator closed on scooter; settled
Pina, Margarita (5-1-11) tree; settled
Andrew, Todd (2-20-13) hit head on beam above Harbor Galley condiment table
Jamaleddine, Wissam (6-24-13) DCA Animation Building sofa

Collapsing Objects
Musolf, Verna (12-14-58) Mark Twain chair
Bailey, Earlene (7-28-64) Casa de Fritos stool
O'Sorup, Sasi (2-25-94) Captain EO chair; settled
Fernandez, Georgeanna (10-4-96) table; settled
Hotzinger, Veronica (4-19-02) toilet
Beamer, Christine (3-9-08) Splash Mountain railing
Zakaryan, Karine (9-12-10) railroad railing; settled
Smallwood, Sherry (12-19-12) folding chair during Candlelight Procession

Tom Sawyer Island
Honeycutt, Elizabeth (8-3-57) fall; dropped
McGarry, Marcie (8-15-57) fall
  Verdict: D
Cummings, Sandra Lee (4-3-58) fell off merry-go-round; settled
Shannon, Marion (6-3-58) fall
Stevenson, Vivian (7-6-58) fall; *MT*
  Verdict: D
Stockler, Katherine (c. 1959) fall
  Verdict: D
Ferris, Grace (8-20-59) fall; dropped following mistrial
Snider, James (8-20-60) merry-go-round fall; settled
Rosenwasser, Seymour (8-22-62) bridge fall
Howie, Wanda (4-10-63) fall
  Verdict: D
Hunter, Brian (7-18-65) hurt in cave
  Verdict: D
Makoutz Jr., Timothy (1969) merry-go-round fall; *MMT*
  Verdict: D
Dixon, Eugene (4-12-70) fall
Russo, Lori Ann (9-30-72) fall
Serradell, Evelyn, & Duarte, Mary (8-17-74) fell on bridge; *MMT*
Ontiveros, Carmen (5-26-75) fell on bridge
Weber, Kyle (8-24-75) fall
Salkin, Karen (8-8-77) fall
  Verdict: D
Good, William (12-2-77) fall

Bowen, Ken (7-29-85) fall
Dwyer, Megan (8-13-86) fall
Linaeus, Joseph (12-3-88) fall
Davis, Mary (12-13-88) fall
Grieg, Gordan (6-9-89) fall
  Verdict: D
Goldin, Alix (4-27-91) fall
Dorman, Barbara (5-14-94) fall
Pedersen, Lucille (12-11-94) fall
  Verdict: D
Patino, Delinda (12-21-00) hit head in cave; settled
Figueroa, Priscilla (1-21-01) lost finger in rifle on fort; settled
Devisser, Hazel (11-7-02) fall
Hawkins, Merrita (4-26-03) fall

Struck by Cast Member
Prestia, Dorothy (6-16-62) hit by saloon worker
  Verdict: D
Norton, Nancy (7-23-65) tea burn
Hawley, Ruth (12-22-74) cart
Silkiewicz, Irene (7-13-76) poles; settled
Roberts (7-19-80) cart
  Verdict: D
Rachowsky, Shelly (8-4-88) cart
Hancock, Cynthia (7-5-90) leaf blower
Ouda, Nagi (1-13-91) cart
Lopez, Deborah (4-26-91) Blue Bayou plate
Vlaovich-Ramirez, Jane (c. 1991)
  Verdict: D
Deturk, Patricia (4-17-92) cart
McNair, Jeff (5-18-92) cart
Wood, Ronald (2-25-95) CD cabinet
Schmidt (7-17-95) umbrella
  Verdict: D
Crosby, Kelly (8-1-99) Blue Bayou chair
  Verdict: P ($10,000)
Hernandez, Rita (8-13-01) hit by Plaza Inn worker
Horning, Mechelle (7-25-02) garbage bin; settled
Bolduc, Christine (6-19-03) motorized cart
Martinez, Annie (4-20-04) struck in eye by worker
Peluso, Janette (9-30-04) struck by worker on ECV; settled
Morales, Leonides (7-16-05) run into by worker; settled
Bays, Dorothy (10-17-05) collided with Plaza Inn waiter; settled
Dickerson, Lena (8-24-06) attacked by dog; settled
Kwon, William (11-13-08) coffee burn at Blue Bayou; settled
Sanchez, Stephanie (12-30-09) dolly
Dunne, Diane (10-10-10) knocked over at DCA; dropped

Characters/Parade
Gurll, Mary (12-30-60) hit by Mad Hatter; *MT*
Lopez, Debbie (1974) slapped by Pooh; *MT*
  Verdict: D

McClain, Connie (6-2-74) hurt by Mary Poppins; *MT*; settled
Mick, Christiaon Susan (4-20-76) assaulted by pig; *MT*; dropped
Levy (3-80) pushed by pig
  Verdict: D
Nissan, Erna (7-4-82) struck by character; dropped
Stormer, Shanta (8-17-86) assaulted by bear; *MT*; dropped
Sewell, Dorothy (6-5-95) fell while fleeing wolf
Guenther, Donna (4-8-96) parade float
Palmatier, Dwight (11-13-04) pushed by Queen of Hearts
  Verdict: D
Perez, Mayra (12-27-04) hit by float; settled
Su, Ronin (11-24-05) hurt by Tweedle Dum or Dee; settled
Urlich, Lauren (5-1-11) hit by Darth Vader; settled
Black, Annelia (8-11-12) White Rabbit discriminated; settled

– Disneyland Attractions –
Adventure Thru Inner Space
Blakely, Cheryl (8-18-67) fall
Tommaso, Helga Ruth (8-6-74) ejected; settled

Alice in Wonderland
Duarte, Leslie Allyson (8-24-63) hit head during power failure; *MT*; settled
Robinson, Thelma (10-1-64) fall; settled
Worth, Thomas (3-16-69) settled
Pierson, Gayle (1-31-71) run over
Sherman, Barbara (6-11-72) fell exiting; settled
Weller, Mark (c. 1977) hurt foot
  Verdict: D
Bankhead, Edna (5-31-77) collision; dropped
Lane, Ethel (10-15-77) collision
Joerger, Bonnie (11-9-77) thrown about; dropped
Duran, Natalia (4-20-78) fell exiting
Glenn, Perry (12-27-78) hurt foot
  Verdict: D
Marlow Jr., Herman (4-4-82) dropped
Banayan, Bob (9-8-85) collision
Almanzan, Theresa (10-23-90) run over; dropped
Soria, Maria (6-29-91) ejected; settled
Dukin, Elaine (3-13-97) hurt foot
  Verdict: P ($23,400)
Borbeck, Blake (12-21-00) hurt foot
Messick, Ruth (5-20-02) dragged

Astro-Jets/Rocket Jets
Lyle, Heide (8-56) hit face
  Verdict: D
Ridinger, Linda (6-13-65) hit face
Murphy, Margaret (8-19-65) hurt knee
  Verdict: D
Haynes, David & Myrna (11-13-77)
  Verdict: D

Reed, Scott (3-25-88) hit head

Autopia
Marshall, Janie Marie (7-20-55) hit curb; *MT*
  Verdict: D
Sumrall Jr., Garland (4-14-56) broke leg on gas pedal
Hagee, Vivian (11-27-57) collision
Corsch, Fridel (4-29-58) hit curb
  Verdict: D
Gelb, Gail (6-7-58) collision; dropped
Heard, Helena La Rosa (7-4-58) hit dash on Jr. Autopia
George, Hazel (12-9-58) collision
Logan, Cheryl (6-21-59)
Marilla, John (7-7-59) fall
  Verdict: D
Knecht, Audry (10-11-59) fall; settled
Dixon, Michael (5-14-60) crushed hand
Brill, Shirley (6-19-60) collision; dropped
Lowy, Lillian (6-26-60) fall; dropped
Catalano, Rose (7-24-60) collision
  Verdict: D
Wells, Myrtle (7-30-60) Jr. Autopia collision
  Verdict: D
Blackford, John (8-13-60) collision
Bijou, Marcella (12-26-60) collision
Barron, Katherine (1961/62) collision
  Verdict: P ($10,000)
Maldonado, Alice (8-5-61) collision
Haberg, Marilyn (12-28-61) settled in mid-trial
Baccanti, Tom Dana (1-7-62) collision
  Verdict: D
Newton, Gene (8-13-62) settled
Grossman, Robert (1962) collision; dropped
Takeda, Nobuko (8-30-62) collision
  Verdict: D
Erwin, Jean Ann (9-22-62) settled
Zupo, Mary Anne (6-27-63) dropped
Dalton, Elizabeth Mae (7-4-63) collision; settled
Swanson, Dorothy (7-13-63) collision
  Verdict: D
Wyatt Jr., Perry & Marie (9-8-63)
  Verdict: P (Perry $1,400, Marie $1,100)
Brannon, Marie (12-28-63) collision; dropped
Donath, Ronald (1-18-64) collision; settled
Haynes, Camille (8-16-64) collision; dropped
Larrabee, Patricia (7-26-65)
Hernandez, Eula Mae (12-25-65) collision; dropped
Olson, Rebecca (1-1-67) Jr. Autopia fall; dropped
Johnston, Marjorie (9-24-67) collision
Paine, Jackolyn (1-26-68) fall
Johnston, Donna (7-29-68) collision; dropped
Ellerbroek, Wendell (3-29-70) fall
Reens, Evelyn (8-2-70) collision
  Verdict: D
Farrin, Frank (4-22-72) collision
Ginsberg, Tamara (8-31-72) injury

Varela, Sandra (5-10-75) collision; *MT*
Verdict: D
Caraveo, Monserrat (8-29-75) fall; settled
Lemons, Alice (3-13-76) fall
Verdict: D
Hakes, D. (8-11-76) collision
Verdict: D
Gardner, Johanna & Redd (9-22-76) collision
Ayala, Dina (10-31-76) dropped
Comeax, Jacqueline (3-27-77) run over
Dillard Jr., Kirk (5-6-77) fall; dropped
Blackshear, Eula (8-4-78) rear-ended by employee-driven car while exiting
Alon, Hanon (5-11-80) injury
Short, Miriam (6-2-80) collision
King, Kimberly (2-14-81) collision
Hurt, Connie Lea (5-23-81) dropped
Thompson, Richard (7-12-82) collision
Verdict: D
Miskulin (c. 1982) collision; arbitrated for $10,900
Sandrini, Ann (7-16-85) collision
Peterson, Esther (8-14-86) hurt exiting
Martinez, Victor (11-22-86) collision
Brandt, Joanne (10-3-87) collision
Garcia, Julia (2-7-88) fall
Grainer, Ryan (7-20-89) collision
Haines, Barbara (12-8-89)
Tiamzon, Susan (5-20-90) collision
Mouradian, Arshakouhie (7-22-90) collision
McLean, Josefa & Juan (2-2-91) collision
Verdict: D
Sawires, Malak (4-10-91) run over
Verdict: D
Clarke, Bertha, & Miller, Hanna (4-12-91) collision
Verdict: D
Tatangelo, George (7-16-91) collision
Verdict: D
Hood, Elinor (8-19-91) hurt hand; dropped
Brunk, Leisa (11-10-91) collision; transferred to small claims
Velasco, Velia (7-12-93) fall
Pineda, Naomi (7-31-94) collision
Fesler, Susan (6-25-00) collision; settled
Funk, Joel (11-11-00) collision

Big Thunder Mountain Railroad
Corey, Joyce (9-21-79) jostled
Verdict: D
Satterberg, Franklin (7-8-81) hurt by guard rail; dropped
Dogra, Anil (6-2-85) car tipped over; dropped
Grigorian, Grigore (6-15-91) ejected
Kreb, Susan (8-7-93) sudden stop
Alvarado, Christina (9-5-03) crash; settled
Becker, Christina (9-5-03) crash; settled
Gutierrez, Vicente (9-5-03) crash; settled
Smith, William & Teresa (9-5-03) crash; settled

Torres, Jamie & Carmen (9-5-03) wrongful death; settled
Van de Keere, Phillip (9-5-03) crash; settled
Cope, Gerald (7-8-04) collision; settled
Shouse, Kristen (2-14-09) hurt exiting
Verdict: D

Buzz Lightyear Astro Blasters
Gates, Gail (6-16-08) fell exiting; settled
Brown, Edward (9-5-08) hurt hand; dropped

Canoes
Wilson, Patti (8-30-60) fell boarding
Verdict: D
Tamayo, Antonia (4-19-64) struck head; dropped
Goettig, Elfriede (7-3-67) fell exiting
Walker, Johnnie Mae (7-30-72) fall
Verdict: D
Armendariz, Robert (4-8-79) fall
Maliszewski, Madeline, & Hogan, Mary Lou (8-10-92) collision with keel boat; settled
Gusman, Brandon (11-25-95) collision
Verdict: D
Jones, Deborah (12-20-03) fall

Casey Jr. Railroad
Williams, Pauline (7-19-61) fell exiting; *MT*; dropped
Shelton, Alice (8-30-69) jostled; settled

Disneyland Railroad
Cook, Ronald (9-15-62) broke leg
Verdict: D
Manchester, Jeff (5-7-10) jostled; settled

Dumbo
James, Lenora (2-4-68) ejected; *MT*
Verdict: D
Green, Paulette (7-20-68) hit face
Hill, Susan (1-21-78) hit by gate; *MT*
Verdict: D

Flying Saucers
Behar, Susana (11-10-62) injury
Verdict: P ($1,100)
True, Myrtle (9-26-63) struck by vehicle; settled
Gonzales, Penelope (3-22-64) her vehicle pushed into wall by employee
Lundin, Gertrude (6-24-64) bumped into railing
Verdict: D
Cusimano, Susie (7-5-64) injury
Verdict: D

Haunted Mansion
Georgiou, Mary (8-20-69) fell boarding
Libertone, Mary (11-27-69) fell exiting
Verdict: D
Timmons, Joy Anne (12-20-69) fell exiting; dropped
Burke, Bernice (1-3-70) ejected
Verdict: D
Byers, Mary (4-25-70) fell exiting
Verdict: D

Cox, Helen (6-20-70) fell exiting
Verdict: D
Bordie, Stephanie (10-3-70) fell exiting
Beaty, Eileen (4-25-71) fall; dropped
Dominguez, Edward (6-18-72) hurt boarding
Schwotzer, Pauline (8-6-72) fell exiting; dismissed
during trial
Sandes, Mary Alice (8-23-73) fell exiting; dropped
Eiser, Frances (9-13-73) fell exiting
Swearingen, Mary (11-10-73) fell exiting
Verdict: P ($2,800)
Long, Edith (4-9-74) fell exiting
Verdict: D
Abdelsayed, Nadi (5-26-74) hurt boarding
Schroeder, Alice (9-5-76) fall
Wildman, Meta (10-8-78) fell exiting
Levesque, Catherine, & MacLellan, Peter (5-16-80)
fell exiting
Verdict: D
Murillo, Fanny (5-2-81) fell boarding; settled
following mistrial
Cahan, Anna (5-17-82) hand crushed
Vinazza, Ofelia (11-2-91) fell exiting
Verdict: D
Vierra-Lambert, Robbie (2-20-94) quadriplegic
pulled out of vehicle
Banks, David (9-23-94) hurt leg
Verdict: D
Samari, Soroush (5-9-95) fell boarding
Verdict: D
Enkelis, Shirley (8-8-95) fell exiting
Miranda, Maria (12-30-99) fall; settled
Wilson, Lori (3-31-01) elevator injury
Isaacson, Jeffrey (12-28-05) hurt knee
Andrade, Vianey (9-7-09) hurt ankle; settled

Indiana Jones Adventure
Katic, Christine (4-9-95) hit mouth
Vasquez, Edmond (6-15-95) hurt back; settled
Jacob, Zipora (7-17-95) brain bleed; *MMT*; settled
Lerner, Sharon (12-26-95) torn rotator cuff; settled
Craig, Kim (1-28-97) fell exiting
Bynum, Deborah (11-28-98) brain bleed; settled
Patino, Regina (4-19-99) brain bleed; settled
Pacheco, Michael (8-13-99) injury
Moreno, Estate of Cristina (6-25-00) brain bleed;
settled
Younger, Elizabeth (12-12-09) hurt shoulder due to
loose seatbelt; settled

It's a Small World
Scott, Gwendolyn (7-4-66) jostled; settled during
trial
Miller, Ruth (7-18-66) collision
Forte, Hilda (3-11-67) fell into water exiting; settled
Boyd, Mary (12-24-67) hurt leg
Verdict: D
Jacob, Rachel (8-70) fell boarding; dropped

Perry, Glenn (8-27-71) collision
Brown, James (6-25-73) fall
Verdict: D
Thanos, Catherine (7-18-73) fall
Rhodes, Arthur (5-10-74) fall; settled
Wulf, Albert (7-31-76) fell boarding
Davis, Donald (10-1-76) crushed thumb; settled
Kakuuchi, Rosie (2-21-77) fell boarding
Sanchez, Lydia (8-16-79) fall
Whie, Cheryl (3-10-88) injury
Helland, Suzanne (3-29-88) fell boarding
Verdict: D
Cardoza, Dora (8-23-89) fell boarding
Dewitt, Ruth (2-9-91) collision
Miller, Lisa (6-19-91) crushed arm; settled
Cawthorne, Cynthia (2-9-92) collision
Bates, Edward (2-27-93) fell exiting
Verdict: D
Iturralde, Violeta (8-28-94) fell boarding; dropped
Williams, Darlene (5-30-01) settled
Shelton-Love, Kimberly (c. 2001) fall
Martinez, Jose (11-27-09) trapped
Verdict: P ($8,000)
Hartsell, Kimberly (4-1-10) crushed foot; settled
Delgado, Anthony (8-23-11) fall

Jungle Cruise
Buchanan-Bates, Anne (4-20-58) fell boarding
Baebler, Clara (7-24-58) fell boarding
Verdict: D
Daly, George (6-26-59) shocked by gunshot; *MT*
Pinon, Esther (7-6-64) fell boarding; dropped
Sheahan, Mary (8-5-64) fell boarding
Margolin, Fannie (8-10-64) fell exiting; settled
Collings, Bessie (10-11-64) fell boarding
Verdict: D
Richardson, Grant (1-8-66) struck by rudder
Gardner, Phyllis (4-19-68) hurt by gunshot; *MT*;
settled
Griffin, Agnes (8-18-68) fell boarding
Verdict: P ($4,000)
Tomino, Dolores (8-13-72) shocked by gunshot; *MT*;
settled
Di Giambattista, Constanza (4-13-75) fell boarding;
dropped
Parsonese, Mary (7-22-82) fell exiting
Verdict: D
Garbett, Blanche (4-8-87) fell boarding
Dejong-Hull, Annette (12-26-88) struck on head by
part of boat
Bender, Gitta (4-17-90)
Greening, Brandon (4-4-91) arm crushed
Unknown (8-92) fell boarding
Verdict: P ($21,120)
Jones, Elizabeth (5-6-95) jostled
Larosa, Nick (8-2-95) scraped leg
Verdict: D
Keane, Susan (6-3-97) fell boarding

Lasry, Helene (6-29-97) fell boarding
Verdict: D
Wagner, Brian (7-12-00) struck head; settled
Kissee, Jonathan (1-3-06) fell exiting
Verdict: D
Perea, Raele (6-9-06) fall
Lee, Jeffrey & Maria (2-7-10) collision; settled
Gillons, Sarah (7-5-12) collision; settled

King Arthur Carrousel
Stickler, Katherine (8-1-59) fall
Verdict: D
Berkowitz, Rose Lee (11-20-60) hurt boarding
Burke, Colleen (6-22-71) fell boarding
Genus, Christine (12-5-76) ejected
Macherdchian (3-23-80) fell exiting
Verdict: D
Vidaurreta, Procespina (11-17-85) fell exiting;
   dropped
Wiler, June (1-4-90) fell exiting; dropped
Dover, Irene (7-18-96) fall
Saatjian, Mary (8-9-93) fall
Verdict: D
Revolorio, Lucia (4-24-05) fall
Duan, Zhiliang (8-10-11) fell exiting; settled
Hernandez, Frances (1-1-12) ejected; settled
Moreno, Matthew (2-17-14) squatting on Carrousel
   next to his daughter when hoof of a horse came
   down on him, trapping his ankle

Mad Tea Party
Steiner, Mildred (7-26-56) dropped
Henle, Mary Jo (7-1-57) jerked
Verdict: D
Smith, Holly (8-11-57) fell entering
Verdict: D
Jensen, Dianne (4-26-58)
Israel, Annette (12-22-58) fall
Brand, Elsie (7-20-59) fall; dropped
Sojack, Arlene (7-10-60)
Wheeler, Charles (4-18-62) fall; dropped
Hutson, Anita (11-11-64) dropped
Maresca, Anna Florence (8-31-67) fall; dropped
Kleinheksel, Mary (6-9-69) jerked
Keidser, Mark (10-5-69) ejected; *MT*; settled
Darash, Denise (2-14-70) ejected; settled
Schultz, Allison (10-3-80) ejected; settled
Beck (6-21-81) fall
Verdict: D
Anderson, Donna & Angela (9-15-89) teacup
   stopped too abruptly
Verdict: D
Dutton, Christopher (12-1-89) ejected
Dosanjh, Inderjit (6-29-94) ejected; *MMT*; dropped
   after mistrial
Thomas, Maxine (10-5-96) fall
Cordropm, Joan (9-22-04) jerked; settled

Main Street Vehicles
Yee, Jacqueline (7-9-57) fell out of Omnibus
Dossman, Johnny (10-3-57) fell from surrey
Verdict: P ($1,000)
Kohl, Sara, & Ure, Edna (1-2-58) surrey capsized;
MT
Verdict: D
Perry, Una (9-26-59) surrey struck by vehicle; *MT*
Marsh, Genevieve (9-10-65) hit head when streetcar
   hit bus; *MT*
Verdict: P ($5,500)
Lee, Chai Pao (8-31-69) collided with trolley horse;
MT
Verdict: D
Walker, Holly (3-17-72) thrown out of Omnibus
Coppock, Mattie Lee (10-12-74) fell out of Omnibus
Verdict: D
Brennan, Wendy (5-2-87) run over by fire engine
Verdict: D
Barry, Ariella (3-15-12) ejected from trolley when
   collided with second trolley

Matterhorn Bobsleds
Mogul, Rose (6-23-59) frightened; *MT*
Verdict: D
Mann, Mary Ellen & Franklin (8-14-59) collision;
   settled
Paiz, Steven (8-14-59) collision; settled
Rawson, Matilda (8-14-59) collision; settled
Hicks, Charles (9-11-59) collision; settled
Mingus, Lawrence (9-12-59) collision; settled
Freed, Homer (9-23-59) collision; settled
Root, Lucille (1-27-60) collision
Verdict: P ($4,200)
Russel, Wyona (6-13-60) hurt back; dropped
Morway, Fern (7-29-60) collision; settled
Schultz, Susan (8-7-60) jostled; settled
Chapman, Gladys (8-28-60) jostled; dropped
Alvarez, Catherine (1-1-61) jostled; settled
Kusch, Lillian (2-25-61) collision; settled
Selner, Minette (7-2-61) jostled; settled
McArthur, Eleanor & John (6-30-61) collision;
   dropped
Rubey, Reed (7-14-61) hurt back
Verdict: D
Krasow, Dolores (9-4-61) hit forehead; settled
Wegner, Irene (7-10-61) jostled
Verdict: D
Arbaugh, Frances (8-15-61)
Williams, Rose Marie & Irus (2-25-62) collision;
   settled
Polin, Martin (12-1-61) jostled
Verdict: D
Peterson, Vernon (7-4-60) jostled; dropped
Schurch, Patricia (5-19-63) collision; settled
Whalen, John (8-17-63) fell exiting; settled
Haurd, Gladys (9-19-63) cut finger; dropped

Kelly, Nancy (8-1-63) frightened; dropped
Webster, Olive (11-30-63) fell exiting
  Verdict: D
Brown, Florence (4-16-64) defective seatbelt; dropped
Osborn, Nancy (4-21-65) collision; settled
Maples, Jack (5-15-64) wrongful death; *MT*; dropped
Figliolino, Mary (8-21-67) collision; settled
O'Neill, Cornelius (6-2-67) collision; settled
Branch, Alma (8-22-68) collision
Cruz, Esther (8-24-69) jostled; settled
Amaya, Dorothy (9-1-69) frightened
Johnson, Debra & Larry (3-20-71) jostled
  Verdict: D
Farretta, William & Sandra (9-26-71) collision
Epperson, J.D. & Gloria (10-30-71) chemical burns from Matterhorn fire; *MT*; settled
Galey, Mary (9-11-72) jostled
Mason Jr., Alfred (9-2-73) jostled; dropped
Cox, Linda & Samuel (10-14-74) collision
Reyes, Charles (12-22-74) collision
Howard, Robert (5-24-75) fell boarding
Thomas, Leona (6-11-75) fell exiting
Snyder, Margie (8-24-75) hurt back; dropped
Leistico, Donovan (7-21-76) fell boarding; dropped
Wagner, Lois (5-5-77) collision
Leslie, Glen (4-28-79) jostled; settled
Mora, Charlotte (1-26-80) ejected; settled
Avila (8-28-81) hurt foot
  Verdict: D
Bennett, Beth (8-2-87) jostled
  Verdict: D
Smith, Roberta (6-5-88) jostled
Seadg, Razieh (3-10-89) broke nose
Yaymadjan, Inga (7-3-94) collision
Wittman, Jenni Marie (6-17-00) struck face
Anderson, Jeremy (5-23-02) struck head
Enriquez, Anita (8-25-02) hurt shoulder
Saravia, Paola (3-6-04) hit head after bobsled allegedly jumped track; settled
Christy, Wanda (5-22-04) jostled
Mulhearn, Pamela (7-22-05) fell exiting; settled
Apodaca Estrada, Gloria & Karen (7-9-08) jostled
Ramirez, Jennyfer (5-26-09) hurt boarding; settled
Shorey, David (8-31-11) crushed by fellow rider; settled

Mickey's Toontown

Holland, Cynthia (10-23-94) jostled on Roger Rabbit's Car Toon Spin
  Verdict: D
Head, Tari (3-15-95) hit knee on slide; *MMT*; settled
Radke, Travis (7-27-95) fell on boat
Zucker, David & Victoria (9-22-00) ejected from Roger Rabbit; settled
Petrick, Julie (8-19-06) fell exiting Gadget's Go Coaster

Mike Fink Keel Boats

Davis, Stephen & Laura (5-17-97) capsized; *MMT*; settled
Martin, Arlene, Alexis & Rosie (5-17-97) capsized; *MMT*; settled

Mr. Toad's Wild Ride

Fowlkes, Theatus (10-29-55) hit by barrels; *MT*
Ricci, Mary (4-20-58) run over
Oller, Jorge (7-3-60) fell exiting
Bilal, Yusuf (10-27-84) run over
Petree, Leah (9-29-90) run over
Fonseca, Cecelia (12-16-97) fell exiting
Hanekroot, Christina (6-12-98) fell exiting
Bennett, Richard (3-24-00) fell entering
Todd, Sherlyn (2001) fell exiting
  Verdict: D
Hamby-Hodges, Rachal (12-8-01) hit head

Monorail

Campbell, Jean (7-31-59) fell on downramp
  Verdict: P ($4,500)
Bensley, June (8-5-59) hurt toe on upramp
  Verdict: D
Feely, Ellen (4-18-60) fell on upramp
Carlson, Tonetta (7-20-67) fell exiting; *MT*; dropped
Tischer, Harry (12-14-86) hurt eye; *MT*
Smith, Benna Jean (1-4-97) seat collapsed
Hookman, Nicholas (8-14-99) struck by door

Motor Boats

Saperstein, Harold (4-12-58) cut on nail
Zikmund, Hattie (7-21-61) fell boarding
  Verdict: P ($4,331.14)
McAlister, Debra (4-24-65) fall
  Verdict: D

Pack Mules

White, Mary Edna (7-21-60) fall; settled
Steinbeck, Josephine (1960)
  Verdict: P
Williams, Pearl (1-16-61) rolled; settled
Duell, Roberta (7-7-62) ejected; settled
Chew, Sharon (8-24-62) rolled; settled
Niemet, Norman (9-23-62) ejected & dragged; *MT*
  Verdict: P ($4,000)
Quigley Jr., James (6-15-64) ejected; settled
Sanborn, Mary (7-20-64) ejected; settled
Jackson, Virgil (c. 1967) settled
Wilkins, Barbara (c. 1969) settled
Hammersley, Marjorie (9-26-71) ejected; *MT*; settled
Eldridge, Betty (5-6-72) ejected; *MT*
  Verdict: P ($41,084.03)
Gallegos, Susan (c. 1973) settled
McKinney, Lafayette (7-29-73) fall
  Verdict: P ($130,000)

PeopleMover

Griffith, Robin, & Trani, Vincent (8-11-67) jostled; dropped
Broyles, Donna (8-17-67) collision; settled
Yama, Estate of Ricky Lee (8-21-67) wrongful death; *MT*
Rosario, Salud (8-29-67) struck foot
Frederickson, Rita (11-3-68) collision; *MT*
Verdict: P ($4,720.55)
Noll, Peggy (11-3-68) collision; settled
Strauss, Larry & Judith (11-3-68) collision; *MT*; settled
Lockhart, Odelia (8-25-71) hurt leg; dropped
DeLuise, Peter (1972) struck foot; *MT*; settled
Ogle, Susan (10-13-72) fall; *MT*
Verdict: D
Franklin, Josephine (7-18-73) struck foot; settled
Sparks, Jody Lee (3-22-74) struck foot; *MT*; settled
Gonzalez, Estate of Gerardo (6-7-80) wrongful death; *MT*
Farley, Caren (8-17-86) jostled
Martinez, Ruth (9-25-87) collision
Ahlers, Glenys (7-14-93) collision
Canty, Rebecca (8-18-94) collision

Peter Pan's Flight

Sims, Effie (10-13-67) ejected
Verdict: P ($5,000)
Salita, Stephen (10-26-75) thrown about; settled
Luna, Manuel (7-18-82) fell exiting
Huff (10-20-83) fall
Verdict: D
Feingold, Idelle (11-1-87)
Gentile, Amy & Edwin (9-26-93) hurt arm
Verdict: D
McAdoo, Diane (6-23-94) fell exiting
Verdict: P ($13,370)
Knutzen, Eugene (9-17-94) ejected
Verdict: D
O'Leary, Neil (6-12-97) fall

Pinocchio's Daring Journey

Razzo, Luzmila (3-8-85) fell exiting
Contabile, Michelle & Michael (3-23-10) fell entering

Pirates of the Caribbean

Illions, Ronald (4-23-67) collision
Sciuto, Rosie (6-26-67) jostled
Ludwin, Linda (8-19-69) jostled
Kane, William (7-2-72) struck in back
Eckfeld, Marylene (10-31-72) collision
Harrington, Jeanne (11-2-72) collision
Tuckness, Juanita (5-11-73) fall
Verdict: D
Welch, Sheila (2-14-74) ejected; settled
Mora, Angel (3-16-74) injury
Poche, Gerald & Leslie (6-25-75) jostled; settled
Nichols, Virginia (10-11-76) crushed leg

Diaz, Celia (4-27-80) fell boarding
Stansbury, Barbara (7-3-84) hurt ankle boarding; dropped
Garcia, Christina & Martin (12-25-85) fell boarding
Verdict: D
Tab, Jinous (11-13-87) collision
Fazio, Patrick (3-23-88)
Gutierrez, Modesto (4-10-88)
Hopkins, Jan (5-6-89) collision
Olin, David (9-1-89)
Ismail, Rabea (1-9-92) collision
Neubauer, Gary & Donna (6-93) collision
Anderson, Julia (7-18-94) fell boarding; settled
McGreevy, Doris (7-18-94) fell boarding; settled
Elliott, Ryan (12-19-01)
Levy, Debra (6-26-06) fall
Osorio, Sandra (5-31-09) fell boarding
Verdict: D
Frye, Michelle (7-16-12) jostled
Verdict: D

Rafts to Tom Sawyer Island

Steuart, Annie (3-29-59) fall
Davidson, Sherry Lynn (5-23-89) collision
Sicairos, Ricardo (4-21-08) fall; dropped

Sailing Ship Columbia

Wright, Patti Ann (8-2-58) shocked by cannon; *MT*; dismissed during trial
Nenonen, Elizabeth (12-28-58) fell boarding
Widman, Pauline (7-19-61) fall; dismissed during trial
Mosher, Virginia (3-4-61) shocked by cannon; *MT*
Gzaiel, Veronique (8-11-89) shocked by cannon; *MT*
Venema, Elizabeth (5-9-92) shocked by cannon; settled during trial

Shooting Gallery

Peyton, Robert (1-28-62) hurt by discharge; settled
John, Dorothy (2-21-65) struck by pellet; *MT*; settled
Petrantoni, Joseph (7-9-68) struck by pellet; *MT*
Verdict: D

Skyway

Vicker, Harold (7-15-66) jostled
Kriete, Marie (8-19-68) fell boarding
Cummins, Angela (8-8-87) collision
Verdict: D
Riedel, Faye (1-21-89) hurt boarding
Charles, Randle (4-17-94) claimed ejected; *MT*; dropped

Snow White's Scary Adventures

Jordan, James (2-8-56) collision; *MT*; settled
Sims, A.E. (7-21-57) hurt foot; dropped
Vera, Evangeline (5-31-76) fell exiting
Nagy, Floresia (8-24-78) collision
McClintock, Ginger (7-3-91) hurt exiting
Cohn, Lisa (10-11-91) collision

McCurdy, Debra (7-24-93) collision; dropped
Lindstrom, Ronald (4-1-96) fell entering; settled
during trial

Space Mountain
Smith, Cyrus (6-8-78) jostled
Stevens, Williams (9-9-78) sudden stop
Walters, Judith (5-13-79) sudden stop
Hoffman Sr., Ronald (8-14-79) wrongful death; *MT*
Gentry, Diane (c. 1980) fall
Geller, Gregory (1-1-80) jostled; dropped
Barton, Gregary (1-31-81) collision
Verdict: D
Ohe, Brian (9-13-81) lap bar bruised leg; dropped
Crowe (11-28-81) hit face
Verdict: D
Scavo, Martha (4-5-82) sudden stop; dropped
Higgins, James (2-19-83) ejected; *MT*
Verdict: D
Miller, Ronald (4-20-84) whiplash
Verdict: D
Addis, Darci (5-1-88) sudden stop; settled
Summers, Leslie Marie (5-23-89) sudden stop
Storll, Bonnie (2-17-91) hurt foot boarding
Tsui, Hank (5-5-91) struck by object
Bennett, James (11-24-91) hit head
Verdict: D
Burnistine, Estate of Antonio (3-92) paralyzed;
settled
Goeske, Nancy (5-15-92)
Verdict: D
Loesche, Paul (5-15-92) merged with Goeske case
Cortes, Aaron (6-14-93) arm crushed; settled
Brinkman, Pamela (6-26-94) collision
Verdict: D
Buchanan, Carol (8-14-94) hurt entering; settled
Sederberg, Gregory (2-18-95) lap bar crushed leg
Verdict: D
Trodick, Sherrin (7-30-96) dropped
Auzene, Michelle (9-29-96) jolted
Rivera, Michael (5-4-97) jammed finger
Verdict: D
Gribovsky, Kathleen (7-14-99) jostled
Mayes, Robert (6-21-00) fell entering
Woodcock, Jonathan & Julie (7-31-00) crash;
settled
Santos, Audra (5-12-01)
Pacheco, Dennis (5-28-01) fall
Sharp, Adriana (8-29-02) collision; dropped
Spight, Russell (6-25-06) hurt exiting; dropped
Hernandez, Raymond (5-4-09) fell exiting; settled
Soffin, Jonathan (12-17-12) struck by debris

Splash Mountain
Tupaz, Maria (10-4-89) sudden stop
Lucero, Sandra (10-6-89) fall
Verdict: D

Coats, Kyoko (6-5-90)
Rivas, Paul (7-7-90) sudden stop
Jacobson, Norma (10-6-91) broken back
Hendrix, Bobbie (11-23-91) collision
Haberman, Mark (6-3-94) fell boarding
Verdict: D
Taylor, Arreta (9-17-94) collision; settled
Chao, Hsiao-Chuan (11-15-94) fell boarding
Verdict: D
Erickson, Brian (1-28-95) collision
Guyaux, Charlotte (6-30-95) fell boarding; settled
Freund, Carole (10-9-96) hit head
Garibay, Olivia (5-23-98) sudden stop
Verdict: D
Avants, Teresa (6-12-98) collision
Verdict: D
Goodman, Jeff (7-18-98) hurt exiting
Eubanks Jr., James (9-7-96) lost finger
Verdict: D
Lynn, Jana (8-20-99) settled
Traina, Yvonne (8-8-00) hurt back; settled
Hennings, Catherine (5-5-00) collision
Mercado, Frank (9-6-02) hurt hand
Moreland, Marilyn (6-9-04) collision
Vuksic, John (10-15-12) hit head

Stagecoach
Hungate, Billie Lou (3-10-57) fall
Verdict: D
Horner, Bert (9-14-57) capsized; *MT*
Verdict: P ($5,000)
Norton, John (9-14-57) thrown; *MT*
Verdict: P ($17,500)
Ruegsegger, Bette (9-14-57) capsized; *MT*; settled

Storybook Land
Wallace, Kathryn (8-7-58) fell boarding
Verdict: D
West, Isabella (8-1-59) foot crushed
Verdict: P ($660.18)
Farabee, Maxine (8-5-61) fell exiting
Verdict: D
Pittman, Mercille (6-4-69) hurt leg
Verdict: D
Rance, Patricia (10-18-78) fell boarding
Piol, Kimberly (1-18-87) fall
Williams, Donnie (7-17-02) fell boarding
Villalobos, Ben (9-20-03) crushed hand
Sais, Carlos (10-6-10) fell boarding; settled

Submarine Voyage
Sherwood, Janet (4-16-60) fall; *MT*
Verdict: P ($36,650)
Kapigan, Roxie (8-2-60) fall
Sterett, Spencer (4-23-61) fall
Fitzjerrells, Mary Louise (7-10-61) pinched hand;
MT
Verdict: P ($32.50)

Sye, Donna (8-20-64) fall; *MT*; settled
Mulhern, Peter (6-28-70) hit by water
Verdict: D
Kohl, Michele (12-28-87) hit by hatch
Hamilton, Gwendolyn (11-15-08) fell boarding

Other

Schilkey, Emma (5-16-58) fell on Satellite View of America moving walkway
Verdict: D
Hovespian, Sara (3-20-71) Circle-Vision fall; *MT*; dropped
Costles, Patricia (3-27-87) jostled on Star Tours
Verdict: D

– Beyond the Berm –
Parking Lot Tram

Goodman, Mildred (12-30-56) tram fall; *MT*
Verdict: D
Valenzuela, Amy (8-12-63) tram
Logsdon, Lucille (8-17-65) tram fall
McCreary, Delores (3-18-67) tram hit planter; *MT*; settled
Schramm, Frieda (8-24-67) tram trip; *MT*
Verdict: D
Woofter, Evelyn (8-16-68) tram fall
Verdict: D
Olivas, Edward (6-22-70) tram sudden stop; dropped
Kennedy, Lillian (7-27-71) tram fall; *MT*
Verdict: D
Geher, Julien (4-28-73) car hit by tram
Choi, Choong Kun & Young Soon (9-5-76) tram hit car
Hagar, Janice (5-10-77) hit by gate; *MT*; dropped
Willis, Mary (4-3-78) tram fall
Aaron, Arnold (7-15-79) tram fall
Ruda, Gil (8-8-80) tram fall; dropped
Sussman (11-22-80) tram fall
Verdict: D
Haminger (4-1-84) tram fall
Verdict: D
Orcel, Jacqueline (8-7-85) tram fall; dropped
Castillo, Celia (1-14-90) fell after exiting tram
Marsh, Kathy (8-25-91) tram fall
Jones, Rosa (6-19-93) tram fall
Roter, Kenneth (12-19-93) tram sudden stop; settled
Gamboa, Carmen (7-11-94) tram fall
Santos, Paula (9-7-95) tram hit pole; settled
Barillas, Esther (8-13-97) tram fall; dropped
Caravageli, Ethena (4-9-00) while waiting to board, hit by metal bar from nearby construction
Garner, Paul (4-23-01) tram fall; settled
Hendricks, Jodee (10-13-02) hit by stroller on tram
Park, Kyung Mia (11-02) tram fall
Qursha, Suzanne (5-31-03) sudden stop
Lara, Kristin (12-09-04) tram fall
Verdict: D

Martinez, Alex (9-2-06) tram fall; settled
Zhao, Qi (2-23-07) tram fall; settled
Gillin, Julia (7-20-09) tram fall; dropped
Grafton, Kourtney (10-11-09) tram fall; dropped
Esquivel, Jasmine (5-7-10) tram fall; settled

Traffic

Sanders, Goldie (11-6-64) wrongful death; *MT*; dropped
Young, Sarah (7-12-70) crash in lot
Verdict: D
Ives, Eloise (6-8-72) crash on West Street
Dyba, Louis & Frances (6-11-72) motorcycle accident
Maus, Robert (4-7-77) motorcycle hit by tram; dropped
Metress, Charles (5-30-79) hit by car in lot; Disneyland cleared
Sutphen, Martha (7-13-79) crash in lot; D cleared
Zamani, Hosein (c. 1980) car crash
Reid, Family of Jennifer Faith (9-14-85) wrongful death; *MT*
Verdict: D
Velasquez, Eileen (10-19-88) crash in lot
Fobair, Heather (8-3-95) hit by car
Morales, Lupe (10-8-97) crash in lot
Ginnings, Bailey (3-4-11) cyclist hit by car

Hotels

McCormick, Travis (12-4-00) HVAC fumes
Bruno, Frances (3-4-11) rough massage; settled
Wayne, Ricky (2012) scabies
Verdict: P ($2,884 split three ways)

Food Issues

Edgington, Doris (7-13-94) food poisoning
Verdict: D
Rosales, David (5-8-99) broke tooth on rock in Redd Rockett pasta; settled
Bastieri, Cathy (7-17-99) food poisoning from Club 33 salad
McFalls, Joshua (6-20-07) room service food poisoning
Verdict: D
Swatkowski, Margaret (7-27-08) choked on souvenir chocolate
Tupper, Sandra (3-24-11) choked on fishbone at Ariel's Grotto
Verdict: D
Ishizaki, Tony (8-20-11) food poisoning from Ralph Brennan burger; settled
Hatton, Brian (2007) food poisoning

Disney California Adventure
California Screamin'

Heber, David (8-9-01) jostled
Verdict: D
Tillman, Nicole (10-5-01) injury
Bippus, Gloria (c. 2002) sudden stop

Gibson, Mary (4-11-79) assaulted on Pirates; dropped

Garcia, Melinda, & Contreras, Alice (4-29-79) false arrest
Verdict: D

Lee, Douglas (10-6-79) false arrest; *MT*; dropped

Brandt, Jennifer & children (7-26-80) wrongful death
Verdict: D

Exler, Andrew (9-13-80) discrimination; *MT*
Verdict: P

Reynolds, Clarence & Ellen (3-7-81) wrongful death; *MT*
Verdict: P ($600,000, then settled)

Holzer, Lena (7-5-81) wrongful death; dropped

Fittro, Patrick Wayne (5-8-82) false arrest; *MT*; settled

Fernandez, Manuel (7-4-82) false arrest
Verdict: D

Sardina, Pietro (7-10-82) false arrest; dropped

Ravindran, Margaret (7-14-82) false arrest; *MT*; settled

Doss, Robert, & Garrett, Michael (2-19-83) false arrest; *MT*
Verdict: D

Campbell, Bruce & Roxanna (5-22-83) false arrest

Penley, Victoria & Kathryn (5-6-84) denied entrance; dropped

Straughan, Bernice (6-3-83) wrongful death; *MT*; Disneyland cleared but co-defendant settled

Dahlenburg, Edward (9-25-84) unlawful picketing

Christo, Mario (9-27-84) false arrest; *MT*; dropped

Kwiatkowska, Barbara Jolanta (4-16-86) false arrest; *MT*

Slobod, Tonya (7-17-86) denied entrance; *MT*
Verdict: P ($250)

Zavala-Hicks, Martha (8-11-86) false arrest; *MT*

Evans, Eric (10-1-86) assault & battery on Michael Jackson impersonator; *MT*; dropped

Camacho, Vincent (1-10-87) assault & battery

Amanaki, Lelei Jione, & Tai, Takase (3-7-87) wrongful death; *MT*

Sanchez, Monica, & Guzman, Eve (6-16-88) false imprisonment

Tran, Nga & Justina (5-8-89) Autopia road rage

Boozer, Lindsey, Melissa, Karen & Lonnie (10-7-89) false arrest; *MT*; settled

Plascencia, Nayeli (2-11-90) struck by bullet; *MT*

Xu (1-9-93) trampled by crowd
Verdict: D

McKellips, Shirley (8-15-93) bumped by guest

Paotello, Edward (6-12-94) pushed from hotel Monorail station
Verdict: D

Davis, Brian (7-7-94) assault & battery, false imprisonment; settled

Paulson, Robin Ruth & children (4-19-95) assault & battery; *MMT*; dropped

Matay, Billie Jean (8-17-95) inadequate security; judge dismissed

Sowards Jr., Samuel & Rhonda (8-20-95) false arrest

Mazza, Mark (10-6-95) false arrest

Roberts, Nicole, & Cleaver, Chad (10-23-95) assault & battery

Lopez, Magali Mena (11-19-95) false arrest

Winters, Denise (2-24-96) false arrest
Verdict: P ($65,000, then settled)

Cortez, Veronica (4-6-96) false arrest

Rogers, Erin (6-7-96) inadequate security

Burton, Lataynia (8-30-96) false arrest; dropped

Menard, Cecille (9-7-96) false arrest; *MMT*; settled

Canada, C. Taylor (9-24-96) false arrest; *MMT*
Verdict: D

Nassief, Edythe (7-29-97) trampled by crowd

Brooks, Ernest (c. 1997) false imprisonment

Bartlow, Teri Kay (c. 2000) false imprisonment

Marler, Christian (3-14-06) inadequate security; dropped

James, Teri (8-10-08) inadequate security allowed Downtown Disney drunk to fall on and break daughter's arm

Cromwell, Sylvia (7-12-09) wrongful detention; settled

Perez, Justine (10-10-10) wrongful detention

Pulido, Heber (6-26-11) trampled by crowd; settled

– Cast Member Issues –
Accidents

Davis, Thomas (3-31-55) labor dispute

Gillibanks, George (6-30-61) noxious fumes; settled

Foote, Judith (8-8-69) tripped on canoe dock
Verdict: D

Stone, William & Marilyn (7-8-74) America Sings wrongful death; *MT*; settled

Pelcak, Carolyn (1-17-78) insurance dispute

Churchill, Garey (3-18-78) put arm through window
Verdict: D

Alexander, Betty (1980) insurance dispute; dropped

Guerrero, Denise (1980) dragged by Space Mountain rocket; settled

Attaman, Gregory (1-14-85) PeopleMover fall

San Angelo, Phillip (6-4-86) fall building Star Tours
Verdict: P (Disney cleared, but $191,054 from co-defendants)

Werle, Keith, & Milniac II, Carl (6-24-89) injured building Splash Mountain

Morgan, Carl (4-11-90) fall renovating PeopleMover

Barnes, Jerry (11-25-91) burned building Fantasmic

Decenzo, Joe (c. 1995) fell building Indiana Jones

Cisneros, Mark (1-6-97) fell renovating PeopleMover; settled

Ortega, Juan, & Gonzales, Randy (4-22-97) burned cutting pipe; settled

Palestino, Juan, & Torres, Arturo (12-15-00) hit by falling gate; settled

Zendejas, Kelley (3-22-01) run over by handcar; settled

Jurisch, Eric (11-30-01) fell rehabbing Jungle Cruise; settled

Pionke, Michael (10-11-02) hit by Omnibus

Tomlmachoff, Peter (10-10-08) tripped on wire; settled

Mistreatment

Wheeler, Kelly (3-69) wrongful termination due to race; *MT*
Verdict: P

St. Pierre, Joseph (c. 1976) wrongful termination

Hellyer Jr., Glenn (8-8-78) wrongful termination

Kloris, Jonas (4-6-79) wrongful termination; dropped

Collins Jr., Clarence (10-82) racial discrimination; *MT*
Verdict: D

Small, Keith (10-22-82) wrongful termination; *MT*
Verdict: D

D'Allura, Joseph (8-14-83) wrongful termination due to retaliation; *MT*
Verdict: D

James, Alfonso (11-28-88) wrongful termination due to race; *MT*

Campbell Nelson (10-89) wrongful termination due to disability; *MT*

Olson, Robert Dale (2-1-90) wrongful termination due to age; *MT*
Verdict: D

D'Amico, Ted (11-11-92) wrongful termination due to age

Winn, Sherrie Lou (1993) sexual harassment; settled

Allen, Laura (1993) sexual harassment; settled

O'Hoyt, Dennis (11-26-94) wrongful termination

Goodwin Jr., Walter (1-31-95) wrongful termination; settled

Smith, William (2-7-95) wrongful termination

Newsome, Janis (1-27-96) wrongful termination due to gender

Lambeth, Michael (8-11-97) wrongful termination due to age

Morales, Jason (c. 1998) sexual harassment

Kean, Ofelia (4-20-98) wrongful termination following injury

Devitis, Chuck; Rowan, Joanne; Jackson, Ted; Lorenz, Mike; McDonald, Robert Jr. (1998-1999) wrongful termination due to age; dropped

Bury, Michael; Willmon, James; Muleady, Robert (1998-2000) wrongful termination due to age (co-plaintiff Hal Williams dropped out before trial)
Verdict: D

Gardner, Peter (11-98) sexual harassment

Klostreich, Robert (1999) wrongful termination for age, retaliation

Long, Don (8-99) wrongful termination due to age
Verdict: D

Delgadillo, Serio, & Valdez, Joe (7-16-99) wrongful termination due to racial discrimination
Verdict: D

South, Heather (7-26-99) wrongful termination, sexual harassment

Nevarez, Gerardo (8-9-00) wrongful termination following injury

Madory, Jacqueline (12-00) wrongful termination; settled

Warner, Sue (c. 2000) wrongful termination

Eatherton, Cortney (2001) wrongful termination due to retaliation; settled

Vargas, Vanessa (c. 2001) sexual harassment

McShea, Jeffrey (10-23-01) wrongful termination & retaliation for requesting sick leave

Overton, Bobby (2002) proposed class action over walk time
Verdict: D

McMillan, Roberta (2002) wrongful termination due to gender, disability; settled

Slater, Terrie Jo (8-7-02) wrongful termination

Williams, Lee (8-9-02) wrongful termination due to disability

Handy, Laela (c. 2003) age, gender, race discrimination; settled

Scales, Lisa (2-10-03) wrongful termination for retaliation

Jiminez, Jose Angel (2004) sexual harassment; settled

Arayasirikul, Sanong (7-04) wrongful termination

Figueroa, Patricia (3-18-05) wrongful termination due to race

White, Jerry (c. 2005) wrongful termination due to disability

Reinartz, Michael (2006) wrongful termination for retaliation

Polselli, Joseph (5-30-06) wrongful termination following injury; settled

Miller, Kimberly (10-29-06) disability discrimination

Erangey, Stephen (2007) wrongful termination due to disability

Galloway, Amber (2007) proposed class action over overtime at Goofy's Kitchen; settled

Nguyen, Chau (2007) wrongful termination

Ruiz, Ana (2007) wrongful termination, sexual harassment

Soto, Deborah (c. 2007) sexual harassment & wrongful termination

Estrella, Stacey (8-29-07) wrongful termination following injury

Guerrero, Ricardo (10-28-07) defamation & slander

Guerrero, Janet (10-28-07) wrongful termination due to gender

Nambiar, Narcira (1-24-08) wrongful termination of late husband due to disability

Lam, Sodajohn, & Danford, Jason (c. 2008) objection to class settlement for underpayment; settled

Ramirez-Cabatbat, Gertrude (c. 2008) wrongful termination

Towns, Don (5-30-08) wrongful termination due to race

Gutierrez, Silveria (2008) wrongful termination due to age

Ramirez-Cabatbat, Gertrude (11-18-08) wrongful termination following injury; settled

Rodriguez, Koren (2009) class action for failure to provide suitable seating

Gordon, Douglas (4-06-09) wrongful termination due to retaliation

Medina, Rafael (5-02-09) wrongful termination for taking off too much time to care for child

Lockhart, Charlene (5-09) wrongful termination due to age

Camarillo, Charles (c. 2009) wrongful termination due to disability

Pinto, Arnaldo, & 6 co-workers (8-09) wrongful termination due to race, disability
Verdict: D

Cobilla, Jose (9-10-09) wrongful termination due to age, disability
Verdict: D

Mulvihill, Jamie (11-2-09) sexual harassment & wrongful termination

Boudlal, Imane (2010) harassment & racial discrimination

Gonzalez, Luis (7-26-10) wrongful termination due to race, retaliation; dropped

Munilla, Silivia (9-22-10) wrongful termination & slander

Grajales, Marycarmen (2-11) sexual harassment & retaliation

Kristi Richards; Iniestra, Jorge; Stern, Josh (2011) proposed class action over privacy concerns

Melendez, Melissa (2011) disability discrimination

Roundtree, Sarah (2011) disability discrimination

Gutierrez, Gabrielle (8-8-11) disability discrimination

Sebreros, Kathleen (9-1-11) wrongful termination due to disability, age, retaliation; settled

Quinn, Randy (10-6-11) wrongful termination due to disability

Rivera, Elvira (10-11-11) assault & wrongful termination due to disability; settled

Gutierrez, Gabrielle (c. 2011) wrongful termination due to age, disability, race

Orellano, Antonio (6-27-12) wrongful termination due to disability

Le, Luoc (2012) sexual harassment & retaliation

Scott, Dayle, & Joseph, Norman (2012) wrongful termination due to age, race

Galvez, Benjamin (2012) class action for underpaying hotel workers

Cesena, Fernando (8-1-12) wrongful termination & discrimination for race, sexuality

Umana, Henry (12-13-12) wrongful termination for requesting time off for new baby; settled

Sewchurn, Sivaramen (3-7-13) wrongful termination due to disability, age, retaliation

Gonzales, Peggy (5-1-13) wrongful termination due to age, disability, race

Romero, Alma (c. 2014) race, age, disability discrimination

Silva, Maria (2-4-14) wrongful termination

Cook, Kimberly (2014) wrongful termination/failure to accommodate morning sickness

– Other Primary Sources –

Ascenzi, Joe, "Attorneys Agree Winning Case against Disneyland Is Tough," *Anaheim Bulletin* (7-24-86)

Herubin, Danielle, "Ride Spinning Again," *OC Register* (7-13-01)

Hicks, Jerry, "Amusement Parks, Often Sued, Are Seldom Beaten in the Courts," *LA Times* (2-28-82)

Himmelberg, Michele, "Disney Lifts Its Veil on Safety," *OC Register* (6-5-02)

Mott, Patrick, "Lawsuits," *OC Register* (8-8-82)

Mulkern, Anne, "Disneyland Arrestees Face Rough Court Ride," *OC Register* (9-22-96)

Saffian, Sarah, "The Hidden Danger of Amusement Parks," *Redbook* (5-00)

Smith, Steven, "Mickey Mouse Suits," *LA Times* (9-28-78)

Walt Disney Parks & Resorts, "Report on Safety" (2002)

Weber, Tracy, "Plaintiffs Suing Disney in for a Rough Ride," *LA Times* (1-31-99)

Woodyard, Chris, "Litigious World After All," *LA Times* (4-16-95)

Zeller, "Mickey's No Mouse in Courtroom," *LA Times* (6-18-81)

Index

— Italicized page number denotes photo

Books by David Koenig

Mouse Tales:
A Behind-the-Ears Look at Disneyland

Mouse Under Glass:
Secrets of Disney Animation & Theme Parks

More Mouse Tales:
A Closer Peek Backstage at Disneyland

Realityland:
True-Life Adventures at Walt Disney World

Danny Kaye:
King of Jesters

The People v. Disneyland:
How Lawsuits & Lawyers Transformed the Magic

For more information on these books or to order your own copies,
contact Bonaventure Press, P.O. Box 51961, Irvine, CA 92619
or visit
www.bonaventurepress.com